CORNELL
UNIVERSITY
LIBRARY

GIFT OF

Prof. Juan E. Reyna

ar V.
1022.

R. W. Bindieck
No 50 East State St
Ithaca
N.Y.

WOMAN'S WORTH

AND WORTHLESSNESS.

WOMAN'S WORTH

AND WORTHLESSNESS.

THE COMPLEMENT TO

"A NEW ATMOSPHERE."

By GAIL HAMILTON, *pseud.*

NEW YORK:
HARPER & BROTHERS, PUBLISHERS,
FRANKLIN SQUARE.
1872.

Entered according to Act of Congress, in the year 1871, by
HARPER & BROTHERS,
In the Office of the Librarian of Congress, at Washington.

PREFACE.

I HAVE called my book "The Complement to a New Atmosphere," to remove, if possible, the misapprehension of those who have given it the honor of their attention as it has appeared from week to week, and who have been disturbed by what has seemed to them a change of views.

Strictly speaking, it is impossible to obtain, and insolent to undertake to present an adequate idea of any subject or object without changing one's views. We are directed by very high authority to walk about Zion, and go round about her, not stand still and stare at her from one point. I suppose Zion looked very different seen from the Mount of Olives and the Fount of Gihon, but it was Zion all the while.

Change of views involves more or less change of opinions—is, indeed, made for the purpose of forming opinion. Looking but casually at Woman Suffrage, I regarded it with indifference. From a careful survey, I can not regard it but with apprehension. The more closely I scrutinize it, the more formidable seems to me the revolution which it implies, the more onerous seem the duties which it imposes. I feel, also, ever more and more vividly, that

"It is not ours to separate
The tangled skein of will and fate;"

and many things which once I would have attributed to cold-blooded malice I would now attribute to partial growth, to imperfect adjustment, and so find it easier to hate, uproot, and cast away the sin, and yet love the sinner—if he is not too hateful! But of any change important enough to be spoken of—supposing any change worth speaking of—I am unconscious. I know that I have never swerved a hair's breadth from my belief that the only way out of our estate of sin and misery is the slow growth of individual excellence, and that it is in the home, in the family—more sacred than any church, the only divine institution—that this excellence must be chiefly nurtured.

Whether such a belief assigns to woman a commanding or a subordinate position in the world's economy I must leave to the judgment of my readers.

GAIL HAMILTON.

CONTENTS.

CHAPTER	PAGE
I. THE STATE OF NATURE	9
II. THE STATE OF [FRENCH] GRACE	24
III. FALLING FROM GRACE	45
IV. THE PURSUIT OF THE FORTY THOUSAND	64
V. THINGS NEEDED AND THINGS WANTED	90
VI. WOMEN AMONG THE PROPHETS	116
VII. DISABILITIES	134
VIII. SERFDOM	154
IX. SERVILE OCCUPATIONS	167
X. HOME TRAINING	180
XI. FEMALE SAGACITY IN POLITICS	191
XII. PRESS-WORK	206
XIII. REPRESENTATIVE REFORM	237
XIV. THE NECESSITY OF FEMALE SUFFRAGE	246
XV. EXEMPTION OR IMPOSITION	264
XVI. THE ATTITUDE OF MEN	272
XVII. RESULTS	276

WOMAN'S WORTH AND WORTHLESSNESS.

I.

THE STATE OF NATURE.

"My dear," I said to my friend Hassan the Turk—Hassan is not his real name; but circumstances, into which a generous public will not, I trust, peer too closely, have made an alias grateful—

"My dear," I said,
"I shall go
To Professor Blot."

"My dear," he replied, limping promptly after me, but in most un-Gallic guise,
"I think you better not
Go near Professor Blot."

"Why should I not?"
"Why should you?"
A door was open, as the missionaries say, and I walked in.
"You men—"
"Now then. All hands on deck!"
"From time immemorial men have been talking about the noble art of cooking. You have descanted on its importance to the material and spiritual interests of society. Without a knowledge of it, a love for it, a skill in it, no woman could long retain her husband's love or the sovereignty of her home. The education that omitted it was but a synonym for inadequacy, not to say uselessness. If a girl could not bake a loaf of bread or boil a pudding, she was a

failure, however lovely or accomplished. You have wailed Jeremiades over female ignorance, and then, taking heart of disgrace, you have broadened out into Jeremiades over American ignorance on this point. You have set against it the tact, toothsomeness, and economy of the French kitchen. In short, you have moralized and demoralized, in season and out of season, and all to no purpose; for how can people learn when there is none to teach? According to your own showing, we are a nation of barbarians in all that relates to the *cuisine;* and of what use is it for the blind to be led by the blind? But here is a chance for you to prove your sincerity. Here comes a high-priest of the mystery. He is not only a man, but a Frenchman. He is the exponent of the highest civilization of the cooking-stove. We may, as it were, lay our hands upon its mane. All that is known we may know. Stand by your principles now. Since knowledge comes, do not let wisdom linger. Electioneer for Professor Blot. Encourage or admonish every woman to attend his lessons. We can not always drink from the fountain-head of knowledge; but when the fountain-head bubbles up at our own door, a dollar a ticket, what doth hinder that we drink our fill?"

"I hinder. I forbid the bans."

"You?"

"Yes, I. In the name of my domestic peace, which is threatened, I protest."

"Why, herein is a marvelous thing."

"That you should spoil a horn in the futile ambition to make a spoon?"

"But the horn is good for nothing."

"That is the beauty of it. Your great charm is that you are of no use. Your ignorance of every thing which no gentleman's library should be without is truly appetizing. One never knows where your absurdity will crop out next;

curiosity is, therefore, always on tip-toe, and life worth living. Now go and make yourself a useful member of society, and you will spoil the whole. Useful members of society are already as the frogs of Egypt for multitude. Do not *you* turn into one!"

"But the true woman, my dear—"

"Hold your tongue, my dear. If you are dissatisfied with your place, and wish to hire out as cook in a genteel family, I will give you a character; but if you wish to live a rational life, pray you keep clear of all these utilities. A hard fate thrusts them upon some of our fellow-mortals; but Heaven has mercifully exempted you, and has given you, moreover, a rare advantage by endowing you with a brilliant inaptitude for every thing useful. Any body can do every thing; but for doing nothing, and doing it with ingenuity, I don't know your equal. The consequence is that you are, if not always an agreeable, at least an available companion. One is sure of you. But go and waste your substance in riotous living under Professor Blot's management, and the spell is broken. You will be forever having an eye on the larder. You will be greedy of receipts, and, instead of eating your meat with gladness and singleness of heart, you will be fretting about the way it is cooked. For Heaven's sake, my dear, spare my old age this pang, and let us trust to Providence for the few years that remain."

Providence has done well by us, it must be confessed. When we set up housekeeping we did it under the auspices of a sweet, gentle, innocent widow just out of the House of Correction, who recorded her vow that she never would drink again, and in a spasm of benevolence we took her in. Unfortunately, we soon began to suspect that her resolution was more comprehensive than at first appeared. She had apparently resolved not only that she would never drink again, but that she would never eat, nor be the cause of eating in others. Her supplies were of the scantiest. The whole house had a gaunt look. Even the cat moaned in her sleep. Our pretty widow was gentle. She was sweet. She was sensitive. But we were starving, and she had to go.

Next came Miss Gilbert's career. Miss Gilbert was profoundly respectable and highly recommended; but wages were not her object so much as a situation in a pious family. I would have preferred to pay wages. Unhappily, piety never was the strong point in our family. I was not uneasy about myself, but I felt that I could not answer for my friend. He maintains that if a man is just, cheerful, helpful, and good-tempered, his fellow-man has no right to demand any further proof of his religion. All the rest lies between the soul and its Maker. He thinks that while promiscuous religious talk is not absolutely incompatible with religion, it is a strong indication of its presence in microscopic proportions, if not its entire absence, and that exactly in correspondence with the depths of one's inner experience is reluctance to display it indiscriminately. I need not say that in these extraordinary whims he receives no countenance from me. So far as talking is a test of piety, I trust I shall never be found wanting. On the strength of my virtue, I ventured to introduce Miss Gilbert upon the scene. She was a stirring, energetic woman, and what is called in some quarters an active Christian, and we could make but little headway against her. The momentum with which she went to evening meetings was appalling. We creep out to evening meetings ourselves sometimes after a modest sort, but with her it was a crusade. The thaws of the opening spring working on country roads had no terror for her. The deeper the mire, the hotter her zeal. She seemed to think there was a virtue in floundering through these sloughs of despond. The sprinklings and splashings of mud stood her for a sort of baptismal regeneration. She made no scruple of letting us know that she considered us cold and dead, ecclesiastically speaking. In fact, her piety was so highly flavored that I thought Hassan would have stoned her, and I bowed her out of the house. She was an excellent woman, and we would contribute liberally toward sending her on a mission to the Cannibal Islands.

Norah appeared next—happy Norah—who came confidently asserting that she could do all sorts of work. Could she cook? No. That was one accomplishment she missed, but she could do every thing else; and cooking—she pronounced the *oo* like *oo* in boot—coooooking she could learn. Norah's crowning fault—and faults she had like Caroline Helstone's curls, in picturesque profusion—but her masterpiece was ingenuity; a too vivid imagination. She improvised blunders with far more ease and rapidity than we could counteract them. We tried to head her off, as farmers say of their cattle; to let conjecture run on before, and ascertain and prevent the mischief she would determine, but to no purpose. Her fertile brain outstripped us all. Who can keep pace with a mind that douses the spider, crock and all, into the dish-water every time it is to be washed? Farewell, Norah! Fare well if you can, oh families who in all coming time shall give your household gods into her keeping! credulous families who open your hearts to her latest declaration that she is a good plain cook! A fine girl was Norah, red-cheeked, brawny-armed, never sulky, with a shoulder for every wheel, but inscrutable in all her ways.

How shall I speak of Rushy—Rushy the imperturbable; the innocent child who came to us in tatters; a little neglected waif, receiving every fate with a sublime serenity that might have sprung from fortitude or from insensibility. She never told her love or hate, but took praise or censure with equal immobility, smiling as brightly and chatting as briskly after the one as after the other. She was formed for literature and society. Her mind was superficial and untrained, but active and intense. She fastened upon novels, newspapers, magazines, and memoirs with the avidity of famine. She waited at table *arrectis auribus*. She complimented the entertaining guest by pausing midway between table and door, dish in hand, head turned, mouth open, eyes fixed upon him, unable to leave the room till she had heard his sentence out. She washed dishes with a slow circular sweep, her face over her shoulder to catch every movement going on outside. And, notwithstanding her leisurely motion, she touched nothing which she did not tear. Her own dress was a curious freak of cohesion. The skirt was ripped till it hung in festoons from the waist; and we amused ourselves by computing the number of miles of torn cloth that would be amassed by one who should collect her rents. But she, in her great content, never seemed conscious that her gown was torn, and when the fact was forced upon her from without, she darned, and patched, and botched after a random zigzag sort exquisitely painful to the average New England mind. She washed floors to some merry mental tune that sent the soap-suds dancing up the mop-board and the wall-paper in the liveliest manner imaginable. She leaned out of the window with the utmost nonchalance at important culinary crises, balancing herself on the sill, and accosting the boys of her acquaintance with unaffected candor and simple good-will. We loved Rushy. As a study, she was invaluable. In good nature, she was inexhaustible. Alas! so were not her employers, and we parted.

Through friendly intervention succeeded then a brief interregnum, during which we had recourse to advertisements —not making, but answering them. Ever before our eyes flitted some ideal Scotch, German, or English girl, faithful, friendly, efficient; such a servant as one so often meets in stories of English country houses; but they never appeared in the advertising columns. Each morning, as we opened the daily paper, hope sprang eternal in the human breast, but only to spring back again. There was no lack of women—middle-aged women, widows of twenty-five, twenty-eight, thirty; young widows, ladies of refinement, ladies of culture, ladies who wanted situations in a small family; housekeepers, to whom a good home was more an object than high wages—but they were sure to end with the fatal words, "Widower preferred." Fatal to us, for neither my friend nor myself was a widower, and we knew no legal way of becoming so. It was one of those arbitrary and unjust disqualifications which, like sex or color in the question of suffrage, no merit can remove. Remonstrance was useless; remedy there was none; what could we do in a market where the demand for widowers was always brisk? I asked my friend why he supposed that class of employers was so attractive. He replied that it was probably owing to the combined influence of lovely woman and grief. Man in his native state, he observed, was a wild animal. Lassoed, tamed, and trained by his wife, he became a useful domestic beast, but at the cost of his trainer, who sank under the arduousness of the task. Grief for her loss still farther subdued and chastened him, rendering the soil, as it were, mellow, and fit for cultivation; so that a man who had loved and lost was more malleable—to change the figure again—than he who had never loved at all.

Very just reasoning, I admitted; and added farther that in him who had loved and lost was this advantage over him who had loved and not lost. She who goes to the latter finds another woman in the case. This woman, this living wife, while she does not make the pies, is yet constantly putting a finger in them, which is worse. And a man is a great deal easier for a housekeeper to get on with than a woman. He has not eyes for every crumb on the carpet, every roll of lint under the stove, every layer of dust behind the sofa, every stain on the spoons, every waste in the pantry. He never knows exactly how far a cup of sugar will go, or how much twelve and a half cents will buy. If he is only fed and starched in a general way, he never suspects any thing is the matter. Yes, I do not wonder that widowers are preferred. I should prefer them myself.

Still we went on wildly answering advertisements, stating our requirements and appliances in such terms as might seem seducing to the advertising mind, till I think there can hardly be a corner of this great republic to which our household belongings (so many stories, so many rooms, furnace in the cellar, chimney that does not smoke, sunshine in the kitchen all day, pump in the sink, six hens and a cat—I know it like the multiplication table) have not penetrated. But to no purpose. Once we thought we had caught her. A woman appeared without any patent predilections for widowers. We sent our six hens and a cat after her by the next mail. We never heard from them again; but on the following day the advertisement appeared with the appended condition that she wished a situation in a genteel family! This was the most unkindest cut of all, and we ceased to haunt the journals.

For we went into the kitchen ourselves. I say *we*, for my friend had small faith in my unassisted reason. I would have preferred to be alone. When you are trying experiments, or meditating doubtful devices, or balancing between opposing systems, few things are more disturbing than a bystander, an over-see-er. I would have liked to order him out of the kitchen; but he had so much at stake in the result, and I knew so little of the processes, that the measure seemed hardly justifiable. It promised to be, on the whole, more satisfactory to give him a retainer, as you might say, and take it out in having him handy to lay the blame of the failures on, particularly as he was enjoying a short space of leisure, and it would not be possible to keep him off.

Should any person read this on whose hands time hangs heavily, who seems to himself to have exhausted the resources of interest, let me respectfully invite him to repair to his own kitchen, and attempt, as our late beloved President used to say, to run the machine. He will, as the poet sings, feel himself new-born. He is the centre of a new order of things. Bread and beef, which have always been to him a momentary and disconnected fact, suddenly take on a history that stretches back into a remote and thrilling past. The savory steak of the breakfast-table, which he was wont to consider a self-evident proposition, represents only the last step of a long process of thought, is the crowning close of a series of scientific experiments. At the same time, nothing more forcibly strikes the contemplative mind than the uncertainties of the kitchen. You are constantly surprised to learn, from painful observation, that like causes do not produce like results. Mathematics and chemistry are fallacious. I remembered some delicious rye muffins I had once eaten in a friend's house. I sent for the receipt. I followed it—one pint of sour milk, one pint of rye flour, eggs, and such things. What happened? Plump, light puffs of muffins such as I had eaten in a foreign clime? No. A panful of little, flat, wrinkled, shrunken, and still shrinking dabs, which, on opening, proved to have been transmuted into rye hasty-pudding. Withered old crones without, molten lava within. I scalded my mouth trying to swallow one or two of the worst ones out of the way before my friend came down. There were some pretty bad ones left. Hassan is a good-natured creature, and he grappled with them manfully, but he did not seem to make much impression on the plateful. I told him I was sure he could eat more if he would give his mind to it—just set up a little resolution ; but he said he had made a remarkably good dinner at the Farmer's Club the week before, and really was not hungry. Afterward I recollected that I had left out the eggs; but it would have made no difference if I had put them in. There needs something more than eggs to heal the breach between a muffin and a volcano. Drop-cakes were next tried. Drop-cakes are a household word in our clan. The memory of the oldest inhabitant does not go back to a time when drop-cakes were not a familiar friend, and I knew all about them —molasses, and rye meal, and flour, and so forth, and dip your hands in warm water before you make it up into cakes. I did every thing precisely in the appointed way, and the mess runs through your fingers faster than you can take it up. Unstable as water. I stood in despair contemplating my ten outstretched fingers, daubed and draped with embryo drop-cake, and looking for all the world like web-feet. "Spoon it out," said Hassan, laconically ; and I spooned it into the pan, making a collective noun of it instead of the regular plural, which was its legitimate character. After ten minutes in the oven, it had not changed a shade. I attempted to turn it, in order to get it into a hotter part of the oven, and perhaps I tipped it the least in life, as the best of cooks might, when out flopped near half of it, rolling down the stove to the floor. Hassan brightened up visibly, and said it was rightly named ; there would be plenty of it left. When we came to eat it we found there was. Perhaps I had forgotten the proportions, but the ingredients were correct. Determining to remember both next time, I studied the receipt for Indian cake till I had learned it by heart. It colored my dreams. I used to wake up in the night repeating it—one cup of flour, two cups of Indian meal, four table-spoonfuls of cream, one table-spoonful of sugar, four table-spoonfuls of flour, two cups of cream, one cup of flour, and forth came a flat, rough, unrisen cake, cracked in every direction, and ridged, and hard—it was like eating raw corn.

"Suppose we forswear these side-issues, and try regular bread," said my friend.

But we were no better off. We had a written receipt, word for word. Every thing was timed and measured with astronomical exactness. Begin at noon with yeast and water. Then yeast, and flour, and water, and rise till night. Then more flour and water, and rise till morning. Then knead and bake. This in general; but the particulars filled three pages of a sheet, which I pinned to the kitchen clock above the kitchen table, and prepared to follow slavishly. I did follow slavishly till the ingredients balked. The very first installment of flour and water refused to rise. Night set in on a contumacious sponge that was not all a sponge. Perhaps it had risen the thousandth part of an inch. No one could affirm it had risen at all. It looked a little scaly at the top, and that was the sole sign of activity. It stood till morning. Still it groveled. We both eyed it in silence; I stuck a knife in. The flour seemed to have settled, and there was a layer of water above it.

"That, I take it," said my friend, "is a very good illustration of the figure which our earth made before the third day —before the waters under the heaven were gathered together into one place, and the dry land appeared. Life is only a wheel within a wheel. Every macrocosm has its microcosm."

I was very sure, I said, that there was such a thing as bread griddle-cakes.

"What man has done man may do," he rejoined, solemnly. "If you can make griddle-cakes out of that muddle, you had better do it at once, for nothing short of divine decrees could evolve bread."

"I wonder how griddle-cakes are made," I half soliloquized.

"With yeast-cakes that will not up."
"But how to cook them? They are not baked, I imagine. Exactly."
"Humanly speaking, they must be cooked on a gridiron."
"Grid-griddle-cakes. Gridiron. Yes, if there is any thing in etymology."

The gridiron always hung by the stove. I took it down and surveyed it.

"What is going to prevent the dough from dropping through the bars?"

"What prevents the flame from getting through the wire netting of Sir Humphry Davy's safety-lamp?"

"The interstices are very much smaller than these."

"So are the particles of flame very much smaller than those of dough. Here is the formula. As fire is to unleavened bread, so is Sir Humphry's lamp to a gridiron. Let us have it mathematically," and he whipped out pencil and paper.

"Fire : W. B. : : S. L. : Grid. There. What can one ask more in a world of uncertainty?"

"My dear, Euclid himself would never convince me that a griddle-cake could be baked on a gridiron. You run up stairs and bring me down the Unabridged. A sudden heat might form a sudden crust, but nothing can prevent the surface from being ridged, since it would not reach the heat till it had fallen through on the stove ; and if it were ridged, it would be a waffle, and no griddle-cake."

"Gridī-ron (i-run)," he came down reading from the big dictionary in his hands, "[W. *greidiaw;* It. *greadaim*, to heat, scorch (just as I said, my dear), roast, and *iron*. See Griddle.]"

"There! now *see* griddle."

"Griddle. Griddle—oh! yes. Griddle is the fellow. W. *greidell*, from *greidiaw*, to heat, singe, scorch. A pan, broad and shallow, for baking cakes. So much for going to head-quarters."

"Oh! and a handle to it. I have seen it dozens of times, only I did not know it was a griddle. Now, where have I seen it? We must just hunt it up, and the problem is solved."

But it was no easy matter to hunt it up. I looked every where I could think of. So did my friend; but as he only looked where I had gone before, he did not forward matters much.

"Now," said the calmer of the two, at length, sitting down with a philosophical air that was akin to despair, "what is the use of going about in this random sort of way? When Leverrier had a planet to discover, he did not jerk his telescope all over the sky at once. He calculated where it ought to be, and then found it quietly."

"Certainly," said my friend; "let us evolve from our moral consciousness the natural habitat of griddles, and then push our researches in that field. To begin by exclusion, it would not be in the china-closet?"

But just then I happened to catch sight of it on the nail where I suppose it had hung for generations, and we made the griddle-cakes. I draw a curtain over the scene that followed.

"I am afraid," says Hassan, carelessly fingering my papers, "that you are putting too fine a point on it. You will be considered as drawing a long bow. No one will think it possible for a New Englander to attain to this state of heathen ignorance even by trying."

"I am glad of it," I answered. "We hear of people who have so strong a love for falsehood that they would rather lie on a twelve-months' note than tell the truth for cash, and I suppose you think I shall come into that class. But, on the contrary, it only shows that one may know so much that he will not be believed even when he confesses ignorance. See the virtue of a good reputation!"

Women, so far as they have come under my observation, have little skill in teaching the art of cooking, even when they can practice it with very admirable results. Their directions are confused and contradictory, vague and inadequate. They begin, perhaps, intelligibly enough, but at the critical point you put a vital question, and are told, "Oh! you must go by your own judgment." They apparently do not know, or do not remember, that judgment is the result of knowledge, and that the very reason why you have recourse to them is that you have no judgment to go by. Or they will give you a detailed and elaborate receipt, which you painfully transfer to your note-book, and are smitten with consternation and despair by the closing remark, uttered as coolly as if it did not deal the death-blow to your hopes, "But, after all, every thing depends on the bake!"

To be sure, the inexperienced craft generally strikes a snag before reaching the baking point; but of what avail, I ask, is the nice selection of ingredients, and the nice adjustment of quantities, if selection and adjustment are alike liable at the last moment to be baffled by the "bake?" All the juice has oozed out of your mince-pies, giving you a kitchen odorous of spices, but leaving you only the ghost of your Thanksgiving pies, because you had "too quick an oven;" while your sponge-cake hollows itself into an ocean-bed of heaviness because you had "too slow an oven." But how can you stay in an oven long enough to find out whether it be quick or slow; and who shall draw the line between quickness and slowness? You presently learn the existence of the difference, for the quick oven scorches and spoils its prey, and the slow oven depresses and demoralizes it; but the knowledge comes too late, and wisdom lingers. Why do we not have thermometers connected with our ovens, and reduce a snap judgment to a mathematical certainty?

Let me put forth suggestions with caution, for our own stove is a victim to misdirected ingenuity. The damper stuck a little, and my friend Hassan, who believes nothing human to be foreign to himself, worked upon it till it stuck fast, and we had to take out the funnel whenever we wished to turn the damper—which was not a modern improvement. Then the blacksmith came and mended it; but Hassan could not let well enough alone. I heard a clanking of chains one morning, as if Sing Sing had been let loose upon us. It was Hassan leading in a man with a string of dampers on his arm—a new invention; something that was to diffuse the airs of Paradise through the whole house. The stove drew perfectly at the time. It had a damper simple of construction and manageable by a child, but because, far back in the pluperfect tense, there had been a slight impediment in its speech, this elaborate machine was to be introduced into our artless old funnel. Wondrous feats were promised. It was going to send the flame here and the smoke there, the heat round a corner, and the smells up chimney. It was put in, and would, I dare say, have been harmless enough, if it could have been let alone; but an ingenious hand was constantly twiddling it, by way of experiment, and filling the room with smoke. One day, when I had the field to myself, I hired the blacksmith to take out the damper, leaving the handle in. It answered admirably. My friend twiddled on, amusing himself, and inconveniencing no one.

II.
THE STATE OF [FRENCH] GRACE.

It was at this epoch that Professor Blot came over the horizon. I caught at him with the gasp and grasp of the drowning. Hassan, as I have said, at first violently opposed any recourse to him; but, supported by a firm faith in my inherent and inalienable incapacity, he presently withdrew his opposition. In fact, after a while, he rather encouraged the Blot scheme, seeming to think the addition of a French element to native inaptitude would lend it a piquancy which it had hitherto lacked.

So all in the pleasant summer weather I went to town to hear Professor Blot. The neighborhood took kindly to the adventure, though evidently mistrustful of this armed intervention from a foreigner. Every face that saw me go by wreathed itself in smiles; yet in the calm still hour, by the moon's pale beams, I sometimes question whether they were not in part smiles of incredulity. "Want to learn how to make one more puddin'!" said my friend the forester, meeting me on my winding way.

"Can this Blot fellow tell us how to get somethin' to cook? that's the point," asked my friend the captain; but that was not my affair. I assisted at the lectures with notebook and spoon, according to directions. I looked, and listened, and tasted. It was marvelous. Every thing happened. Nothing failed. Nothing went uncooked. Nothing collapsed. Nobody was anxious. It was that plump, *jolie* French cook. She gave a caressing pat, a dextrous dab, a spirited stir, and every atom melted into its place and became a viand. Some of us loftily sheathed ourselves in nonchalance, and tasted with a nil-admirari air. Should a haughty world suppose that we had not as good things every day at home? Others of us were crushed to the dust, and admired indiscriminately. A woman at my elbow went into raptures over the joint which there had not been time completely to roast.

"Ugh!" said the professor, shrugging his shoulders in disgust; "that ees not half done!" I was vexed that she should have made such a display of American ignorance to a foreigner, though I should not myself have known it was underdone if he had not said so; and I, on the principle that a fault confessed is half atoned for, remarked, deprecatingly, "Alas! we are such barbarians in this country that we don't know when our food is cooked and when it isn't."

"Alas, mees," responded the unhappy professor, "that ees too true."

I did not expect so ready and unqualified an assent.

One could but pity the man who had not only to teach, but create a public opinion to receive his teachings; who had not only to concoct his viands, but to train our palates to appreciate them. I concealed my ignorance as carefully as possible; but it is useless to deny that to backwoods eyes and ears, not to say nose and mouth, some of his modes and results were at least uncommon. I copied with exemplary docility directions to pour white wine on chicken, but I saw in my mind's eye the demure gravity with which my neighbors would receive such an announcement. Unresistingly I chopped up mushrooms with every other dish; but I thought of my friend the forester swinging his axe on the strength of the toad-stools he had eaten, and I fancied that even Hassan would suspend, *naso adunco*, that little bunch of see-sawn-ing which seemed to pepper every dish. But I yielded to no misgivings, and carried home my notebook in triumph at the close of the lectures. My friend displayed a languid curiosity as to my opinion. I told him I thought Professor Blot was a good cook, but that he did not understand French. At least his pronunciation was different from that to which I had been accustomed. He asked me if I had possessed myself of the general principles of cooking. I said I thought I had. He begged me to repeat them. I replied that the fundamental requisite to good cooking was a French cook. He said the knowledge of that fact alone was worth the whole price of the lectures. "Go on." I added, "*Si monumentum quæris, in spice,*" and handed him my note-book. He slowly turned the leaves, held the book right side up, wrong side up, and diagonally in succession, and asked where it began. I answered, on a venture, that it began at the beginning, of course. He said a man would have to stand inside a mill-wheel in motion to read it. I was obliged to admit that it did need an editor. There was a great quantity of valuable material in an undigested state, with an inexhaustible amount of bay leaf and garlic scattered through it.

"It begins at the beginning, does it?" said my friend. "Let us, then, begin there." And he fastened upon the inside of the first cover, and read, in a monotonous, inexpressive, unintelligent tone,

"'Bay leaf at druggist's.

"'Every dish look at once in a while to see how it goes.

"'Chicken when one horn—'"

"It is not horn," I interrupted.

"What is it, then?" passing me the book.

"It looks like a horn," I said, after a silent contemplation, "but it must mean hour."

He read on :

"'Two stalks parsley half onion—

"'Stuck in it.

"'One or two cloves half bay leaf—

'Skim it.' Skim what?
"'Half tea-spoonful butter h—ty [Humpty-dumpty—I could make nothing of it myself]—flour mix together a little juice and stir to melt and mix—take off onion cloves and bay leaf—odd mixture.' I should think it was!"
"*Add* mixture!" I explained.
"Add what mixture?"
"Why, the mixture you have just been making!"
"Add it to what?"
"To the mixture you had been making before you began this. Why, the chicken!"
"'Little lemon-juice—shake.
"'One yolk with—no, into—beaten—into bestow—into vesture—' What is that word?"
I studied it attentively, but was unable to decipher it.
"Never mind," I said; "go on."
"Your chicken seems to have come to an end, my dear."
"Oh no; there must be more. He can't end in that yolk."
"No; he more naturally begins there. Still, if I were called upon to pronounce an opinion on this particular chicken, I should say that by the time he reached this stage he was no chicken!"
In hot pursuit of the missing chicken we turned page after page, but the only vestige of his creation was an entry of—

Then Sputters { Fricassee chicken entrée.
Wash—put in toast-pan—just cover with cold water
salt cover the pan.

This certainly was not the original fowl, but a distinct and subsequent individual, while the cabalistic marginal note was quite unintelligible. There was nothing for it but to take high moral ground at once, and assume that the chicken was off the stage before the yolk was brought on. That egg was broken into some other dish.

"Yes," Hassan said; "that last shake probably finished him prematurely. What next?"

"To explain precisely how this hop, skip, and jump came about. In the beginning, Professor Blot wrote the whole dinner on the blackboard. Then he cooked it on the range. We had consequently to make history and to write history at one and the same moment, and were constantly darting from point to point. When it was time to put salt in the pudding he made a note of it; and immediately there was a bay leaf to be stuck in an onion, and we turned the page and made a note of that. Then, before you had fairly seen how a bay leaf would look in an onion, you were directed to put butter in the pudding; so you dropped your bay leaf, and turned back to the pudding again. Thus you were kept ever on the stretch. Is it any wonder if you sometimes flavored the pudding-sauce with parsley, or scattered sugar on the roast? It is certainly some such mistake which sent that yolk on its wanderings. Find now a definite programme for a regular dinner. There are plenty of them. Here is one that looks systematic. Read that straight through."

"'Riz au lait.

"'Fish caper sauce.

"'Beef piquante sauce.

"'Croquettes.' (A game dinner certainly.)

"'Potatoes à la Française.

"'Plat au beurre.

"'Petites bouchées à la crême.

"'Pie.' (How that one little English word shines among all these foreign folk, like a good deed in a naughty world!)

"'Crême pâtissière.' Is that all?"

"Now you will find a page devoted to each one of these dishes. Somewhere. You must look till you find it."

"Sure enough. Here is—

"'Fish caper sauce.'

"Let us see, said the blind man.

"'Set on fire just cover with water—always put a table-s vinegar to a pound of (boil) fish—salt caper sauce—½ table-s butter—same flour—1 gill warm water on fire—stir salt and pepper to taste—a little water in which fish has cooked—caper in sauce just before serving.'

"That is certainly very direct and intelligible. I like that—especially capering in the sauce. It reminds one of bucolics: and in the vats of Luna this year the must shall foam round the white feet of laughing girls. A New England housewife dancing in the fish-sauce must make a sauce piquante.

"'Potatoes entremet à la Française fillets.' What is fillets?"

"Fillets? Curl-papers? It has a familiar sound, but I do not at this moment recall its kitchen range."

"Potatoes in curl-papers. They must be lady-fingers."

"There was something in curl-papers, if it was not potatoes. I think it was mutton-chops. Read on. Perhaps the sequel will show."

"Here, again, we seem to come to an untimely end."

I instituted a personal investigation, but could discover no clew. The thread was broken off short.

"When I was in the middle of one of the most interesting dishes—"

"Then the sauce was not the only thing you capered in!"

"While I was lost in contemplation of the simmering and steaming, I suddenly awoke to the fact that a caterpillar was creeping over my dress. I struck him off with my note-book into the aisle, but with unparalleled resolution he kept constantly heading my way, so that I was forced to divide my already overstrained attention between the cooking and the caterpillar, and had no sooner jotted down one item than I dropped pencil, took up parasol, and poked back caterpillar. I assure you the intense mental effort gave me a headache. Those unfinished potatoes mark the spot where that caterpillar thrust his head in. Every gap you may fill up with caterpillar."

"Charge the deficit, then, to him. Here is a page of what seem to be general directions:

"'Never use soda sal c of t c pepper (here) parsley for fish and chicken.

"'Plants easily grown.

"'Veal must be overdone.

"'Broth—stir again—spoonful of gravy.

"'All kinds of fat strain—

"'And put in stone jars.'

"This is somewhat unintelligible to me, but I suppose you understand it?"

"Y-e-s. But here is a long, fair page, that looks as if it would run smooth. 'Broth!' That is an important matter. Professor Blot puts broth into every thing."

"'Three lbs. lean beef—must be fresh never more than 2 oz. bones with lb. meat—no bones best put it in soup-kettle or sauce-pan—'"

I could not help interrupting the reading to announce a discovery. There is a species of large dipper in family use. We always called it Ursa Major. It was interesting to learn from Professor Blot that it was a sauce-pan. One is familiar with sauce-pans in literature, but it is delightful to know that one has a personal acquaintance with them. *Ah! la belle chose que de savoir quelque chose!*

But when I defended from the dictionary, which is one of our most important kitchen utensils, my life-long impression that all pans were milk-pans, broad and shallow, and that nothing with a handle could properly be called a pan, Hassan immediately quoted warming-pans and the Panhandle of geography against me!

"Go on," I said, seeing he was disposed to trifle.

"'Cover with 3 qts. cold water—set on good fire in about ½ hour boil—then remove kettle don't boil much—skim scum.' (That apt alliteration's artful aid reminds me of a Magazine story named 'Snip Snap.') 'If it has boiled unaware gill cold water and skin ½ middle-sized carrot ½ as much turnip 1 leek small onion with 2 cloves stuck in it 2 stalks parsley 1 celery 1 bay leaf salt and pepper keep simming—'"

"Simmering," I corrected under my breath, too much pleased at so long a run of smooth sailing to break it for any slight deviation.

"'For 5 hours—no boil for rich broth have 2 qts. water poor 2 qts.'"

"You have not read that right. It can not be two quarts for both rich broth and poor."

"Look before you leap to such a conclusion."

"It was the caterpillar," I said, after a prolonged examination.

"That is the most responsible caterpillar that ever crawled. Well—

"'Two qts. water—no fat—no bones must be clean.' How is that?"

"My dear, you punctuate with your elbows."

"My dear, I follow your punctuation to the letter, to the smallest Abyssinian quirk."

"But can you not see that, weary and worn, not to say saturated and suffocated with savors, one's brain might become a little muddled; and can not you bring your reason to the aid of your eyes; and does it not stand to reason that bones must be clean for soup, and that there must not be any bones?"

"Nothing easier. Hereafter, then, I follow my unassisted reason in punctuating your bones.

" 'Take off meat—put bottom paste for pie 4 oz. flour and knead with 2 oz. butter—knead—' "

"You are surely off the track again."

"Not in the least."

"Is there no dividing-line?"

"If there is, it is equatorial and invisible."

"But do you not see that you have suddenly emerged from the broth, and fallen plump into a pan of pastry?"

"There is no way," he replied, slowly turning the leaves, and looking up and down the pages with great solemnity—"there is no way out of that broth *except* plumping into the flour and butter."

Alas! it was, as Professor Blot remarked, "too true." After "put" came "bottom paste;" and the page went on from bad to worse in this random fashion:

"In crockery—

"Longer it keeps, always put—

"The quicker you cool it the—

"Then strain the broth and done."

Hassan suggested that it might be read like Hebrew, from right to left. He builded better than he knew, for by reading it from bottom to top it was easy to unearth the meaning. Some sudden emergency had deranged the ordinary stratification, and interjected the trap rock of the pastry-pan. Farther explanation it was impossible to give. However, the broth was done. There was comfort in that.

Similarly it seemed as if a blight had fallen on all my receipts. Professor Blot had cooked them through before my very eyes, and I had watched them with an intelligent interest, and transferred them to my note-book with conscientious fidelity; but the trail of the serpent was over them all. A hiatus, a disjointure, a confusion was sure to develop itself at the vital points, and destroy the value of the whole. And by as much as the important circumstance was left out, the unimportant one was sure to be in. The particular ingredient necessary to round and perfect a dish was not to be found; but in letters of living light was sure to appear the warning that roast beef and stuffed turkey must not be served together! As if people with our income were in the least danger of suffering from a conjunction of roast beef and stuffed turkey!

"But you may have it à la mode," added the notes, with grim sarcasm.

"Soup," prescribes the same discriminating monitor, giving a bill of fare for a dinner—

"Soup.

"Radishes, sardines, melons, hors d'œuvres.

"Fish on one end.

"Butcher's meat, chicken and game.

"Purée, with meat or fish.

"Vegetables.

"Dessert (cheese first)."

An unexceptionable dinner, no doubt, if one could command it. But what, save total depravity, could account for the careful record of all these luxuries, and a total failure to secure the simplest directions for the preparation of a single dish?

Were Professor Blot's lectures, then, a failure? As the wise do not need them, if the ignorant can not assimilate them, of what avail are they? Of the greatest in the world. Their moral uses are incalculable. They relieve your imagination. They give you a certain confidence, an acquaintance with modes of operation, a positive and comforting assurance that causes will produce effects. It *is* possible—your own eyes bear you witness—for meats and vegetables, fishes and puddings, to glide along parallel lines harmoniously and majestically to the table. A raw, red joint goes into the oven; a crisp, delicate roast comes out.

"You might see the same thing at home," suggests the practical mind. But you do *not* see the same thing at home. Nothing lures you to the sight. Very likely the sight is not there, and if it be, you do not care to see it. You might assiduously frequent twenty kitchens without being sure that you were not learning what a truer knowledge of the mysterious art will force you to unlearn. But good company, novelty, immunity from grease-spots and burns, and, best of all, a perfect confidence in the source of knowledge, make these lectures both entertaining and instructive. You leave them feeling that if you should ever be obliged to fight it out on that line, you will know how to sight your guns; and this, of itself, is no small part of the battle. Your ideal has a shape, your ambition a goal. You are not necessarily master of arts, but you know in what direction to advance in order to become one. Moreover, the processes are carried on so neatly and sweetly that, you may say, children cry for them. And this is a benefit whose value is not to be spoken. Cooking wears so winning an air, it opens a field for so much skill, it displays results so agreeable, that your old repugnance changes unawares into interest, into admiration, into impatience, and you burn to shoulder your crutch and show how fields are won.

For example:

It is a very simple thing to break an egg. He who has enthusiastically climbed up hay-mows, and across the great beam, to rifle hens' nests, and come down with half a dozen eggs in his pockets, and then forgotten them—he knows, to his consternation, how easy it is to break an egg. But to break it over the cake-pan, to break it in a regular equatorial line, without shattering the shell, and scattering the bits in the sugar, or daubing your fingers with the stringy white, is quite another thing. Of what nature, then, must be that task which the cookery-books assign when, piling Ossa on

Pelion, they bid you beat the yolks and whites separately? It is like those sarcastic receipts for making hare-soup—first catch your hare; or for capturing birds—put salt on their tails. You can beat the yolks and the whites well enough when they are once apart, but how separate two fluids inseparably mixed? Who shall say to the white, "Come forth!" and to the yolk, "Keep back!" Who does not know that by the laws of matter, when the shell is broken, the two fluids come gulping out together? No. Whenever a receipt talks in that wild way, the only resource for weak human nature is to follow the example of the Scotch divine in the presence of a scriptural difficulty—"Look it square in the face and pass on."

But French skill laughs at human nature, and is a match for universal law. That round-cheeked cook solved the insoluble. With one white arm-sweep, like Juno on Ida—say rather by one little peck outside, such as the future chick would have made within, could he have been spared till his set time was come—she smote the shell into two little cups, and, by pouring the yolk back and forth, divided as deftly the yellow gold from the liquid crystal as the blue sea stands divided from the burning beach. Of course, now you have seen it done, you want to do it yourself. But be not rash. Seeing is believing, but it is not doing. Shall I ever forget how she snatched the whites from the Celtic scullion who, at her directions, was beating them, but with that slow, awkward, uncertain movement which belongs to the natural man; and how, with a preternatural swiftness not devoid of grace, and dazzling to the naked eye, she whipped them into a froth and foam, into a sea of lightness and whiteness, or ever the surprised blood had faded from the Celtic cheek?

So, though possibility is far remote from accomplishment, Professor Blot seemed to throw a new light into the kitchen, or, leaving out the adjective, he threw light upon the darkness hitherto visible. "All hope abandon, ye who enter here," had appeared to me as fit a motto for the kitchen door as for the one over which it was originally inscribed; but when I next passed into that loveless realm it was with an enthusiasm and a buoyancy which had hitherto been a stranger there. I was determined no more to creep timidly along the coast, as in the days of my ignorance. Professor Blot was a mariner's compass, in the confidence engendered of which one could strike out boldly into the open sea.

"No more pottering with drop-cakes and rye muffins," I said. "Professor Blot washed his hands of all such trivialities. I shall plunge at once into the middle of things. I shall undertake that most formidable of feats, 'a regular dinner.' Roast beef and plum-pudding.

"'He either fears his fate too much,
Or his deserts are small,
That dares not put it to the touch
To win or lose it all.'"

"If my desserts were all that will be small," said my friend, "I think I should be able to meet my fate undaunted!"

Professor Blot's cook had a scullion. I appointed my friend my scullion. He stipulated for a salary. I refused it, and offered wages small but sufficient, and capable of indefinite enlargement according to increase of services. He was accessible in point of price, but impregnable in point of technicalities. What objection had I to a *salary?*

It was too fine for the thing.

Not at all. It was peculiarly appropriate. Salary, sal, salt, salt-money—money given you to buy your salt—your necessary outlay; thence money for your services. What more fit than that money awarded you for kitchen-service should be salary—salt-money?

What's in a name? "Sal, salt, salt-money," I said, "for him who just earns his salt." He made a brilliant scullion.

I stationed him at the end of the table, intrenched behind the cookery-books for purposes of reference, if memory or judgment should fail me. We had an ample library of this entertaining literature; for, whenever there was an interregnum in our culinary kingdom, and it became necessary for me to make a descent into the kitchen, I always signalized my advent by the purchase of a new cookery-book. To these must be added, in the present exigency, the undigested mass of the notes of Professor Blot's lectures.

The experiment of the dinner was completely successful, thanks to French tact and mother-wit. The beef stopped at the precise point where continuance would have changed completeness into superfluity. I do not mean to say that there were no false steps. I do not mean to say that it was an easy matter to get the dripping-pan out of the oven and upon the table without spilling liquor or burning fingers. I do not mean to say that when I would fain have turned the meat over in the pan it did not slip from my hands and splash the fat on my face and dress; nor that, when I would have basted it, the fat did not have a way of running outside the pan instead of inside. "Basting it!" said my scullion; "you mean bathing it."

"Not at all. Who ever heard of meat being bathed? The original cow might be bathed; but when the cow has been reconstructed into roast beef, we baste her."

"When a cow has been reconstructed into leather she may possibly be basted with a waxed end, but to drench her with hot fat is a new use for a sewing-machine."

"There is no good in talking. I know it by mnemonics. When Professor Blot spoke of it, I connected it at once with basting a hem."

"And is there the smallest resemblance between basting a hem and basting a joint?"

"No; that is why I remembered it."

"Very convincing. It must be basting, because it is exactly the opposite of basting. Like the village of Gilmanton Iron-works, so called, according to living tradition, because there are no iron-works there."

"But, my dear, get the best—get Webster's, and see."

"Why have recourse to fallible man, when the light of unassisted reason is sufficient? You admit that your word in no sense represents the process. How with my word? You pour the hot fat over the meat. It is a bath. And what, pray, is the name of this receptacle?"

"The dripping-pan, you mean?"

"Why dripping-pan, if not because the liquid drops into it—the liquid left of the bath? What are the remnants of basting? Bits of thread. Your dripping-pan, then, ought to be called a rag-bag. Your own words condemn you. Philology is a swift witness against you. Discussion is fruitless. If you have bathed your meat enough, perhaps you are ready to return it to the oven."

"Quite. Open the door. I think it is thoroughly basted."

I have said that Hassan was a brilliant scullion. He was too brilliant. I often sighed for a little silent stupidity. We read of the advantage of skilled over unskilled labor, and the benefits to be derived from the universal dissemination of letters. I should be sorry to be even remotely instrumental in putting back the hand on the dial-plate of progress; but if there is any thing out of place, impertinent, and, as housekeepers say, "trying," it is erudition in the kitchen. Philology is a good thing; but of what temper must that mortal be made who can patiently bide a philological dispute over a half-cooked joint with the clock galloping steadfastly toward the dinner hour? What you want in the kitchen—in fact, what you want in all manner of service, is not literature, not argument, but prompt, unquestioning, automatic obedience. Those persons who, instead of doing what you tell them, give you a thousand clever and ingenious reasons for not doing it, may be very enlightened citizens, and a constant proof and reminder of our superiority to the ignorant and down-trodden masses of the Old World, but they are very unprofitable servants.

The examples I have given are but a few out of many cases in which my scullion marred an otherwise unexceptionable career by the fruitless, ill timed, and pertinacious display of intelligence. I shudder to think of the scenes that will ensue should our great and glorious republic ever reach that stage of intellectual development toward which we are constantly and eagerly trying to advance her.

But we have not yet reached it, and I am therefore probably correct in assuming that it is not generally known that a dripping-pan is broader than it is long, and the handles are at the wrong ends. If you hold on by them you can hardly avoid burning at least one of your wrists when you put the pan in the oven. I thought at this time it had been out so long it would not be hot, and that the meat had shrunk so much in cooking it would not be heavy. So I undertook to carry the pan to the stove, holding one end in both hands. Alas! I had miscalculated my strength and my endurance, or else it was both hotter and heavier than I had anticipated. I advanced in a straight line to the stove, as a stone goes down a precipice, with ever-accelerated velocity, while the dripping-pan seemed to be sliding with disastrous swiftness down an invisible inclined plane. Hassan was at that moment, as Milton remarks, squat like a toad close at the oven door, holding it open. He saw the ruin impending, caught the danger in an instant, gave a flying leap into the air, and barely escaped a lapful of meat and gravy; for I missed aim, and, instead of shooting my charge into the oven, dumped it a few inches short, striking the ground a little to leeward of my friend. Only one end of the dripping-pan rested on the floor, as I clung with the grasp of despair to the other, regardless of hot iron. Thus the meat, having glided plump to the farther end of the pan, staid there, and only the grease sputtered out upon the floor. "Call the cat," I commanded, sententiously; and Hassan was too grateful for his hair-breadth escape to waste words; so we three speedily repaired damages; and the cat, licking her paws with deep content, congratulated herself that it is an ill wind which blows nobody any good.

Simultaneously with the meat, I conducted a host of vegetables to a harmonious end. It was like a novel with several distinct plots, all tending to one conclusion. You go a little way with one, and then take another. Peas, and beans, and beets, and carrots, and radishes, and potatoes. The scullion said he thought there were too many things on the stove. I told him Professor Blot had things on the stove. He questioned if roast beef took kindly to carrots. I said that was not in the bond; that Professor Blot had his stove covered with sauce-pans, and, to do the same, we must have the carrots. In preparing the radishes I had an impression that the whole was not cooked. I asked the scullion if he knew which part was to be cooked. He said he believed radishes were not generally cooked at all. I said there was standing-room on the stove for another sauce-pan, and our radishes must be cooked. He said he would consult Mrs. Putnam on that point. He did so; but Mrs. Putnam preserved an unbroken silence, and we inferred it must have been a poor year for radishes when she made her cookery-book. In looking for the radishes we came upon the beets; and I was struck with a mild consternation at learning that they must not be cut before boiling. I had carefully peeled them all before putting them in the sauce-pan. Potatoes were nicer to be peeled, and the question naturally arose to the inquiring mind why not beets? It is true, Professor Blot forbade even to peel potatoes before boiling, as their nourishment lies close underneath the skin, which should be removed only by a sort of caressing urgency, and not rudely severed with a knife. But I have boiled potatoes from infancy, peeling them first; and if there is one point on which I feel competent to hold an opinion, it is this. So I peeled every thing but the peas and beans, and waited for the water to boil. It is incredible how long it takes water to boil when you are waiting for it. I asked the scullion if he had ever heard of a kind of water that was impervious to fire. He said he had heard of the next best thing—a letter that would not burn; or, he thought, this might be a lineal descendant of the curse of Kehama: The water shall see thee, and know thee, and fly thee, and the winds shall not touch thee when they pass by thee. But it was not. It began to sing presently, and then it began to dance, and then, obeying Professor Blot's directions of "the first boiling," I thrust in my tubers and legumes, all hard and untoothsome as they were, and waited the wonderful chemistry of the fire. The scullion said I should indefinitely postpone the dinner because I kept lifting the covers to look at the things. But Professor Blot kept looking at things. It was an ecstatic moment when they began to grow soft. It seemed hardly possible that my feeble hands should have succeeded in turning these hard, characterless, inert substances into familiar, delicious vegetables, each with its own individuality. But that was what they did turn into, and with great rapidity, after they had once set about it. In fact, they all seemed to have hit upon the same moment to be done and dished up. Besides, there was the table to set; and at the last gasp I recollected the gravy, and was torn with conflicting emotions. With great presence of mind I clapped on a spider of water, gave the scullion a bowl of flour-thickening to stir, and told him to call me just before the water was going to boil. He asked how should he know when the water was going to boil. I said, tell by the clock. There are dozens of clocks lying about the house, and as each runs on its own account, when one is not striking another is, so we can always know the time at any hour of the day or night. Presently he put his head into the dining-room door, and told me to come and make the gravy. The water was bullatura—about to boil. I went out and stirred in the thickening, sprinkled on salt, and told him to keep stirring till it boiled again, to make it thick. It was not long before he was protruding his head through the doorway once more, and asking, with a strong Hibernian accent, " Does not gr-r-ase make gravy?"

" Grace?" I queried.

" Gr-r-r-ase, mum."

" What do you mean?"

" To look at it from a scientific point of view," he said, relinquishing the Hibernian and assuming the professorial manner, " is water the natural basis of gravy?"

Now water is a great ingredient in our cooking. Hassan often remarks that he does not know how we should get on without a well to go to. If the milk falls short, there is always the pump handy. Certainly it was not for nothing that we advertised a " pump in the sink." Still, contemplating this useful liquid as the fundamental idea of gravy, I was conscious of an incongruity. I stirred it abstractedly, taking up a spoonful now and then, and pouring it back again. " Seems as if it *is* not dark enough," I remarked, doubtfully.

" Perhaps it will boil down."

" It has been boiling up some time, if that has any thing to do with it."

" Really, do you suppose it *is* gravy? Why not starch?"

" The event must determine."

" I wish you would just taste it."

"No, my dear; fancy how stiff my manners would become in case it is starch."

"Look at Mrs. Putnam."

"She hides, like Galatea, among the rushes."

"No directions for gravy?"

"Not a direction, neither under meats nor miscellaneouses."

"See starch, then."

"The starch, too, is an eclipse."

"Very well," I said, with a sudden inspiration, and snatched off the spider. "What is not in the cookery-books shall not be on my table. Gravies are universally admitted to be unwholesome, and Professor Blot says no flour should be put into gravy."

So that was happily settled. Only my scullion says he shall never cease to regret that we did not let the mysterious substance go on and see what would come of it.

The pudding was a plum-pudding; not an English plum-pudding—for I have understood that in the arts of the table the English are hardly less barbarous than ourselves—but an American Thanksgiving plum-pudding, made the night beforehand of bread, and butter, and milk, and eggs; only I left out the butter and eggs, because, if the pudding should prove a failure, it would be a pity to lose them too; though, as I observed to my scullion, it must be good, because there were nothing but good things in it—a layer of bread, a layer of raisins, a layer of sugar, and soak in milk overnight; the next day add more milk and bake it. It baked curiously. It seemed somehow not to have passed the point where bread ceases to be bread and becomes pudding. It was not a homogeneous mass, but lay in regular strata—primary, tertiary, old red sandstone—only the different strata were not petrified, but the opposite—pap-ified, you might say, except here and there hard places, a sort of trap rock. But the scullion said he liked the hard places. In making the sauce I followed Mrs. Putnam, only putting water and flour where she said wine and sugar, to diminish the loss in case of failure. Every thing was very good, as it had to be, since there was nothing in it but what was good. And the remainder was made over into a custard-pudding next day, which looked far more like a custard-pudding than the plum-pudding looked like a plum-pudding, which was encouraging.

III.
FALLING FROM GRACE.

IF I could be sure that only men would read these short and simple annals of the poor, and if there were any way by which men could be forced to read them, I would go on indefinitely. Women in their daily life breathe airs all too redolent of the kitchen-range, and one would not willingly run the risk of adding the fatal straw to the camel's burden by filling their literature with the fumes of roast and stew. But if the men—the men who are so unwearied in pressing upon women the claims of cookery, who never tire of telling us that the way to a man's heart winds around his palate —an elevated and doubtless sufficiently accurate view of masculine affection; at least, if men do not quarrel with it, women need not—could these men be doomed by some inevitable sentence to sit on a bench all day and read, or, still better, hear read to them by their wives and daughters, whatever I should write on the subject, I should feel that I had something still to live for. And oh! with what ease could I, and with what alacrity would I, draw out this linked sweetness to twice, and thrice, and four times its present length, and with what matchless ecstasy should I witness the writhings of fatigue which it would cause! No inquisitor gloating over the tortures of his heretical victim, no Nero fiddling and feeding the fires of Rome, no spider watching with fierce, still intensity his whirling lines dependent that bespeak an entangled fly, should rise to a higher rapture of joy than would swell this exultant heart at being made the instrument in the hands of Providence of dealing out exact poetic justice to a generation of culprits! How should each successive experiment be portrayed with a more than pre-Raphaelitic fidelity! Nulla dies sine lineâ? Nulla hour, nulla moment while passion stirs this mortal frame! No device, no attempt, no failure, even, without its page, not to say its chapter. The cream toast that began so bravely and ended so scaly and weakly should have its diagnosis and its prognosis—whatever they may be—with an enthusiasm of detail. The cold sauce that was kneaded and kneaded, and that swelled and swelled till the mouse threatened to become an elephant, should have its impartial history, with all the causes that led to it, and all the results that sprang from it, and all the things that might have happened if the things that did happen had happened the other way, according to the style of the most approved historians. Nor should patience fail me to speak of that momentous day when, smitten with ambition and high resolve, I bolted the doors, lowered the window-shades, and boiled soft custard into a residuum to which the most confirmed Swedenborgian would be forced to *hope* there was nothing corresponding in the spirit world, and then incautiously poured it into the best glass pitcher, which immediately threatened to betray its secret by cracking with appalling detonations, and which was hastily bound roundabout with a strong cord hidden under the decoration of red, white, and blue ribbon, to keep the molten metal from oozing out, and how I wished afterward that it had oozed out, for there was too much to be hidden, and it was too bad to be eaten. What agonies I suffered in convoying that custard from pillar to post to keep it out of harm's and Hassan's way! And no sooner was it snuggled up on the top shelf of the most unfrequented closet in Dan than you were sure to hear a pair of boots squeaking around in that vicinity, and then some pretext had to be invented to call them off, and give me a chance to transfer the prodigy to an equally undreamed-of cupboard in Beersheba. If the Cardiff giant gave its depositors half the trouble that my custard gave me, it must have been but a sorry joke for them, for it is heart-rending to throw sugar and eggs, like physic, to the dogs, and for the first few days I had a lively hope that it might settle down into a marketable commodity.

Still fixing with my glittering eye my wretched victims, I would tell them the Tale of the Boiled Dish—as country people love to call that dinner of herbs *and* stalled ox, old and salt, prolific of perfumes lingering and pervasive like musk, horresco referens, but dear to the bucolic heart. How tough was the skin of the parsneps, and how one had to dig to get it off. And what a dreadful noise the cabbages made when one touched them!

"And how many turnips would you have?" I queried, innocently, basket in hand, going down into l'Inferno to get them.

"What is a turnip?" asked the scullion, with an Indian war-club, as it were.

To which, undaunted and free, I made answer: "A turnip is a fusiform, napiform root, brassica rapa, depressed globose, contracted into a slender radicle, radical leaves lyrate, cauline ones incised, upper entire, amplexicaul."

"There is no necessity for flinging all your early botany at me," he said, somewhat abashed, fleeing when resisted, after the manner of his kind. "I want to know how big is a turnip."

"How long is a rope? What are the solid contents of a strip of pork?"

This was a fair hit. He had made himself merry not long before because I left orders with the butcher for a strip of pork, which he considered equivalent to ordering a piece of meat, or any other abstraction. He was a good deal taken aback at being told authoritatively what I had indeed learned only half an hour previous, and what, no doubt, the larger number of my readers are living to this day in heathen ignorance of—that a strip of pork is a technical phrase. I might—so intricate is the science of the kitchen—have gone through life myself in Cimmerian darkness but for the merest accident, turned to account by such an inquiring and reflective mind as educed the law of the universe from the fall of an apple.

"You cut up pork into strips from four to five inches wide," said my informant, with ill-concealed scorn, "and that is 'a strip of pork' the world over."

"Oh! the animal is served up in strips, then," trying to look intelligent; for it is as much as your life is worth not to know every thing in presence of that most unrelenting of tyrants, "a good housekeeper."

"No; only the middlings."

Worse and worse.

"The middlings?" faintly, in hopes that some hint may, unsought, be won that will throw a light on the middlings. But none comes.

"And what, pray, are the middlings?"

"Why, that is the middlings. The strips are the middlings. You ask for the middlings, and the butcher will say, 'How much do you want?' And you say you will take a strip."

"That is, the strips are the species, and the middlings the genus?"

"Fiddlesticks!" says your good housekeeper, who has more wisdom in her own conceit, and more contempt for all other accomplishments without her own than ten men that can render a reason.

Full well you laugh with counterfeited glee, and return to your *cochon*, determined to exhaust this department of science, now you are on it, so that you can henceforth hold up your head in good society.

"But it seems that all pork is not strips and middlings."

"Of course not. There are the shoulders, and the leg, and the lard, and the leaves."

One and two you know by the light of unassisted reason. Number three you see through a glass darkly. But you go scrambling around in your mind to find what *leaves* can mean as pertaining to swine.

And you have to ask, after all.

"Leaves? Why, leaves comes out of the inside of the spare-rib. There's nobody that knows any thing but knows what the spare-rib is."

Of course you would be likely to inquire after this mild hint.

"But that is not telling what leaves are."

"Leaves is what you try up for the lard."

"And the middlings is all besides these—all the Internal Improvements?"

"Yes. What you want to salt is middlings."

There it is again, you see. Nothing is said about salt till the last moment, when you supposed your understanding of the subject complete, and then suddenly a Dead Sea is rolled in upon you.

And, as if this were not enough, ere yet the ink was dry upon these pages, I made a call upon a friend high in official and social position, and while we were deep in the discussion of fixed fate, free-will, foreknowledge absolute, his wife, one of those inveterate housekeepers before stigmatized, an excellent woman in every other respect, but conceited and domineering to the last degree in point of housekeeping, cut in with—

"There! David has come. Now stop your harangue, and go down with him and salt the pork."

Meekly he bowed his head, as only a man can who has been thoroughly subdued by a long course of domestic discipline, and murmured, helplessly,

"Is there any thing except the pork to be salted?"

Here I pricked up my ears, determined to distinguish myself by interposing some casual remark to show my lady that I was well "up" on the subject; but my budding ambition was instantaneously frostbitten by her branching off into a disquisition on *sausage-meat*, which had not been dreamed of in my philosophy. Thus ever, when you fancy yourself to be nearing the summit of your aim, do hills on hills and Alps on Alps arise. And after sausage-meat come souse, and head-cheese, and pig's feet, and haslet, and what not, till you feel yourself trampled under foot of a whole herd of swine. Now, if these things are done in a green tree, what shall be done in a dry? If there is so much to be known about the most despised of all the animals that are admitted to a gentleman's table, who shall fathom the depths of science wherein fish, flesh, and fowl of good repute lie pickled? Yet, unless you know all these things, you are no housekeeper—you have "no faculty." It is not simply to roast your meat, but to understand the moral nature, so to speak, of the beast whence it is taken—all the special fitnesses of its special parts for special uses—all its special needs in point of preservation—all the adaptations of its times and seasons to the revolutions of the earth on its axis and the stars in their courses. Thus the good housekeeper must, like Lord Bacon, take all knowledge to be her province. She sees, as did Cicero, that all the arts which pertain to humanity have, as it were, a common chain binding them to her kitchen stove. Yet so unequal are the ways of justice and the demands of our artificial society, that she who hesitates in a single one of these arts is lost; while Mr. Henry Ward Beecher, by his own confession, wipes the dishes with a newspaper when his wife is away, and Professor Blot, as these eyes have seen, tosses them on a sofa without washing at all. And no dog barks.

That severe virtue which presides over the American newspaper finds a noble exercise of its powers in the following paragraph, which appears in an eminently religious newspaper:

"Many young ladies in our day look on kitchen-work as so much drudgery, to be shunned whenever possible. It may possibly inspire some of them to better thoughts to know that the royal family of England consider excellence in this department as an important womanly virtue. An exchange says:

"'But Queen Victoria, the highest gentlewoman in the land, did, down to the lamented death of the prince, pay daily visits of inspection to her kitchen, pantry, confectionery, still-room, and was proud of and did herself show those rooms to her visitors when staying at the castle; and, carrying out the recognized principles of female duty, model kitchens were constructed at Windsor and Osborne, where all the princesses, from the eldest downward, have passed a portion of each day in acquiring a knowledge of the various duties of domestic economy in the management of a household. In their model kitchen the princesses have daily practiced the art of cookery, and also confectionery in all its various branches. There is a small store-room adjoining each kitchen, where each princess in turn gives out the stores, weighing or measuring each article, and making an entry thereof in a book kept for the purpose; besides which the princesses make bread; and that is not all—they have a dairy where they churn butter and make cheese.'"

After so signal a rebuke, it can not be expected that the evil in question will ever again show its head. If the royal family of England count kitchen-work an important womanly virtue, that settles the question. No American young lady can henceforth consider it drudgery. And how charming is the logic to which the impulsive but inconclusive female mind is here treated! Queen Victoria pays daily visits of inspection to her kitchen and pantry, therefore American young ladies should love to work in theirs. Queen Victoria is proud of her rooms, and does herself show them to her visitors—arduous toil! Therefore American young ladies must delight to bake, and brew, and scrub. 'Tis as like as my fingers to my fingers.

And the princesses, too—virtuous creatures—have model kitchens, in which they work a portion of each day. But pray, now, Messieurs Censors of American young women, what occupies these exemplary princesses in their toy kitchens? Do they, let us say, rise betimes in the morning, shake down the coal-stove, sift the ashes, bring in the kindlings, build the fire, pump the water, put on the tea-kettle, broil the steak, toss the omelet, bake the corn-cake, make the coffee, set the table, wash the dishes, sweep the floor, polish the stove, trim the lamps every morning of the three hundred and sixty-five? Conscript fathers, do you not know perfectly well that what these young princesses do is simply to play at work? They take the kitchen just as they take music—in lessons. They have their model kitchens and an array of well-trained servants, and are instructed in the culinary arts by skillful teachers; and they amuse themselves and gratify their friends by practicing occasionally what they have learned. There is no more resemblance between their kitchen-work and the kitchen-work of the great majority of American households than there is between their embroidery and the slop-making of the needle-woman who sews for dear life fourteen hours out of the twenty-four. It is not necessary to be an inmate of kings' palaces to know this. The light of nature teaches so much. Do not presume so far upon the fatuity of your young countrywomen. It hurts you, and does not amuse them. There is not a girl in America who would not be willing to do all the housework that

Queen Victoria and her daughters perform, if she could do it from the same motives and with the same machinery.

We have heard a great deal from time to time of the domesticity of English ladies of birth and breeding. Many is the duchess, and countess, and baroness who has gone down the columns of the American newspaper into her kitchen and store-room to give orders, and keep accounts, and supervise her household arrangements, and who has consequently been held up as an example to the negligent housekeepers of our own unhappy land. I never did put any great faith in these stories; and here comes an Englishman in the London Daily News to help mine unbelief. He is traveling in America, and, speaking of the "residents of most of the three-window stone houses" in New York, he says:

"If she [the wife] has a carriage, she drives in the Park in the afternoon; and in the evening she either receives visits at home or visits at the house of some friend. *She generally is her own housekeeper, and she occupies herself far more with housekeeping affairs than an English lady in the same social position.*

"Cooks here receive about twenty-five dollars a month; and, on the whole, dinners are better than with us. *This is mainly due to the wives themselves frequently visiting the kitchen, and having some knowledge of cookery.*"

I spare my gallant countrymen all comment upon this simple statement, choosing rather to leave them to their own awakened consciences and detected guilt. And, such is the depravity of the masculine human heart, and such its unscrupulousness in the use of means, that if we were as familiar with English newspapers as with our own, we should doubtless find the Catos of the English press just as forward as our own in shaming their countrywomen with the domestic virtues of their transatlantic sisters!

Housekeeping with well-trained, or at least well-disposed servants, is the only way of life tolerable to an adult Christian; but any woman who enjoys housekeeping with only her own self for maid-of-all-work discovers thereby some radical organic defect. It is well enough for a short time, while the exhilaration of the novelty lasts; and even after the exhilaration and the novelty are over, a little of it is wholesome for the future conduct of life. Indeed, I think no one who has not some practical acquaintance with it, not in its holiday garb, but in its working dress, is ever quite master of the situation. To go down into the kitchen after breakfast, to have Mary bring you all the ingredients for your cake or your dessert, and after the dainty work is done leave the "clearing up" for her—this is occasionally an amusement. But you need to feel the iron enter into your own soul, to bear the responsibility of the whole day, to see the awful regularity with which the breakfast-hour, and the dinner-hour, and the supper-hour come, and the awful irregularity with which the breakfast, and the dinner, and the supper rise up to meet them, to watch all the niceties of mixing and baking, and then to front all the horrors of pots, and kettles, and spiders, and skillets—in short, you need to experience the numberless vexations and the irritating fatigues in order to know what service to exact of your servants, what completeness to expect, what shortcomings to forgive.

Some of the reproaches wherewithal we reproach our forefathers—meaning in this instance our foremothers—are directed against customs which, I am persuaded, have their rise in this dreadful and fearful burden of housework. We have all ridiculed or denounced the farm-houses, open on the kitchen side, but solemnly shut up as to the best rooms; and we—those of us who are men—write essays and deliver lectures to show how much better and more cheerful it is to throw open the whole house to the free play of sun and breeze. I regret to admit that I have joined in these shortsighted diatribes myself. I desire to make public recantation, and do hereby declare and affirm that, so far from denouncing the custom, my only wonder is that women who perform their own house-work do not shut up their houses altogether and live in the barn-chamber. Who would not a thousand times rather eat his meat with gladness and singleness of heart on a haystack, and serenely toss the fragments down to the stalled ox below, than roast the stalled ox himself and eat him in never so gorgeous a dining-room, with the dishes to wash and the floor to sweep afterward? For, in the first case, the stalled ox would be a cheerful and soothing companion, in the other an irritating and inexorable tyrant. While you were devouring his body, he would be devouring your soul.

It is simply impossible—listen now, I pray, all knights of high and low degree, marching along, thousandscore strong, great-hearted gentlemen singing this song of woman's sphereicity—it is simply impossible for any woman to do the work of her household and make her life what a woman's life ought to be. This is a rule that admits of no exception and no modification. The machinery of the family is so complicated and so exacting that one woman can not have the sole charge of it without neglecting other and equally important matters. The duties which a woman owes to society, and to the moral and spiritual part of her household, are just as imperative as those which she owes to its physical comfort. And if she alone ministers to the latter, the former must be neglected, and the latter will hardly be thoroughly accomplished. I know all about our noble grandmothers. I have heard of them before. I think we could run a race with them any day. But if we can not, whose fault is it? If the women of to-day are puny, fragile, degenerate, are they not the grandchildren of their grandmothers —bearing such constitutions as their grandmothers could transmit? It was the duty of those venerable ladies not only to be strong themselves, but to see to it that their children were strong. A sturdy race should leave a sturdy race. It was far more their duty to give to their children vigorous minds, stalwart bodies, healthy nerves, firm principles, than it was to spin, and weave, and make butter and cheese all day. We should have got along just as well with less linen laid up in lavender; and if our grandmothers could only have waited, we would have woven them more cloth in a day than their hand-looms would turn out in a lifetime. But there is no royal road to a healthy manhood and womanhood. Nothing less costly than human life goes into the construction of human life. We should have more reason to be grateful to our ancestors if they had given up their superfluous industries, called off their energy from its perishable objects, and let more of their soul and strength flow leisurely in to build up the soul and strength of the generations that were to come after them. Nobody is to blame for being born weak. If this generation of women is feeble compared with its hardy and laborious grandmothers, it is simply because the grandmothers put so much of their vitality, their physical nerve and moral fibre, into their churning and spinning, that they had but an insufficient quantity left wherewithal to endow their children, and so they wrought us evil.

One would not willingly quarrel with his grandmothers. All agree in awarding them praise for heroic qualities. They fought a good fight—perhaps the best they could under the circumstances with their light. We would gladly overlook all in their lives that was defective, and fasten our eyes only on that which was noble. But when their fault is distinctly pointed out as their virtue, when their necessity is exalted into our ensample, when their narrowness is held up to our ambition, we must say that it was fault, and need, and narrowness, grandmother or no grandmother. Indeed those excellent gentlewomen, no doubt, long before this have seen the error of their ways, and, if they could find voice, would be the first to avow that they did set too great store by chests of sheets, and bureaus of blankets, and pillow-cases of stockings, and stacks of provisions; and that if it were given them to live life over again, they would endeavor rather to lay up treasure in the bodies, and brains, and hearts of their children, where moth and mildew do not corrupt, which time does not dissipate nor use destroy, and whereof we stand in sorer need than of purple, or scarlet, or fine-twined linen.

A long way this side of our grandmothers we find bustling, energetic women, who would laugh to scorn the idea that they needed any help in transacting their household business. But then, dear ladies, the laugh is not wholly on your side. We in our turn, we incapables, laugh to scorn your idea of life, or, if we do not laugh, we lament. We think you utterly fail to form any conception of the true motives, methods, and ends of the family and of society. We think you attain the less only by sacrificing the greater—that all this strain of the muscles destroys the play of the mind. Sometimes your work is really but half done. You rush through your house with a touch and go. You have not even an ideal of domestic comfort, of mere material purity. You apparently have great executive ability, but its finest feat is in covering your manifold defects with a superficial decency. Any person could do her housework who could be content with not doing it. Or, again, you are a marvel of thoroughness. You are all "faculty." You are the town talk for thrift and industry. You rise while it is yet dark, and pride yourself on having your breakfast eaten and cleared away before six o'clock. All very well, if you think it is a cheerful thing to do in our climate. Yours may be an extreme case, but it is like Byron's gentle hill—the cape of a long ridge of such. You are at the extreme, but there are many following you at a greater or less distance. But tell us what you do with your time after you have thus taken it by the forelock. Are you really any happier? Do you walk on a higher plane than we who like to begin the day with sunshine? Look at it, good friend. Is there not something left out, after all? Is your influence upon your husband elevating and spiritualizing? Do you help him to rise above his material occupations into the regions of thought and sentiment? Do you study into the hidden nature of your children? Do you thread with loving watch the labyrinths of their little life, that you may get the clew whereby to guide them through no winding paths into a happy and honorable maturity? And as they come up into youth, into young manhood and maidenhood, are you still to them the personification of what is most wise, and winning, and worthy in human character?

Are you of the first consideration in your house? While you are thinking and planning for the others, are they thinking first of you? Is your approbation the confirmation, and your disapproval the veto, of every new plan? Is your house a familiar resting-place for weary pilgrims? Do the young people of your circle like your society, come to you for advice or sympathy, for careless chit-chat and serious conversation? Do men and women of mark frequent your house, drawn by some unseen attraction? Do you make of your home a little sunny spot of greenery in the great wilderness of the world, where the jaded may find rest, and the sorrowing consolation, and the inert stimulus, and the merry free play—whence every one goes out a little fresher, a little brighter, a little happier than he came in?

And look at yourself. Alas! your hands are bulging at

the joints, hard in the palms, rough as to the finger-ends, spreading, unshapely, and discolored, active enough in work, but ruined for delicacy and grace. But a woman's hand should be soft, and white, and supple. Heavens! what heresy is this! What laudation of luxury, and idleness, and general worthlessness! Let me say it again, then. A woman's hand should be white, and soft, and supple, and the robbery of grace and beauty which it has suffered only marks the loss of so much grace and beauty out of womanhood. I do not say that a woman may not do worse than have hard hands, and a face and form disfigured by toil. If it is a question of life or death, of dishonorable dependence or deforming labor, there is but one choice. Rather there is no choice. It is better for a woman to sacrifice her soul through her body, than to sacrifice her soul outright and spare her beauty. In the first case, she may hope to save something from the wreck; in the second, all that is valuable goes down together. But it is none the less sacrifice. If you must destroy comeliness and grace by hard work, there is virtue in doing it as quietly and cheerfully as may be. If you do it without the spur of necessity, there is no virtue in it at all. And let it be ever remembered and rehearsed, that all labor that wears upon the physical frame, or mental or nervous power of woman, whether it be indoor or outdoor labor, is so much taken away from her children. Whatever deteriorates her deteriorates her offspring. Through inherited vigor she may stand all the wear and tear after a fashion, but there is imminent danger that her children will not live out half their days, or will vex their allotted time with an attenuated existence. Nothing but tranquillity, and high health, and happy spirits, added to the royal souls of mothers, can give us the brave, grand race that is to mark and make the Golden Year.

The perfect woman is as beautiful as she is strong, as

tender as she is sensible. She is calm, deliberate, dignified, leisurely. She is gay, graceful, sprightly, sympathetic. She is severe upon occasion, and upon occasion playful. She has fancies, dreams, romances, ideas. Sometimes her skies are clear, like the cloudless blue of winter; but sometimes they are hazy and vague, like the Indian summer afternoon. She is never idle, but she sometimes seems to be. She uses her hands, but she never abuses them. She commands her children and her household after her, but she does not drudge for them. She administers the government of her kingdom, she *looketh* well to the ways of her family, but she never eats her bread in the sweat of her brow. Her mind is in every corner of her house, but her face shines chiefly where husband, and children, and friends sit in the light thereof. She organizes neatness, and order, and comfort, but they are merely the foundation whereon rises the temple of her home, beautiful for situation, the joy of the whole earth.

Thus at least we comfort ourselves, Hassan and I, for our foes the housekeepers, who look down upon us.

Since it can not be denied that our housekeeping flagged wonderfully after the first few days. The inspiration seemed to flutter and fade as we receded from Professor Blot, and left us stranded upon a cruel shore of bare flat facts. What is there to the kitchen after the novelty is over? When you have once baked a potato well, that is the end of it. While the world stands there can be no improvement. As like as two peas in a pod, says the proverb. As like as two thousand peas out of a pod. To boil pease to-day is to boil pease to-morrow, and the next day, and forever, till their salt has lost its savor, and their freshness its flavor, and your soul loathes the sound of boiled pease. When Sally Lunn has once made a creditable appearance at the breakfast-table, you desire to wash your hands of that femme passée for all time. The only revival of interest comes with a new guest. They tell you—the good moral books of Advice to Young Housekeepers, and Mothers' Aids—that you ought to serve yourself just as you serve your company. You will then be always ready to welcome and enjoy your guests. It is a good rule enough; but, though the spirit be willing, the flesh is weak; and I have found that agreeable and exhilarating guests are the only spur which the clear spirit doth raise to get any kind of a meal after the first two or three times. It creates life even under the jacket of a baked potato to think that somebody you love will eat it. There is real pleasure in making your table inviting—in bringing out for your friend something a little remote from every-day uses—something a little finer, a little rarer than is cast into the common lot. But for your own self, bless me! let us gnaw any sort of a crust, and have done with it. What is the odds? You get a dinner for the family; it is gone in the twinkling of an eye, and you reflect with dismay that you must pace the same tread-mill to-morrow. Or it is let severely alone, and you know that something is burned, or water-soaked, or under-done, and are equally brought to confusion.

Hassan's enthusiasm ebbed as rapidly as mine. He brought down newspapers, and read them surreptitiously behind his pile of cook-books. Then he waxed bolder, and began to read them aloud to me. We all know it is nice to be read aloud to when you are rattling about amidst the crockery. You are likely to have a great deal of sympathy with the Cuban insurrectionists, and be mightily interested in the Suez Canal, when the chocolate is boiling, and the oatmeal is burning, and all the outside doors are slamming. Finally Hassan showed symptoms of deserting the kitchen altogether.

"Come, it is half past seven, and I *must* go and get breakfast," I say, decidedly, after many futile attempts.

"Don't rush," says Hassan. "You have oceans of time."
"But it is half past seven."
"And we breakfast at nine. You have a good hour yet."
"But there are the eggs to boil, and the toast to make—"
"It takes just three minutes for the eggs to boil, and allow five more for the toast."

And then he goes into a mathematical calculation, showing by the rule of three that fifteen minutes is enough to get all the breakfast in. And so it is—in his brain—nowhere else; for, though I never can detect any error in his figures, it is a matter of experience that breakfast never comes in fifteen minutes.

And your neighbor does—dear little kind-hearted woman! But she *will* come round by the back door, where you are already immeasurably perplexed because the tea-kettle will not boil. Now it is not of the least consequence how kind-hearted people are; they ought never to come in by the back door. I am agonizing over the tea-kettle; but that is not suspicious, for it is past ten; and if she surmises cooking she will think it is dinner. You can always christen a meal according to the hour it hits nearest. We trip around the field of neighborhood gossip with a celerity which she probably does not understand. And the water *will* not boil. And I can not go into the dining-room to set the table. And the clock is ticking on toward half past ten. She is a dear little woman—but if she only would go! Does she not see how abstracted and incoherent I am? For my underthought will protrude into my surface talk. I expect every moment Hassan will come breezing in with, "How do you make it on the breakfast?" And then we are lost. Already I hear his tramp emerging from his lair. Light breaks. "Mrs. Smith, I wish you would go out with me and take a look at our beans. I am afraid they are frost-killed." Under-reflection, "She won't come in again." And she doesn't.

My interest in the beans falls away as soon as she is launched on them, and I gradually edge toward the house, drawing her after me. Will she pass through or by the door? Oh joy! she makes as if she would go farther. "Won't you come in, Mrs. Smith?" Hypocrite that I am—but how can you help it? "No, thank you; I believe I must be going." And, released at last, I make another descent on the tea-kettle, and suddenly remember that I forgot to put in the wood upon the kindlings, and the reason why the water does not boil is that the fire went out half an hour ago.

Such is life—in the kitchen. Professor Blot may garland it with roses, and put a bouquet of see-sawn-ing in its hand; but the grinning, mocking, hideous skeleton is still there, and will not be lectured or lessoned away.

IV.
THE PURSUIT OF THE FORTY THOUSAND.

"This will never do," said Hassan.

"No," I replied; "it is flying in the face of Providence."

I did not know to what he was referring; but it is always safe to strike in with an acquiescing remark.

"Something is about to give way, and we must have a woman. There are lots of them."

"Forty thousand in the city of New York, with nothing to do but come out in the newspapers every year making shirts at six cents apiece or die."

"And thirty thousand in Massachusetts."

"And me with the whole world to reconstruct on entirely new principles, and can't get at it for the barricades of bread-and-butter that rise around me."

"Exactly, my dear. You might cry with the sons of the prophets, 'There is death in the pot!' for you, while to these forty thousand it might be life, let alone that our planet would immediately turn into a self-luminous body if you could but have free play for a few minutes."

"What is the good of talking? The facts remain. No hypothesis regarding a millennium relieves in the smallest degree the pressure of existing circumstances. Doubtless the Golden Age awaits our laggard steps; but at present we are hungry."

"It is always well, however, to take a dispassionate view of the situation. Put the case, now, you were cast away on a desert island alone, with plenty of flour, and sugar, and mutton-chops, but with no one to cook them—all your specific dislikes and all your generic inaptitudes in full vigor. What should you do?"

"I should advertise."

"A Daniel come to judgment!"

"And now you have put the idea into my mind, why should we not advertise as it is? I think we are as near being stranded on a stern and rock-bound coast as we are likely ever to be."

"What good did our former advertising do us?"

"None at all, because we did not advertise. We were merely passive recipients of the arbitrary wants of others. We only answered advertisements. I believe our misfortunes are a judgment upon us for attempting to help ourselves, and turning a deaf ear to the forty thousand women in New York who are crying for bread, and the thirty thousand of Massachusetts, who may be a little better off, but who, doubtless, must stint themselves in butter. Let us be no longer selfish, but humane. Let us advertise."

"There is a possibility that these seventy thousand may not be regular subscribers to the newspapers."

"But at the houses of their hard-hearted employers a newspaper will be furnished them to wrap around the work they are to carry home; and, bending over their needle at midnight, their eyes will fall on the advertisement, which will bring to their weary hearts a glimpse of refuge; they will deny themselves a loaf of bread to buy a postage-stamp and a sheet of paper to send us a letter; receiving which, we shall immediately remit their fare, and thus secure a servant for ourselves, with the happy consciousness that we have drawn an overburdened fellow-mortal out of the Slough of Despond."

"Bring me my pen," cried Hassan. "We will advertise instantly."

We sent immediately to our weekly religious and our daily profane newspaper:

WANTED—In the country, thirty miles from Elysium, a woman to do the housework for a family of two persons.

I was about to add, instinctively, "Widow preferred," but recollected myself in time. We must delay that adjunct till our Chinese brethren favor us with their company in greater numbers than at present.

I was very desirous that Hassan should engage a private secretary to read and answer the letters which our advertisement would elicit. If only a half, or even a thirtieth of those thirty thousand women should happen to see this advertisement in the paper that wraps their work, under what piles of correspondence should we groan! But Hassan thought that, as the eight-hour law was not yet in force, if we should rise early and write late, we might perhaps dispose of the bulk of the correspondence ourselves.

It turned out that he was right. Our secular advertisement brought us seven answers; our religious advertisement one; so that, with an eight-hour law and a letter an hour, our private secretary would have had just a day's work.

Even the eight letters were seven too many for us. We suffered from an embarrassment of riches. The eight writers were all excellent housekeepers, neat, economical, versed in cookery, all that heart could desire. How eagerly, if vainly, we wished we were eight families instead of one, or that we were rich enough to keep eight servants! But when our respondents appeared upon the scene, we were startled to observe that they all had ailments, and most of them infants. Apparently the talismanic words "in the country" had put out of sight the fact that there might be work to do. I asked Hassan if there was any thing in the advertisement that looked as if we were designing to establish a Hospital for Incurables or a Home for Little Wanderers. It would appear that some of our characteristic benevolence must have crept unawares into the paper, thus to have drawn out the maimed, the halt, and the blind. Perhaps the poor creatures thought a breath of country air would cure them. Things came to such a pass, finally, that Hassan bade me henceforth not to seek of our applicants their qualifications for the situation, but to ask them in the beginning what were their complaints. I never before had so realizing a sense of the scriptural truth that we are fearfully and wonderfully made. Never knew I how complicated an invention was the human organism till I thus saw the number of diseases that could prey upon it. Our religious respondent was too far off for a personal interview; and, in the faint hope that she might not have mistaken us for an Infirmary, we sent to a relative living in her city to know if he could ascertain the character and capacity of Priscilla Marquesa. He replied promptly that he knew Priscilla well; that she was, in fact, one of his own patients; that she usually rallied a little in the summer, and during these revivals she might be capable of taking care of her own chamber. We might rely upon it that she would not require much waiting on, except in winter.

We were neither of us good nurses, and there is no doctor in the village. We therefore declined to assume the responsibility of Priscilla's health.

Mary Ann seemed to be the least fragile and the most promising, and she had only one orphan nephew of three years to bring with her. We engaged Mary Ann. She was to come a week from Wednesday—orphan nephew—two dollars a week—stay a fortnight on trial; and we were then to decide on future arrangements. So we had our household wheels freshly oiled to run smoothly on Wednesday morning. Tuesday night Mary Ann sent word that her brother had decided to keep house again, and wanted her, and she could not come. Penelope stood next on the list for eligibility, and we turned to Penelope. Penelope had many disorders, but no children. Penelope replied instantly that she would come. The arrangement was the same as before—a fortnight's trial previous to the definite engagement. She was to come next Monday. "Is it an engagement?" "Yes, it is an engagement," says Penelope; "and I never break my word." Friday comes a letter from Penelope, saying only this and nothing more: "I have concluded not to work for you."

"It *is* the curse of Kehama," I said to Hassan. "The orphans shall see thee, and know thee, and fly thee. The aunts shall not touch thee when they pass by thee."

The next was a stout Irish lassie. She surveyed us coolly and critically from garret to cellar. We seemed to find favor in her eyes. She was graciously pleased to remark that the house was pleasant and *convanient* for work, though I must admit that never did the ceilings seem so low, or the carpets so faded, or the whole aspect of the establishment so ungenteel, as while undergoing her inspection. But she condescended to our low estate. She was very good-natured, and said she would come Sunday night. The Wednesday after I caught a glimpse of her Magenta gown among the poplars a quarter of a mile off, and in process of time our little lad brought word that Ellen told him to tell us she had got a place in the city.

But Elfleda came. Oh, heavens! Elfleda is the kind that always comes. Poor dear! with her dark, drawn face, her thin, bent figure, her unrestful eyes, her poor, wan, puny baby boy! How many bones do the physiologists tell us there are in the human system? Two hundred and something? I have not a doubt of it. Elfleda had them all, and every one ached; and, what is remarkable, not only had each one its separate and peculiar twinge, but there seemed to be also a sort of double-back-acting machinery by which they all ached in concert with an entirely distinct and well-defined pang. We did not find it out till she was safely housed under our roof; then we discovered, to our dismay, that she creaked every time she moved. I do think—but I never suggested it to her—that all the lubricating oil must have been washed out of her joints by the multiplicity of her douches and sitz baths. What *are* douches and sitz baths, I wonder? I only know that we seemed to be living under a dispensation of them, and our tubs never got a holiday while she was with us. Do I seem to be making a mock at misfortune? Alas! I pitied her from the bottom of my heart. But why should one drown one's self alive? Neither the sufferings of the body nor the sins of the soul can be swept away by a flood. Because you have a pump in the sink, need you live under the pump-nose?

Elfleda's conversation was cheerful and instructive, equally divided between minute and graphic descriptions of the diseases with which she had grappled and the remedies thereunto appertaining, and the diseases, remedies, and virtues of her departed consort. And what a temper she had! We always spoke of her as "the angel." I constantly kept her before Hassan as a model and a rebuke. When she was in the very act of holding forth upon her pet themes you could interrupt her without ruffling in the least that saintly temper. This was a fortunate discovery for me. Of course we are all brought up to hold it impolite to interrupt an interlocutor, or even abruptly to change the subject upon which he is discoursing. It requires sometimes no small degree of ingenuity to construct a gently-inclined plane along which to conduct him imperceptibly from his subject to your own. A goodly amount of such carpentry was performed with Elfleda during the early days of our connection, but it was love's labor lost, for she could step from one subject directly upon another without the least apparent moral jerk or jar. Picture the heavenly-mindedness of a woman who, having lovingly led her story along through the febrile, symptomatic stages, and finally got the most malignant small-pox under full headway, will allow you to break in, just as the malady is about to break out, with, " Now let us have one pan of hot biscuit for breakfast, and the rest in loaves. And is there milk enough for the chocolate ?"

Yes. And that martyr would let go the small-pox, turn right about face, and immediately begin to descant upon chocolate and biscuit, and the peculiar varieties of both—which had been dear to her late espoused saint—with as much sweetness and fervor as if that had been the subject she started out on. And all the while I am surreptitiously slipping through the door, and edging through the dining-room, and backing up stairs, she following unconsciously with her innocent gush of talk, and me responding hypocritically with "Yes!" and "Why!" and unmeaning smiles, till my foot is on the top stair, when I shatter her remainder biscuit with a sudden "Good-night, Elfleda!" and dart out of sight. "Good-night!" replies the cherub, cheerful and content, and trots back to baby and biscuits.

But those biscuits were the perfection of delicacy. They would have enraptured Matthew Arnold with their "sweetness and light." And she somehow gilded their refined gold by painting their lily whiteness with butter before she put them in the oven, so that their crust was a delicious crisp.

Her clear-starching was as perfect as her biscuit, and would rival the frosty Caucasus. Her honesty would have snuffed out the candle of Diogenes. Her neatness was, as I have before intimated, a heavy drain upon the tubs. What could our grief be? Alas! An unconquerable incapacity neutralized every advantage. Breakfast was delicious, but it never came. Dinner was the Head-Centre of delay. Washing drizzled along till Thursday, and the last of the ironing dawdled up stairs on Sunday morning. You were sure of nothing. The breakfast dishes gathered in the sink, swelled with relays from the dinner-table, and finally overflowed upon the kitchen chairs. Imagine the thrill of horror that would curdle a New England village at rumor of such doings! True, we lived; but nothing was finished. As gossips say, the work was never "done up." Yet that saintly temper did not fail. You might go down at ten o'clock of a July night and find her with a red-hot fire, a crate of unwashed crockery, and a soul as serene as if she were only listening to the songs of nightingales. Her furious fires, raging through the long summer days, told fearfully upon our fuel. I walked over to my friend, the soft-voiced forester, and begged him to replenish our exhausted wood-house.

"You don't mean to say your wood is all gone?"

"Indeed I do."

"Not all that I cut up last winter and put into the barn?"

"Every stick of it. We have been living off the old fence these three days, and have now begun on the pitchforks and hoe-handles."

"Well, I won't say you're extravagant, but, by gorry! you've done well."

Poor, dear Elfleda!

In this irritable, exacting, rampageous world it would seem hardly credible that there could be such a thing as not having temper enough; but if there be such a thing, its name is Elfleda. It was impossible to keep her, and equally impossible—if I may employ a euphuistic Gallicism—to disembarrass one's self of her. You can not scold a mother of children. That sacred suffering and service interpose a barrier which no superiority of position, attainment, or character can break down or override. To any gentle hint of dissatisfaction Elfleda presented a voluble and valid excuse, or a flood of tears, heart-rent and heart-rending. What can you do? The baby—and this was a constant, solid comfort—waxed fat, and kicked. Abundant sunshine, pure air, and fresh milk puffed out his thin, sad, pitiful cheeks into laughing, dimpled, charming plumpness. He crept outdoors, delighted, among the birds, and bugs, and hop-toads, whenever a door was left open. He took contented little naps on the piazza, while the cat and hens gathered in friendly conclave to claw and peck the gingerbread from his chubby fists. He went through a lung fever on the door-step, and throve mightily in all ways; and Elfleda turned a deaf ear to any suggestions of departure, as if they had been temptations of the adversary. No one could have the heart to set her adrift on the great wide wild world again, and we bestirred ourselves to find her a harbor. We recommended her to all the neighbors in every capacity under heaven, from wet-nurse to Universalist minister, and they snapped their fingers at us. We cut down her wages to starvation rate. There is no available villainy in the calendar of crime which I did not perpetrate against her, and all in vain. If a new hospital had not been opened in a neighboring county, I believe her boy would have cast his first vote in our town in spite of us. That hospital may or may not be an eleemosynary or a pecuniary success, but it was our salvation; and if we ever inherit a fortune, we mean to put that establishment on a princely foundation. The first mention of it suggested a way of escape for Elfleda. If there be any inherent and eternal fitness of things, Elfleda and a hospital were made for each other. If there be any inherent unfitness, it lay between Elfleda and ourselves; for Hassan and I both distinctly remember that our last sensation of illness was when we were teething. The prospect of rioting in douches and sitz baths, of unlimited revels among fevers and lotions, blue pills and bluer patients, touched the weak spot in Elfleda's character; and as I painted in glowing colors the gay and festive scenes on which she would enter if she could become nurse or matron in such an institution, the light actually sparkled in her faded eyes, and her poor thin hair seemed to crinkle with ecstasy. So she went to glory, as you may say.

But I was not thus to be baffled. If the forty thousand would not come to me, I would go to the forty thousand. Any thing is better than to sit moaning among the fleshpots of Egypt, with thirty thousand women starving over the needle in Massachusetts, and forty thousand more in New York.

I arose and went to Boston.

I inquired for thirty thousand anxious and aimless women making shirts at six cents a piece. People stared, and directed me to the employment offices.

The first one was presided over by a lady, tall, slender, delicate, and refined in appearance—a pretty, gentle woman of culture and character apparently; but the air she breathed was horrible for any human being, let alone a lady. However, there is a choice in features; and when you go on a mission of this sort, you can give up your nose and take to your eyes. The domain over which this sovereign lady presided was two rooms—one very large, the other smaller. Every seat in the larger room was occupied by women wanting places. The smaller room was frequented, and sometimes thronged, by women wanting servants. The situation was appalling. It was my first experience of an employment office. I paused at the open door between the two rooms, and looked in upon the congregated waiting-women. Such an array of coarse, ignorant, unintelligent, unhelpful faces; such stolid indifference; such unshrinking self-assertion; such rude, brawny, worthless womanhood! My very heart and soul misgave me—misgave me for home, and family, and country, and future. Who can make a home with such raw material as this in the heart of it? It was not mere domestic inefficiency that confounded me, but a far deeper—an organic, inherent incapacity that seemed not soluble, nor malleable, nor pliable, nor able in any way to be wrought, by any known agent in moral chemistry, mechanics, or alchemy, into a sympathetic member of a Christian family. Of the scores that sat there, silent, chatting, listless, watchful, not one but seemed bold or stupid, crude, repellant, and utterly alien. I speak only of appearances. Doubtless under the harsh exterior were the germs of gentleness, fidelity, truth, modesty, courage — all human and womanly qualities, but dwarfed and crowded out of sight by unrelenting circumstance, by bitterly cruel fate. Doubtless patience and self-sacrifice, uncalculating love and uncomplaining sorrow, had mellowed and moulded many a poor soul before me. But all that I *saw* was an army of Amazons, who seemed conscious alike of their strength and their worthlessness, and equally to exult in both. It was as if they knew their inadequacy to household service, yet knew also that the call for household servants was so exceeding great and bitter a cry that it quite drowned any call for improvement on their part. They were blundering, awkward, and incompetent; but they are all we can get, and they know it. They control the market, and we must take them not simply with the grain of salt, but with the whole pillar of it. I was shocked to find suddenly springing up in my heart a sort of hate and hostility toward them. A distaste for republicanism and individual liberty, a longing for an absolute monarchy came over me, in which I should be absolute monarch. I hungered to have authority over them, rank, rampant weeds as they were; to transplant them and train them, with hoe, and knife, and trowel, and trellis, into sightly flowers, and wholesome, honest vegetables. Why should they be allowed this wild, vicious growth? Wages?

These clumsy, unskillful fingers, these inert, heavy brains demanding wages, when they should be only too thankful to be tolerated under tuition! Oh for one hour of tyranny— one hour of autocratic, irresponsible power, such as we knew in the halcyon days of slavery, to make these unprofitable servants feel their ignorance, and force them to overcome it! But the spirit of Seventy-six, the instincts of three generations of freedom, came quickly back, and suggested that moral disease is not to be homeopathically treated. It is tyranny that has wrought the mischief which tyranny can not cure. It is slavery, not liberty, that gave these sluggish brains and stolid faces. More than this, it is liberty's late-coming that brings this irritating exultation, this brazen and ill-timed content with ignorance and inefficiency. Over and over came to me the still small voice, "God hath made of one blood, one blood, one blood, all the nations of the earth." One blood. I pinched my own poor useless hands black and blue in the effort to impress upon them that they were one blood—one blood with the big, bare, sinewy, shapeless hands around me. And religion, patriotism, and pinching, all together, they did not more than half feel it. The other half kept saying, "Head of fine gold, feet of iron and clay. *We* are the head of fine gold; *you* are the iron and the clay."

I should be sorry even to be thought pandering in the smallest degree to class prejudices, and I know that mistresses are often as much to blame as maids for the disorder and misrule that prevail in our domestic kingdoms; but certainly the mistresses that I saw at this employment office were innocent-looking women enough—such women as I would not have hesitated to take service with were I in search of a situation. Some of them were evidently ladies of wealth and fashion; some—most of them—apparently of modest means and mien. There was, at least, no display of imperiousness, unreasonableness, inconsiderateness, or any form of bad manners. On the contrary, the signs of cultivation and courtesy were as marked in the one room as was their absence in the other. Equally marked, also, was the difference between the wants of mistress and maid. The former seemed chiefly concerned about qualifications; the latter regarded only price. These servants betrayed no misgiving of their ability to fulfill any duty whatever—indeed, no conscience or consciousness of the existence of such a thing as duty or faith in service. The main question was, "What do you pay?" On two points they were invulnerable. They would not budge an inch into the country, and they would not budge an inch any where for less than three dollars a week. This I learned by listening before making inquiries of my own. One lady was very desirous to secure a certain girl whose look pleased her, and she tried to move the obdurate Milesian heart by representing her family as small and the work light; but it availed nothing when she was obliged to add, "But my husband says he can not pay more than two dollars and a half a week."

I must here turn aside from the high road to enter my protest against this form of speech. It is a slight matter in itself, but it indicates and fosters a wrong state of affairs in the household. "My husband says *he* can not pay!" Is the husband, then, one firm, and the wife another, or are they joint members of the same company? Does the husband own the establishment and disburse the income, as an irresponsible monarch, and is the wife simply his subordinate? If so, she is just as much to blame as he. The husband is, or ought to be, the active partner in the business management of the concern, and the wife must, of course, depend chiefly upon his word for knowledge of its financial condition. But that knowledge, once communicated to her, is her own. That financial condition, whatever it be, is hers as much as his; and it is as much beneath her dignity to say to her servant, "My husband says he can only pay so much," as it would be beneath her husband's dignity to dismiss his clerk on the ground that "My wife says she can only pay you so much." If the husband has been delegated to hire the servant, it is proper enough; it is, at least, not severely reprehensible for him to arrogate to himself a little semblance of authority, and, having received due instructions from his wife, to say, "*I* will pay thus and so." If the wife is transacting the business herself, no power on earth should be strong enough to make her say any thing but "*I* will do this and that." Where husband and wife stand toward each other as they ought, these little matters adjust themselves without friction. My remarks are intended for the ninety-and-nine whose relations to each other need to be reconstructed.

The few men who came into this employment office on domestic errand bent made but a sorry figure. They looked and felt so out of place that one could but pity them. They stood around with their hats in their hands, trying not to be in the way—the great, innocent, helpless, good-natured, good-for-nothing creatures; shrinking up into corners, swept past by silks, drowned in flounces and laces, holding their hats high above their heads in the last gasp of self-sacrifice, awed by the mistresses, cowed by the maids, and utterly ground into insignificance. One, a country clergyman, was attempting, with a very moderate degree of success, to measure swords with a swarthy middle-aged woman, short, stout, indescribably hard-featured, and unrelenting. His educated and slightly professional voice, toned down to the requirements of the occasion, mingled pathetically with her harsh, unmitigated monotone. Doubtless he fancied he was securing a servant, but the unprejudiced by-stander could but admire at the assurance with which she was securing him.

She carried things with a high hand. He made a feeble effort to engage her on trial for two dollars and a half. But, oh no! oh no! This was a thing not dreamed of in my lady's philosophy. It was three dollars a week or nothing. And having guaranteed all her vested rights to attend church and not to attend children, her evenings out, and other constitutional prerogatives, he walked off with his prize. I pictured to myself the dismay with which some worn woman, dainty housekeeper, careful mother, delicate lady, would see her husband marching into the house with this tawny barbarian in tow.

The beauty of it was, that by the time it came my turn, I was ready. They would not go into the country, would they? Heavens! No country that I knew any thing about would hold them! The gentle-faced queen-mother circulated through her droning hive, and brought up to me one and another of her unpromising subjects who were supposed not to have insurmountable objections to "going into the country."

"An' what is yer pay, mum?" begin my interlocutors.

To which, with all the suavity I can summon, I make response, "That will depend entirely on what you do. If you suit me, I will pay you the full price. If you do not suit me, I shall not care for your services at all."

This seems to strike them as an entirely new view of the subject. The idea of suitability seems never to have found lodgment in their brains, and they are not prepared for it. They go nowhere on probation. They serve no apprenticeship.

"What is your family, mum?" inquires one, when she has recovered breath from the surprise of learning that there is a power of choice on the other side.

"*I* am my family," is the impressive reply. (*L'empire c'est moi!*)

"Likely you don't have much company."

I do not know why she considers it likely I don't have much company, unless she has conceived as unfavorable an opinion of me as I have of her, and I assure her solemnly that I have all the company I can get. It is needless to say we part with mutual satisfaction.

Certainly my thirty thousand women are not starving in this office.

We went to another intelligence office with no better success. The lady abbess was a florid, flourishing woman, admirably adapted to her calling, and not backward in expressing her mind freely to both classes of her customers, in a manner pleasant to witness, though it bore no visible fruit. Neither persuasion nor denunciation could induce her girls to go into the country. And while we were yet speaking, a buxom maiden came up, and reported herself in the market.

"Why, you have but just gone!" exclaimed madam, in surprise. "Couldn't you find the place?"

"Yes, mum. But the lady would not pay but two dollars and a half, and I wouldn't stay for that."

"More fool you!" was the pithy comment, as the girl was summarily dispatched to the waiting-room again.

Evidently an intelligence office is the last place in the world to look for intelligence. We must push our researches on a higher plane. Is there not a Christian Young Woman's Home, or some such benevolent invention, where young women from the country can find a cheap, comfortable, and respectable boarding-house while they are looking for employment? This is the place where working-women of the better class would be likely to resort for the suppression of starvation. Irish women do not starve. Look at their color and their muscles! It is our high-spirited American women who follow that occupation. Look at their lack of color and muscle! He that goeth in search of the rich and powerful Irish shall, of course, not prosper; but he that followeth after Americans shall have poverty enough on his hands to employ all his resources in its relief.

We sought and found the Home for Christian Young Women. A single Christian young woman was sitting in a comfortable room, waiting the hegira of young women from the country, which had evidently not yet begun. I laid my errand before her. She did not *know* of any person now who would be willing to engage in household service, though they did sometimes have applications for work of that sort. Generally the young women who came to them wanted employment in stores and offices as saleswomen, book-keepers, and copyists.

"Where do the thirty thousand starving sewing-women mostly go to?" I asked, steadfastly.

"To heaven, let us hope," said Hassan, under his breath.

The Christian young woman, who was a very nice person too, looked at me inquiringly. I explained the secondary object of my search. She smiled, comprehending the situation at once, and said she knew there were rumors of a great deal of suffering, which undoubtedly did exist, and which ought not to exist. But the girls would go into shops, and would not go into families, and what could you do?

Unquestionably nothing—only look over the Home, which was still in the experimental stage, and which was decent enough, so far as decency consists with sleeping four in a room, and which was apparently planned and conducted with the honest intent to be useful. We gave it the meed of our approbation, if that can be called approbation which is founded on an examination so slight; and having agreed that the Grand Army of the Starving did not rendezvous here, we were on the point of leaving, when we were called back by the announcement that a woman had just come in who might prove to be precisely what we wanted. She was a tall, muscular Christian, with high cheek-bones, and great facility in the use of language, and was accompanied by a young Christian of the same persuasion, perhaps fourteen or fifteen years old. The two forces were marshaled face to face, and, in reply to the first tentative inquiry, she poured forth torrents of information. She had been accustomed to living out, and, in fact, was then living out; but she wished to change her place. She would tell us the whole story, for she had nothing to keep back. She worked for a living, and she wasn't ashamed of it. She came from up country. Her father was well off, but the fact was he was penurious. And then she had a step-mother, who made matters worse, and she could not live in any peace at home. And her father died and made a will ("Made a will and died," muttered Hassan; but it was a pebble against the tide), leaving her something—no great—not enough to support her. But her step-mother would do nothing for her, because she had a will—would not even let her live in the house. And she had this child to support, and she had to work to help out. She could do housework best, because the child could stay with her. It was her sister's child; her sister was dead, and she had always taken care of the girl since she was a baby. She was a lawful, legitimate child, and as good a girl as ever stepped, and had never been away from her. She was fourteen years old, and must have an education; and she wanted to be where the child could live with her and go to school. It was suggested that the girl might get a place near her aunt, where she might work enough to earn her board and go to school at the same time. But no; they had never been separated, and she must have the girl with her where she could see to her. People might impose upon a girl of that age if they had the chance. Her price was three dollars a week, and the girl thrown in. What she should like was to keep house for a widower or an old bach.

They were easier to get along with, and would not mind the child so much.

I mentally thanked the Jewess for teaching me that word, and vocally suggested that it was impossible for me to furnish either of those qualifications. She smiled grimly, and admitted the imperativeness of the situation. Hassan, with his hand over his mouth, wished me to ask her whether she should prefer to have the girl taught in a Female Seminary, or by a governess engaged at the house; but it did not seem worth while to go into particulars while the generals were so far beyond our reach, and he was afraid to speak himself. So we came away, leaving the Christian young women to their fate, though Hassan, when he had recovered his spirits, courage, and freedom in the open air, remarked that he did not think this woman was very young or very Christian. I know that she was exhaustive. One would as soon have a whirlwind in the kitchen.

"Well?" queried Hassan, when we had walked on several minutes in silence.

"New York next," I replied. "I will find those thirty thousand starving women, or perish in the attempt."

"Forty thousand is the New York figure," he suggested, being, like the minute-hand, quick at figures.

I wrote to the editor of the best-tempered, the best-mannered, and the most trustworthy daily newspaper in the city of New York:

"DEAR SIR,—A few weeks ago I saw in your paper the annual statement that there were forty thousand women in New York making shirts at six cents apiece, and otherwise starving over the needle. If you will put me in communication with those women, I will speedily find a comfortable and respectable home for one of them, so that you will have only thirty-nine thousand nine hundred and ninety-nine to carry over to next year. Very respectfully, etc., etc."

His reply came promptly. Could I tell in what issue of

their paper the statement referred to appeared? If so, they would endeavor to look up the matter and give me the earliest possible information.

I could not give the exact date, but it was only a few weeks before.

He expressed great regret, but it would be impossible for them to do any thing without definite information on that point.

Five peas sat in a pod, says Hans Christian Andersen. They were green, and the pod was green, and therefore they thought the whole world was green. The fable is of New York editors. But the rural mind knows that forty thousand women *in articulo mortis* do not suddenly drop out of the universe like a penknife lost from your pocket.

I arose and went to New York.

I descended boldly upon the awful lair of a New York daily newspaper editor, who professes himself, and is generally believed to be, the busiest person in the known world, except the father of all mischief.

I do not expect to be believed if I say that he was sitting with his feet upon a chair, reading a newspaper, doubtless admiring one of his own editorials. Therefore I do not say it; but I know what I saw.

He took down his feet instantly, and stood upon them, evidently feeling that his hour had come. New York editors, I fancy, are not accustomed to being called upon to confront their assertions in this summary fashion.

I accosted him without apology or remorse.

"You said in your excellent paper"—so much granted to the spirit of courtesy—"a few weeks ago that there were forty thousand women at the point of death and the needle. Unless they are by this time all dead or fed, I will thank you to introduce me to a few scores of them."

He ran his fingers through his hair—beautiful hair it was,

too, and abundant, in spite of the severe toil of the brain beneath—in a perplexed, abstracted way, and began, hesitatingly, "If you could give me the date of the paper that made the statement—"

But I was familiar with that old refrain, and replied, unflinchingly,

"I can not give it to you. But this thing is not done in a corner. Forty thousand gaunt, famine-stricken women can not come to the surface momentarily, like earth-worms after a shower, and then disappear from the day. If they swarmed the streets, or the cellars, or the garrets of New York three weeks ago, they swarm them now. They can not march into your newspaper forty thousand strong, and leave no trace. Tell me where to find them."

Poor fellow, I pitied him, as a tender-hearted inquisitor may be supposed to have pitied St. Lawrence on his gridiron. He ran both hands this time through his magnificent hair. He leaned his tortured head on his hands, and his elbows on the table. He folded his bonnie brow in horizontal and perpendicular wrinkles till it looked like a distressed chess-board. And then he started up with a bright, happy smile, and invited me home to dinner!

Rather than let go my hold upon him, I went.

We sailed and sailed up the beautiful river as serenely as if there were no women in the world. The editor expected his wife to meet us at the landing with the ponies, but she was not there. "Something has detained her," he said; and, after waiting a while, he went to the livery-stable and hired a coach. We had been ten minutes on our land journey when the editor's little son cried, "There's mamma!"

She was just late enough to have caused the trouble and the extra carriage, and not late enough to imply any serious cause of detention. Now, I thought, he will be vexed, though he is too polite to show it.

"Why, so it is!" he exclaimed, warmly. "Poor little mamma!" and jumped out and gave her his own seat, and drove the ponies home himself alone, or with some man, while we rode royally companioned.

I forgave him his forty thousand women on the spot.

If every man in the world would be thoroughly good to the one woman whom God has given him, there would be no forty thousand, or forty scores, left to fight the bitter battle in outer darkness.

Four-and-twenty hours lasted that dinner and its concomitants—four-and-twenty hours of paradise in a little stone eyrie—if that is not too violent a word—perched high up among the rocky Palisades. The lordly, lovely river wound slowly and smoothly by, and lost itself in the brilliant hues of autumn woods and the hazy purple of distant skies. Slender skiffs shot athwart from bank to bank, and lazy boats drifted down the gentle current far beneath our feet. The stars came glowing out one by one, and the city lights twinkled across the water, hardly less brilliant and beautiful —stars of hidden, happy homes.

What have want and famine to do in this perfect world?

The night-air freshens and sharpens, but within, upon the ample, hospitable hearth, leaps and sparkles, flickers, and fades, and leaps again, the boundless cheer of a hard-wood fire. Children play quietly about the room—real little girls, healthy and wholesome, in honest clothes, shy and silent, watchful and bright, whispering softly among themselves, and breaking out into half-hushed but wholly irrepressible laughs. Cogently entreated, little miss finds courage to exhibit her gymnastics on the hearth-rug before a very select and appreciative assembly, who enjoy exceedingly her skill in turning a somersault; whereupon Miss Roly Poly, fired with a noble ambition to emulate the feats of her older sister, must needs throw her somersault also, and proceeds to roll her chubby person into a delicious little puff-ball, and squirms around sidewise in a series of most astonishing and laughter-provoking wriggles, flattering herself all the while that she is turning heels over head, which is the only turn she does *not* make, bless her sweet innocence! The next best thing to her gymnastics is her devotion. "Bend your head, Roly Poly," says her papa, when he is about to say grace before meat. And if Roly Poly is too intent on her stranger neighbor, papa merely takes her by the nape of the neck and chucks her silky head into her plate till the words of thanksgiving are ended, which is an Aid to Devotion at once simple and effective; and Roly Poly takes it all in good part, sucking her thumb with silent steadfastness through the whole, nothing doubting herself to be in the line of the true apostolic succession.

After the glory of the dark comes the glory of the dawn, and then long rambles in the gorgeous woods, and long lingering on the sunny, warm rocks above the rolling river, and then down, down, down the steep cliff, through tangled shrubbery and over treacherous rocks, to the water's edge. And farewell, charming host and hostess, rosy cheeks, dimpled fingers, Roly Poly—good-by! And may no hard fate ever bring you out from your summer nook among the birds and breezes to swell the dreadful ranks of the unfriended and unsheltered!

We resumed search for the forty thousand women, but we never found them. It would be impolite and illogical to affirm that they did not exist. I only declare that they were not visible to the naked eye of the rural districts. At every turn one came upon ladies whose patience and temper were worn thin and threadbare by unfaithful workwomen; ladies whose plans were laid, whose engagements were made weeks beforehand, and who found both deranged and destroyed because their seamstresses failed to come. Worse than this, these seamstresses not only failed to meet their appointments, but they sent no excuse, no explanation, not even a notice. It was simply that nine o'clock, ten o'clock, twelve o'clock failed to bring them. I said, "Men would manage these things better. Men would dismiss a clerk who was so grossly negligent and unfaithful. You are really aiding and abetting misconduct. Why do you not teach punctuality and promptness by hiring other persons to do your work, instead of condoning them by submissively waiting till Madame La Sempstress is ready to come to you?"

"It would be just as bad," they said, "with the next one. The delay would simply be repeated. Besides, we do not know where to go for other assistance. All the women who are worth any thing are engaged weeks ahead. It is less vexatious, on the whole, to concentrate your patience on one person than to diffuse it over a dozen, since, unfortunately, each fresh draught upon vexation creates a new supply."

I must confess that I mistrusted these reports. Such a state of things seemed to me incredible. It must be apathy, supineness, indolence on the part of these city ladies, I thought. It is that *laissez faire* which will presently corrode the character, subvert our institutions, eat the heart out of our republic, and make mischief generally. Let us see what an influx of energy, determination, and courage from the green pastures of New England can accomplish. I visited in person the places where unemployed women might be supposed to congregate—rooms which were used, not as intelligence offices, but as a sort of sewing agency, where women's and children's garments were put out for manufacture and brought in for sale; rooms which were under the supervision of benevolent and intelligent persons, whose object was less commercial than philanthropic. But it was to no purpose. Not a little finger was to be had for love or money. There were the coats and garments which the Dorcases had made and were about to make, but no Dorcas stood ready to serve a waiting world.

"Do you never have applications from women who want work?" I asked.

"Occasionally we do, but we do not happen to have any on the slate now."

Yet one would suppose that a whole nest of slates would not be able to contain the names that should be written.

"Do the working-women *know* that there is such an agency as this in existence?"

The young woman smiled at my pertinacity and eagerness, and thought it was pretty generally known, as the agency was no very new establishment. Continuing to look over her books, she found that one good seamstress, who was at work in a remote part of the city, was near the close of her engagement, and, unless she had subsequently formed a new one, I could very likely secure her, if I would take the trouble to go so far.

What is trouble when it comes in the shape of coach or horse-car to him who would save an unprotected woman from starvation and dishonor?

"Starvation and dishonor!" echoed my indurated New Yorker. "You will find that she will be engaged three weeks ahead, and then we shall renew our probation of waiting."

But the energy of the farming sections prevailed, and we found the young woman, who thoughtfully counted her fingers—"with a hundred needles exquisitely pricked"—and then replied that she could come to the rescue "three weeks from next Monday." So, it will be seen, the farming sections quick upflew, and kicked the beam.

This, as our friends Swinburne and the ancient Greeks remark, was the end of that hunting. Mark the perfect man, and you will behold that he never pushes his forces beyond the verge of hope for the sake of a futile consistency. The starving women were relinquished to foreordained obscurity, and the exploring expedition devoted the remainder of their lives to moral reflections, of which the following are chief.

V.
THINGS NEEDED AND THINGS WANTED.

THINGS are worth all they are good for. The primary use of the heavy silken curtain is, by richness of texture, and beauty of color, and grace of fold, to give to the room an air of elegance, comfort, and repose. But if a little child of the house has set its clothes on fire, the costly curtain can be put to no higher, no more economical use than to wrap it around the little form and stifle the threatening flame. As between folding the curtain away, to become creased and stained in some antique chest, or leaving it unmarred in all its drawing-room magnificence, and devoting it in emergency to rough but vital service, there can be no question.

The parable is of woman. Her first cause, so to speak, and her actual uses, would hardly suggest each other; and in the press of the latter the former has been largely overlooked. Her primary value is not only foreign to, but is absolutely incompatible with physical toil, manual labor, commercial industry. If we are to judge of design by results, she was not made for it. Physically, mentally, and morally, she was made for directly the opposite. Nature and revelation agree in this. You may not believe the Bible, but you can not doubt your own eyes. You may never have learned to use your eyes, but there is the Bible. It was man who was doomed to eat his bread in the sweat of his face. Woman's bread was to be found for her. A thousandfold more awful in its requirements, perhaps a thousand-fold more sweet in its rewards, was the work of woman. To wrest from the earth shelter, and food, and warmth, to make straight in the desert a highway for the human race, is the appointed duty of man. To nurture the race thus physically provided for into grace, and purity, and strength, is the duty of woman. Yet duty is a cold word to use, and a worthless word at best. For, in the ideal family—which one need not have the gates ajar the smallest crack to know must be the type of heavenly life, if there be any heaven—in the ideal family the man's most abounding joy, the mainspring and hope of his career, is planning and working for his family; while the woman moves hither and thither, transmuting all coarse metal into gold by the unconscious alchemy of her love, without thought of duty. Indeed, there is generally no such thing as duty to the people who really do it. They simply take life as it comes, meeting, not shirking its demands, whether pleasant or unpleasant; and that is pretty much all there is of it.

Speaking broadly, the difference between the Conservatives and the Radicals on the "Woman Question" is one of degree, not of kind; of shadow, not substance; of subordinate, not of primary interest. The Conservatives think that the Radicals are trying to make woman over into a kind of man, and so they are. But the Conservatives think that they themselves are trying to keep woman woman, which they are not. They are simply trying to keep woman the kind of man she already is. No organization has yet been effected, no convention has been called to make her woman, or to remove the hinderances which prevent her from becoming woman, for nature is so strong that it does not need cultivation in this direction. It only wants the absence of restraint. Take away from woman the necessity of being any kind of a man—and a poor kind it must always be—and she never will grow into any thing but a woman. Here and there men have tried the experiment; mostly, it is probable, without knowing it. No ambition to solve a social or psychical problem animated them; but their own native delicacy, their alert mental power, the strong man's spirit born in them and kept unspoiled, set them unconsciously in the right path. Of their own instinct, following their own bent, they did their work, and left the woman, perhaps made the woman free to do hers. Without recognizing the process, the world sees the result in grand, gracious women; in bright, wild, strong-natured children; in free, eager, vigorous home-life. But these men do not organize. They do not even combine. I scarcely know if they have ever spoken. The speakers on the "Woman's Rights" side demand that woman shall have man's advantage to do man's work. The opposing speakers demand that she shall continue to do man's work with woman's disadvantages. But the true woman's right is not to do man's work at all. The Radicals demand that women shall support themselves by having an opportunity to do man's work, and receive therefor man's wages. Their opponents practically maintain that women shall support themselves by doing man's work, and receiving therefor whatever man shall choose to allow them; but the true woman's right is not to support herself at all. I mean this in the broadest, most palpable sense. Women ought to be supported by men. The building can never stand firm until we begin on this foundation. I do not mean simply that women ought never to be forced to get their own living, as the phrase goes, but that the living which is got for them should be one of ease and comfort. A woman is not supported by her husband, or her father, or her brother when she works as hard in the house as he does out of it. To receive service without paying wages may be robbery; it is certainly not conferring support. Stone walls do not a prison make, but neither do they make a paradise. Solitary confinement within a narrow house does not change hard labor into useful leisure.

So great is popular ignorance of the true nature and final

cause of woman, that she who was supported as she ought to be would be considered by the masses, and even by many who tower above the masses, to be supported in idleness. By far the larger part of the peculiar, the really appropriate, the only economical work of woman lies within a sphere well-nigh invisible to the common vision. No woman is free to live the life which she ought to live, to accomplish for the world the work which she was fashioned to accomplish, until to the carnal eye she seems to have pretty nearly nothing at all to do. So, when it is scornfully said, as a summing up of the absurdity of the thing, "You would then turn women into mere dolls, and have them live in idleness!" I answer, Yes. Perhaps, on the whole, that is as near as we can get at it to begin with. So commercial, so mercenary, so altogether material is the value set upon woman in the ordinary estimation, that the nearest approach we can make to a common understanding of her real value is to sweep away the old standards and begin new. Dispense with every thing that is usually considered woman's work, and we shall then, at least, be able to set our faces toward the Zion that will come with the discovery of her real work. Given a clean balance-sheet, and we will see what accounts can be figured up. Given a woman-race with hands unshackled, with time unmortgaged, and we shall be on the high road to ascertain what bountiful provision Nature has made for the sustenance and cherishing of her children.

But upon this subject women seem to be very nearly as much in the dark as men. From the public speeches and public writings of women, you would gather that women had only to choose between idleness on the one side, or man's work on the other. It is either an Oriental life, inane, supine, selfish, or one of manifest, tangible, wage-winning business. They believe in the dignity of labor—man's labor, but they do not believe in the existence of woman's work.

They admit that the mother has special exemptions, but they hold motherhood to be an incident, a vocation, and that, outside of this incident, women are men. Many women are right on this matter, but they are right silently, instinctively, subjectively, through experience and the inner light. What women preach and teach in public is the view which has been held and taught by men time out of mind.

Perhaps it is not too late to say that this book is intended exclusively for women. Men may consider themselves not only discharged from any fancied obligation to read it, but respectfully requested not to read it; for to them it will be but a savor of death unto death. The truth which it contains, and which it is hoped may be wholesome when applied in the proper quarter, will only minister to their self-love, and tend to turn away their eyes from beholding their own vanities, and fix them upon the vanities of women, a result which is beneficial to neither.

To women only let me suggest that, in planning for the world as it ought to be, we should never forget the world as it is. If woman has never yet been ranked according to the real standard of valuation, we may yet make the most of her according to the lower standards. Always remembering that a state of repose, ease, leisure is that for which woman was divinely designed, let us lay aside for the present all thought of what would be necessary or unnecessary for her in that condition, and speak only of women as they are in this hard, exacting present stage of the world's progress. Granting and affirming that woman ought to live outside of the laws of trade, it is none the less true that, if she puts herself, or is brought by society within the scope of those laws, she must conform to them. Granting and asserting that woman ought not to do man's work, it is none the less true that, if she does it, she must do it in man's way, or suffer the consequences. The products of her toil, the value of her labor, must be brought into direct comparison with those of man, and be judged solely by their worth, not by the weakness surmounted in the doing.

⌐The ignorance, the inexactness, the untrustworthiness, the unbusiness-like ways of women are appalling when you look at them from a commercial point of view. Men are as bad as they can be, one is sometimes tempted to say, but apparently they can not be so bad as women in these respects. Long ages of experience have at least educated them into a consciousness of the difference between yes and no, but women have yet to learn that they are not one and the same word. The carpenter promises to finish your new porch by a certain time. He runs weeks behindhand; and when, at length, the porch is finished, the rain weeps in at every seam, and pours in at every joint. But he has the grace to be ashamed. He knows that it is poor work and tardy work, and he takes care to bring in his bill when you are not at home.

But women look you blandly in the face and are not ashamed. They seem to lack a moral sense, or a mental perception, or whatever the faculty is which makes one capable of contracting an engagement. They do not comprehend its nature. It has for them no more binding force than a rope of sand. They break it with a serene unconsciousness that any thing is broken, or that there was any thing to break. I do not refer now to the female portion of our foreign population. No one expects to find there a scrupulous adherence to truth. But the Anglo-Saxon race is, I believe, considered to be beyond all other races truthful; and when a well-dressed and respectable American woman who knows how to read and write, and belongs to the Church, and goes to the sewing society, and changes her gown in the afternoon—when she promises to go east, and calmly turns about and walks west, and does not see that there is any discrepancy, does not tear her hair or send in her confession to the Church, you say at once that here is missionary ground. Such a woman, after as much deliberation as she may choose, engages, without condition, to come into your service on a certain day, to remain for a fortnight on trial, and then to decide whether she will continue or relinquish it. This is not an ordeal so severe that human nature can not be expected to meet it. It is not a promise for life, but for a fortnight. Yet, a day or two before the appointed time, she sends you word that she shall not come, because her son wants her to keep house for him! She does not see that her word is of more consequence than her wish, let alone her son's. She does not see that, even if she repented of her bargain, it is too late to withdraw from it. She does not see that her engagement to a stranger is a reason why she can not make an engagement with her son, but that her wish to make an engagement with her son is no reason why she should cancel her engagement with the stranger. The very slightness of her promise increases the enormity of breaking it. It is but a small thing for the son's housekeeping to be a fortnight delayed, and her engagement only lasts so long. Doubtless a request on her part for a release from the promise would be instantly granted, but she does not value her word highly enough to make that little exertion to keep it.

A young woman, bright, sensible, and American, makes a similar promise, and breaks it in a similar manner, except that she gives no reason at all. She simply and succinctly says, "I have concluded not to work for you." But she had formally concluded and engaged that she would work for you. To a person properly constituted or properly taught, an engagement could not have two conclusions.

When the first promise was made, there was an end of the matter. It was no longer an open question. It had passed beyond her control. No matter how much she might regret the decision, a woman who comprehends the nature of an engagement would not recall it. It takes two persons to make a bargain, says the adage, and it takes two honorably to break it.

Still further, to show how completely childish they are in recognition or non-recognition of obligation, these very persons will come to you, and, repenting themselves of their change of mind, ask you a second time to take them into your service, just as innocently as if no display of Punic faith had ever been made!

Now the first thing which I would do toward the amelioration of the condition of woman—the redress of her wrongs, and the enforcement of her rights—the very first measure I would adopt to enable her to obtain an honorable independence, when an honorable dependence was not possible—would be to imbue her with a sense of the sacredness of an engagement. First, last, and always is the obligation to keep one's word. He who shall abide in the tabernacle of the Lord is he that sweareth even to his own hurt, and changeth not. Do what you say you will do. Come when you say you will come. Go when you promise to go. Be as slow as you choose about making an engagement; refuse altogether to bind yourself, if you will; but, when you have bound yourself, let nothing whatever induce you to break the bond. If you have engaged to teach a school at five dollars a week, and find afterward that you can get another school at ten; if you have engaged to do housework at two dollars a week, and another place is offered you at three; if you have contracted to do a certain quantity of machine-sewing at two cents a yard, and learn presently that your next neighbor is doing the same sort at three—you may represent the case to your employers, and get a release from your engagement if you can, though even so much one should be slow to do. But without such a release you should no more withdraw from your bargain than you should drown yourself. The wisdom of the bargain is not a thing to be taken into the account. The fact of the bargain is all you have to consider. Do your work promptly and thoroughly—as promptly and thoroughly as if the terms were brilliantly satisfactory—and make a wiser bargain next time; but this debt pay to the uttermost farthing, as scrupulously as if you were sent into the world for nothing else.

When women have once become thoroughly possessed with the importance of keeping their word, the next step toward improving their condition is to improve the quality of their work. Of all the evils which womankind endure, the part which law can cause or cure is infinitesimal compared with that which is caused by their own inefficiency. I think it is not too much to say that good work *always* brings good price. There is always room high up. No matter whether it be serving, or cooking, or writing, or painting, real service is always in demand. But women, like men, must do the work which the world wants done, and not simply the work which they want to do. It is not more certain that two and two make four, than that she who can do well what people wish to have done will always find employment. One reason why woman's work is so little sought and so poorly paid is that it is so good for nothing. I am at this moment so far from joining in the general outcry concerning the low wages of women, that it seems to me in a large majority of cases women are overpaid. They receive more money than they fairly earn. The raw, rough, unskilled, untidy Irish servant in a New England kitchen is paid three dollars a week for diffusing discomfort through the house. A boy leaves a high-school well educated, well mannered, eager to learn, to become useful, to please his employers, and goes into the wholesale store, pays his own board, finds his own clothes, receives little or nothing in wages, but is too thankful to be admitted to the house and give his services for the sake of learning the art or the trade. Where will you find a woman, ever so ignorant, who is willing to give a single month's time to learning the arts of cooking or the ways of her employers? Ten to one she does not care to learn either. She is concerned only to get through the day after any fashion whatever, and receive her wages. Will any one venture to say that the New England house-servant is underpaid?

This, indeed, seems to run against what has before been said—that good work is necessary to good pay. But it only shows that in our country the demand for work is so great that even poor work receives good pay, and it makes still more unreasonable the clamor against the low wages of women.

A capable servant is perfect master of the situation. A good cook may be sure of twenty dollars a month the year round, through all her active life, and a comfortable home for her old age. She can be sure of consideration, respect, and kindness, and it is not at all unsafe for her to be often tyrannical and capricious. There is no more free and independent citizen than a trusty servant. It would sometimes not be far wrong to say there is no more absolute master. It is often amusing to see the proprietorship which a loyal servant assumes of a loyal household. Such a relation may become one of the most satisfactory relations of life. And, in face of all this, in face of the alleged suffering of women for want of work to do, and the certain suffering of women from overmuch work to be done, there are not wanting those who will rise up and attempt to heal the hurt of the daughter of my people by reference to social equality. In a paper devoted to the interests of women, a woman tells us of two ladies who "called at a private house in Brooklyn in search of board. On being told that the mother and daughter did the housework, they instantly decided not to remain, for it would be impossible for them to think of sitting at the same table with persons employed in such labor.

"In one of our New England cities lives a lady whose name I should like to give, but do not feel at liberty to do so. She said she wished no servants in her house who were not as good, or who knew less than she. You may be sure she has no difficulty in getting good help when she wants it. When her maid-servants have finished their work for the day, they put on their pretty clothes, and go into the parlor to entertain and be entertained. They sit at the same table with their mistress, and are treated in every respect as her equal. She has in her employ two women who have served her for thirty-five years. Her husband died not long since. He willed each of these servants five thousand dollars, and, in case they outlive his wife, the use of a house during life. Who will arise and make the appropriate comments on these two cases?"

I do not know whether my comments will be the "appropriate" ones expected; but, to my thinking, these incidents put women in the precise attitude of the person who should refuse to be saved from drowning by a man who had not been introduced. We are questioning how to rescue women from spoliation and starvation, and find that the trouble, after all, is not that woman is starving, but that she can not dine with her mistress! This may be a grievance, but it has no place in the discussion of woman's rights, and to bring it in seems childish and trivial. Do men dine with their employers, or refuse to work if they must eat by themselves? Here is a relay of carpenters—skilled workmen, owners of property, singers and players upon instruments, intelligent, reading, thinking men, and they eat their dinner in the barn or the cellar, and make merry. They would make still merrier if you should suggest to them that the fact had any significance in point of political economy. It is worse than foolish, it is mischievous, to bring up such facts as arguments on the woman question. They mislead. They divert attention from the real question. The demand is justice, and we discuss taste. Even as a matter of taste, there are two sides. For me, I have not the smallest admiration for the woman who makes a point of having her "help" eat and sit with her. She may be every thing that is charming, but this circumstance by no means proves it. It does not show or indicate that she is any more just, or generous, or sensible than the woman who prefers to eat alone. It is far stronger presumptive evidence of lack of discrimination and delicacy than of any thing else. A woman may be an excellent servant, and not an agreeable companion. Most women, too, have companionship enough without hiring it. Servants may be superior to their mistresses, but sitting in the parlor does not prove it. The persons who hire workmen or workwomen, not for their fitness to do the work required, but their general availability as companions, may please themselves and benefit individuals, but they contribute little to the solution of the labor problem. Women are not to be blamed for being natural aristocrats, but it is unfortunate that they should be led to nurse this aristocratic tendency at the expense of their comfort and prosperity. If a girl has a choice of places, she is right and wise in choosing the one most to her taste; and that she should choose the one where her position will be highest is creditable to her; but to cry out that she is starving because she can not find one to her taste is not right, nor wise, nor creditable. So, if a mistress can get plenty of her equals to serve her, she would be foolish to go unserved, and to make an ado about her sufferings, because she insists on having inferiors, and can not find them; but when inferiors are many, and their wail for work is loud and bitter, she is entirely wise in consulting her own inclination as to whether they shall assist at her meals in the English or the French sense of the word.

The mischief of it is that, when such things are brought forward as grievances, a wicked and perverse generation will immediately conclude that all grievances are of the same nature, and the plaintiff is summarily dismissed with costs. No one blames or ought to blame a woman for wishing to stand well in the world ; but disappointed ambition and baffled endeavor are as common to men as to women, and real or fancied inequality of rank is a poor ground for social revolution.

There is the great army of sewing-women, who, beyond question, are wretchedly paid. Equally beyond question is the wretchedness of their sewing. A good seamstress is as scarce as a good cook, and as sure of good wages. How many of these women, who make shirts at six cents apiece, know how to fashion under-garments tastefully, to cut them economically, to sew them neatly and strongly? What they do is the coarsest and most mechanical kind of sewing. When it comes to what is called family sewing, they are utterly deficient. There are plenty of mothers who would be eager to engage their services if their services were worth engaging. Women at the heads of households are put to great inconvenience and annoyance for want of competent help at the needle ; and the help which they get is often so clumsy, shabby, and ineffective, that it is a question whether it ought not to be called a hinderance. Let all women who design, or who are forced to earn their living by their needle, become skilled needle-women. Let them learn how to cut, and fit, and make all manner of clothing, outer and inner, coarse and fine, and then let us see whether they will be obliged to work at six cents a shirt.

But it is said they have no opportunity to learn this. They are poor, and have neither time nor teachers for any thing but the plainest work. This may be true, but it has nothing whatever to do with the question. The world does not ask how its servants came to be ignorant, but are they wise? It wants ability, not reasons for inability. It may not be a woman's fault that her work is poor, but she must not expect to get the same price for it as if it were good. This law is inexorable. Man did not make it, and man can not unmake it.

Here also comes in the necessity of doing the work which society wants done. There is just so much serving to be done; so much family sewing, that needs trained hands; so much slop-work sewing, that untrained hands can make shift to do. The trained hands are few, and they command the market. They are called fashionable milliners or dressmakers. They open shops; they set up clothing establishments; they ask great, perhaps exorbitant prices, and they make fortunes. The untrained hands are many, and are at the mercy of the market. They must take what they can get. Because they are many, there is competition; and starvation wages follow. There being only so much coarse work to be done, the greater the number of workers, the greater the subdivision of wages. There being so much fine work to do, the fewer the workmen, the larger the portion of wages to each one. If the woman is dissatisfied with making shirts at six cents apiece, let her make dresses at fifteen dollars. But she does not know how. What, then, is she complaining of? Must the employer who wants shirts, and does not want dresses, pay for one and receive the other? No, it is said; but the employer who wants shirts made should pay a living price. Not in the least. Whether the price be living or dead is no affair of his. It is his solely to pay the sum necessary to get his work done. It is not a question of morality; it is a question of market price. You have no more right to demand of a man that he shall pay twelve cents for work which he can buy at six, than he has to demand of you that you shall pay twelve dollars a barrel for flour when you can get it for five. Morality, and philanthropy, and sentimentality are entirely out of place here. They may come in to relieve individual suffering, but they contribute nothing to the solution of the problem. We pay for things what they are worth. Extra price for extra quality. Extra price for common quality may be charity or short-sightedness, but it is not trade. Trade is a law unto itself. It needs no outside interference. The fashionable dress-maker or the noted lawyer demands exorbitant prices. The remedy is at hand—you need not employ them. If they are really exorbitant, the withdrawal of patronage will speedily bring them to terms. If they are so skillful that you must employ them, then their terms are not exorbitant. For their signal skill they have a right to demand signal wages; and you have no more right to say that they shall bring their style and their sagacity to a cheaper market, than you have to demand that the owner of a coal-mine shall distribute his coal around among the poor, or sell it to working-men at half price.

The suit lately brought by a dress-maker to recover the amount of her bill from a customer exactly illustrates my meaning. Judging from the evidence, I have no doubt the charges were extortionate up to the verge of fraud; but so powerful is a reputation for skill, that, on the strength of it, a woman may dare to risk her reputation for honesty. I am sorry that a woman should thus abuse her gift, but I am heartily glad when she is so skillful in any honorable calling that she controls the market, and dares charge high prices. She has precisely the same right to do it that the great lawyer has to charge high fees. He does not necessarily bestow more thought on his cases than his lowlier brother, but he is paid for his ability to do more work with less thought. The city dress-maker puts no more stitches into her gown than the country dress-maker, but she charges for the *Je-ne-sais quoi*—which is born, not made. Of course, she may make fraudulent charges; she may want an extra fifty dollars on Saturday night, glance over her account-book, and assess that sum upon two or three of her rich and careless customers. Or she may make false entries and render false accounts, believing that her customers would sooner pay privately than contest publicly. That is simple dishonesty. So the hotel-keeper charges carriage-hire to guests who have ordered no carriage. If they protest, he says it was a mistake, and remits the fine. If they do not notice it, he gains his five or ten dollars. It is only a mode of theft. But it is not theft for a woman to put upon her work as high a valuation as it will bear. It is public as well as personal service. Every woman who demands a high price on what she has to sell, and gets it, benefits every other woman who has any thing to sell. Nor does she injure any one; for the woman who can not afford to buy her dresses and bonnets can make her own. Style is a luxury, not a necessity. A woman is under no obligation to wear a Worth gown, nor is there real bitterness to the pain of going through life without it.

There has been much talk lately about raising the wages of the women who are employed in the United States Treasury, and those senators and representatives who favored the measure are spoken of as friendly to the woman cause, and those who opposed it as being ungallant. Such talk is well enough for badinage, but it can never rise to the level of argument. Nothing seems clearer or fairer than that for the same work women ought to be paid the same wages as men. But it is a commercial ought, not a moral ought.

If trade says No, it is not the province of morals to say Yes. It is not the province of morals to have any say about it. Morality has not to make the rules of trade, but it may help to keep them. It has not to regulate the price of labor or of merchandise, though it may enforce the fair and prompt payment of that price. It does not prescribe the terms of the contract, though it demands that there shall be no concealment of conditions, no evasion of meaning, no violation of pledges. Women ought to receive the same wages for the same work as men, if they can get it. But the ought is to be enforced by the power of women, not extracted from the compassion of men. Until then, nothing is gained. A single employer here or there may be moved by conscientious scruples to pay men and women the same wages; but, so long as it turns on a man's conscience, it is local, temporary, not to be depended on. It is no more a victory for the "woman's cause" than when a man gives a poor woman a dollar in the street. Women-workers have gained no vantage-ground until they are in a condition to dictate terms instead of receiving bounty.

The United States government is like any private employer, except that it has only a derivative power, and is therefore more limited in action. If a private employer chooses, from conscientious motives, to pay nine hundred dollars for work that can be equally well done for six, he has a right to gratify himself. He pays the cost out of his own pocket, and it is nobody's affair but his own. I question if the government has a right to pay more than the market-price for labor. It is not spending its own money, but that of the people. It is not set up in business for itself, but is the agent of the people. It may not transcend its proper bounds in trying social experiments to some extent; but there are certain principles which seem to be settled, and which have therefore passed beyond the province of experiment, and one of these is the eternity and self-sufficiency o. the law of demand and supply. The question of work and wages is not to be tampered with. It needs only to be left alone to adjust itself. The government is concerned only to get its work well done. It should employ the best of servants, and pay the price which it is obliged to pay. It has no right to put its wages so low that it can secure only incompetent servants, and it has no right to put its wages any higher than is necessary to secure the best service. If it pays the Treasury women so little that only inferior women offer themselves, and, in consequence, only inferior work is done, it is an unfaithful steward, a squanderer of the people's money. If at the price it now pays it secures perfect and permanent service, has it a right to pay more, out of deference to an abstract idea, whether that idea be justice or mercy? It is no reason against a rise in salary that women can be found who will work at the low wages. Probably no salary in the country can be reduced so low that some man or woman will not be ready to take the office, but the salary may be made so small that only a very poor sort of person will think it worth while. Such reduction would be the worst kind of extravagance. Neither is it necessarily a reason for the rise of salary that the women will otherwise resign, since there may be twice as many women in waiting who would perform the work equally well; and, unless the change would amount to more than the desired increase of salary, government would have no right to grant the increase.

An argument brought forward against the proposed increase of salary is that the women themselves did not desire it, and had sent in requests to members of Congress not to grant it; but this also is vanity. The most thoughtless person must surmise that people never really want less money than they can honestly get; and when a workman petitions for smaller wages, it is an indirect way of gaining some other object. So in this case it appears, upon close questioning, that the outside pressure upon the Treasury is already so great that the occupants have all they can do to hold their own, and, if the salary be increased, they fear they will succumb and be swept away altogether. But this is turning the world upside down indeed. One would not blame the women. It is not to be expected that a weak swimmer, struggling against the tide, should be philosophical, but it would be blameworthy indeed if cool, grave, dispassionate legislators should frame a law on such pretexts.

Whichever way the question is decided by government is of no general importance so long as it is decided by government. When women can demand of their employers a fixed price, and can afford to leave them unless that price is paid, the victory is gained, the staff is in their own hands. Then their price will be paid, and they will have no more complaints to make of injustice. But any liberality or any increase of wages that comes only from an employer's sense of justice or benevolent disposition is of no more account in the solution of the problem than so much money bestowed in charity. It is another form of dependence. It is not a step toward independence.

One would suppose, from what he hears, that the great and crying want of women is work; or, as it is sometimes put, a fair day's wages for a fair day's work; or, again, freedom to do whatever she is capable of doing. This is not so. What women want is not work, but the wages of work; not freedom to work, but freedom to receive money without working. There is plenty to do now, but they will not do it. They wish to live like women, and be paid like men. I do not blame them for this. It is as natural as it is to be born. They can no more help it than they can help being women. They would not be women if it were otherwise.

They were made to spend money, not to earn it. They take kindly, because instinctively, to spending money, and hardly, because enforcedly, to earning it. But all the same it remains that when they become men they must put away womanish things, and when they undertake to earn money they become men.

If women want work, what doth hinder them from getting it? They flock to the school-houses for situations as teachers till there are twenty applications for every vacancy, and in some instances I know there are twice and thrice that number. They press against the doors of the government offices, and for one who is received scores are sent disappointed away. They will be clerks, copyists, amanuenses, any thing which promises light employment, permits tasteful dress, and bestows even a moderate remuneration; and for this they will wait, and pray, and suffer. But to the fields that are really ripe for harvest the laborers are distressingly few. It has been dinned and dinned into the ears of women that the place where they are wanted is the kitchen, but into the kitchen they will not go. They are sorely needed in the sewing-room, but the sewing-room is to them an abomination. They have no taste for these things, it is said. But have they any inborn taste for copying deeds? Is there any thing especially agreeable in counting greenbacks till your fingers bleed? It seems degrading to a girl of good education to assume the business of cooking or clear-starching, but there is a call for ten times as much mind, skill, judgment, wisdom in managing a cooking, or an ironing, or a sewing department, as is required to count money or copy letters.

Sick-nursing is an occupation the most honorable, important, and remunerative. The demand for nurses is constant and urgent. They receive whatever they choose to ask. No skill, no training, no education, no refinement is thrown away here. And it is a calling peculiarly womanly; so much so, indeed, that only the money earned puts it in the sphere of man. One would suppose that women would rush to it. On the contrary, they assiduously keep out of it. The scarcity is so great that the need is always pressing, often distressing, and not infrequently fatal. Life is lost, health and happiness are destroyed, and mourners go about the streets from sheer and simple lack of careful and intelligent nursing. Delicate, sensitive women, in critical and dangerous illness, with every sense preternaturally acute, and power of resistance weakened by suffering, are consigned to ignorant, superstitious, garrulous, obtuse, untidy, snuff-taking old women, whose very presence would be enough to make a well person sick. If sudden and severe disease makes too heavy draughts upon the healthy,

"East and west, and south and north,
The messenger rides fast,"

and often and long they ride in vain. The patient not only suffers from being tended by worn-out friends, but he suffers unspeakably from anxiety on their account. Instead of being quiet, and giving his sole strength to recovery, he is constantly kept back and kept down by feeling himself a burden upon those he loves. And the greater their mutual love, the greater their uneasiness. It is amazing to hear this outcry for a wider sphere and greater opportunities for woman, while her sphere is already a thousand times wider than she spans, and her opportunities a thousand-fold greater than she has ever attempted to measure. Every sphere under the sun is open to her but the do-nothing sphere. Every imaginable opportunity is offered her except the opportunity to sow tares and reap wheat. The cry for work, the clamor for a career, are the cry and clamor of weakness. Strong eyes see work, and strong hands do it, and say nothing about it. She who is equal to a career enters upon a career, and there is no flourish of trumpets. Be sure she who complains of obstacles is not the victim of obstacles.

I do not blame women for wishing to live easy and dress well, but I do blame them for thinking it more dignified to whine and complain than to live laboriously and dress coarsely. I rejoice in every woman who conquers fate and compels deference, but I do not rejoice in those who are neither strong enough for a calm victory or a dignified submission. It is well if a woman has the power of self-direction—feels no fear and asks no favor; but there are thousands of women who have no especial bent to any thing, but who have general adaptations that might make them useful, prosperous, and honored if they would only give their energies to work, instead of to getting money without work.

On the supposition that women want work, various schemes are devised to furnish it. I have heard talk of a plan which is to supply women with small farms in the vicinity of a large city, which farms they are to occupy rent free for a certain time, at the expense of the state, and whereon they are to support themselves by raising small fruits for the market. It is found that the poor women will not go into the country, but persistently cling to the city, and this device is brought forward as a sort of compromise.

One would be slow to oppose any thing which looked to the amelioration of poverty, lest haply he be found to fight against God; but it must be confessed that women in the country, who are wearing out their lives with overwork, and their nerves with the awkwardness and ignorance of housemaids, look with coldness upon such a scheme. "What right," they say to the authorities, "have you to tax us to assist women whom we would pay handsomely to assist us? These women object to going into the country. There are few of us who would object to a residence in the city or suburbs, but we are obliged to live in the country, and we can not see why we should be called upon to release others from the same necessity."

These suffering countrywomen may be right or wrong, but there are reasons which seem to make such well-meant plans chimerical. In the first place, it is wrong to suppose that farming, or even householding, does not need brain. A woman can not raise strawberries by instinct any more than she can make dresses. Of the two, I fancy it would be far easier to learn how to sew than how to carry on a farm with judgment. To take a woman from helpless poverty—and that is the only kind of poverty we are speaking of, for poverty that can help itself is not poverty—to put such a woman at the head of a house and a farm, without knowledge and without experience, seems not only injudicious, but unwarrantable. She who is not faithful over a few things should not be made ruler over many things, especially at other people's expense. She who has not sense enough, or spirit, or efficiency, or whatever you may call it, to set herself to profitable work, in a country where profitable work is as plenty as it is here, has not sense enough to be put at the head of an enterprise which requires so much as does horticulture or agriculture. Farms for women? Why, it demands science to drive a pair of oxen! The ox knoweth its owner, and if that owner be a nervous, unobserving, unreasoning, undecided, inefficient woman, do you think the ox will not speedily find it out? Moreover, though work in a garden looks light, and even romantic, in the columns of the agricultural newspaper, I think it will be found more severe and more wearing than work within doors. The flowers that grow in print grow gayly, with scarcely the soiling of a lady's finger in the cultivation; but the flowers that grow in gardens grow under the old dispensation, by the sweat of somebody's brow. How much more potatoes and beets! That brow ought to be a man's, even if the brain behind it be a woman's. Something may come of setting women at work in the fields, but I do not believe the class of women whom it is the intention thus to aid have the skill to manage or the strength to till a farm.

The women who own and cultivate land, and make it profitable, are not those whose sufferings induce the compassionate to claim for them state aid. They are women of nerve, and ingenuity, and independence. Would it not be a less costly, less hazardous, and less objectionable experiment to seek to perfect the weaker sisters in certain mechanical work, which makes no unusual draught on their mind or their strength, but which does require patience, accuracy, care, and practice? Would it not be better to enter the domains which women have overrun, but not occupied, rather than those into which they have not yet penetrated? Outdoor work has hitherto fallen to man, and indoor work to woman, yet men do even indoor work better than women. There are thousands of female cooks, and the large majority of them are bunglers. There are not a great many male cooks, but they are generally good. I admit that I make these assertions necessarily from a limited induction —rather as impressions than as positive knowledge; but let them go for what they are worth. I believe there are few who will not confess that a man-servant at the table, at the door, at the cooking, and the sweeping, is not only "better style," but is a more efficient member of the household staff. You are more sure that the work will be promptly, thoroughly, and quietly done with a man at the fore than a woman. This is not in the smallest degree a statement in a woman's disfavor. It only goes, with many other things, to show that women were not made for toil, whether indoors or out. Men were made for both, and, therefore, when men and women compete, men must always win. But, if women can not compete with men in those fields of which they have held undisturbed possession for generations, how can they hope to do so in those which have been hitherto occupied by men? If men, as soon as they begin to do what women have always been doing, bear away the palm, how can women hope to hold their own where men have all the advantage of superior strength and practice? Failing in a business where they have much experience but little capital, they would embark in a business where they have less capital and no experience at all. Since, now, women's need is so imperative, would it not be better to take them where they are, and perfect them in those matters wherein they have made a beginning?

It is not to be expected that women hard pressed by the exigencies of life should have leisure to be broadly wise. The poor seamstress is absorbed in getting her work done in season to pay the rent, and to her a suburban house and an acre of land rent-free must seem a paradise. The ignorant girls who organize disorder in our kitchens and discomfort in our houses are hardly to be blamed, for no one has taught them the arts of order and comfort. It is but natural that women who are actually suffering should snatch at any hope of relief, and should send up a great and bitter cry for relief when they have no hope. But the men and women who arise as leaders to these people are under the strongest obligations to be wise. If it is ever lawful to be inconsequent and inconclusive, it is not before an audience to whom wrong doctrine means immediate and disastrous wrong-doing. It has never been demonstrated that any person has suffered in mind, body, or estate from our long delay in discovering the undulatory theory of light; and, if one day some new philosopher shall arise and put this theory to rout by irrefragable proof that light is a fixed and solid body, it is difficult to see how our happiness or well-being is to be consciously enhanced thereby. But if the women of this country are suffering because they can not or will not work, and if the Prophetess Deborah arises and tells them that they are suffering because their selfish employers will not pay them, or selfish society will not employ them, Deborah does them immediate and serious harm. Double harm, for she takes their attention away from the only direction in which relief can come to them, and fastens it upon a spot from which permanent relief can never come. And because she is a woman and a friend she does her sad work all the more effectually.

VI.
WOMEN AMONG THE PROPHETS.

OBSERVING the shiftlessness—I do not know any more comprehensive word—which characterizes so many working-women, and which shows the point of the Scripture, "The destruction of the poor is their poverty," I noticed one day that a woman was advertised to address the working-women in one of our large cities. I had never heard a woman lecture—in public, and had no special sympathy with the feeling that would prompt a woman to do so. Yet one can hardly take note of the distress of the poor, and see how surely that distress is brought about by their ignorance of ways and means, without longing to lift up his voice in suggestion and assistance. No, it is no wonder that a woman of ability and benevolence, gifted with power of speech, should find all her native reluctance overborne by a strong desire to serve the feeble and impoverished. And what an opportunity! One of the largest halls in one of the largest cities in the country, filled with men and women—working-women largely—favorably inclined to the speaker, and listening to her voice as that of a friend and a superior. Will she use the eloquence, the wit, the pathos, the imagination which have been so freely attributed to her, in enforcing upon these struggling women the importance of excellence, of thoroughness, of punctuality; the indispensableness of keeping an engagement, the necessity of doing what work presents itself? Will she show them that it is skill which wins? Will she hint to them any way by which they can learn what they do not know, or improve upon what they do know, or transfer their goods to better markets, or take advantage of the markets that exist? Alas! I had time to think of this, and much more. The lecture was advertised to begin at eight in one paper, and in another at half past seven. I inwardly fear that it is some womanish inaccuracy that has caused this discrepancy; but perhaps it is some man's blundering. Let us hope so; at any rate, let us say so. To make sure, we are on the spot soon after seven. The half hour comes and goes. So much, then, is proved: the lecture begins at eight. Eight arrives, and the lecturer does not. Five minutes past eight, and an audience of thousands waiting; ten minutes past eight, and thousands of working-women waiting. It is to be feared something dreadful has happened—or hoped. Seventeen minutes past eight, and a lady comes forward on the platform and says, "Miss Lecturer hopes you will excuse her. She only arrived on the last train, and has been very busy." And, without farther preamble, the lecturer takes up her parable.

Who does not see that in the very beginning, before a word was spoken, the lecturer had done those working-women a greater mischief than all her talk could undo? In one of their worst habits she had directly confirmed them. Stronger than by any spoken language she had said to them, "It is of no consequence that you keep your engagements. Engagements are not of any account. Punctuality is an unimportant matter. Strict promptness has nothing to do with business. It is just the same to dawdle along fifteen minutes behind time as it is to be exact to the minute."

Understand, her crime was not in being late. If the introducing lady had said, "The train in which Miss Lecturer came was thrown from the track, and detained seventeen minutes," or, "She tore her gown in coming out of the house, and was obliged to go back and change it," the evil would have been avoided; but the excuse given was no excuse at all, and was a lesson in unpunctuality. The lady had made an appointment to address five thousand persons say at eight o'clock. Why did she leave home in the last train if the last train would not enable her to meet that appointment? If her course were unavoidable, she should have said so; if it were avoidable, she should not have taken it. It is an insult to any audience to keep them waiting. To an audience of working-women, assembled for the amelioration of their condition, it is an irreparable injury.

After the hungry sheep had a shepherd to look up to, how were they fed?

It is impossible to give an analysis or an outline of the lecture. It had apparently no plan. It had certainly no coherence. It consisted of a collection of remarks bearing something of the same relation to its subject as did Mr. Artemus Ward's lecture to his "Babes in the Wood." This is not necessarily a defect. It would be difficult sometimes to find the central point of Mr. Ralph Waldo Emerson's lectures, yet no one would choose he should wander in paths less devious. A large part of the lecture consisted in the enunciation of truths which no one doubts, and the announcement of facts which are universally received. The time has come to act. Women are not so well off to be freed from responsibility. The highest motto in life is "Onward and upward." Women must work in order to be healthy. As things are, women often marry for a living, which is very dishonorable; and thousands of souls are steeped in the blackness of darkness because—it was not very clear why; but, as far as one could make out, because things are as they are. Manual labor is not liked by men or women. Masons receive four dollars a day, and clerks two; yet there are many thousands more clerks than masons in New York. Wherefore make labor honorable. Reverence masons as much as you do clerks. Myriads of women are living in a dreadful condition in New York. They might have been ministers or lawyers if they had received a proper training. As it is, their life is drinking away at the point of the needle. And so on, and so on. But what of it?

And yet these generalities were the best of it. When it came to particular application, the case was pitiable. The Hartford Insurance Company was taken to task for not insuring the lives of women as well as those of men. "Are not women liable to be killed as well as men?" asks the lecturer, eloquently. But would any wise man or woman have us believe that an insurance company is conducted on any other principle than that of making money?—is impelled, for instance, by a prejudice against women? There needs no ghost, it would seem, to tell us that, if a company will not insure the lives of women, it is simply because they do not find their account in it, and not because they have a blind belief that women do not die, or a depraved indifference as to whether they die or not. No reform seems more hopeless than an attempt to reform insurance companies in this respect; and we shall secure equal rights to life, liberty, and the pursuit of happiness a thousand years before we shall secure equal rights to life-insurance from these stiff-necked and uncircumcised corporations, unless we can convince them that they will declare greater dividends by such equality!

Another practical suggestion in the lecture was that, as higher salaries are paid to male clerks in Washington than to female, the male clerks should relinquish their desks to women, go West, and till the land. Granting this to be an excellent recommendation to the young men, what was its value in a lecture to working-women? Was any one of them likely to be helped out of her difficulties by it? What sorrow of a woman is soothed or what struggle softened by her being told that some man ought to give her his twelve-hundred-dollar office, and retire to the backwoods—unless he marches to the backwoods?

Suppose he does; is the case decidedly gained? Is it certain that the country would be better for the change? Could the clerical work of the government, with certain advantage, be taken out of the hands that have always held it, and put into those that have never tried it to any large extent, and have not always been successful even in their limited trials?

And if young men will be clerks, and will not be masons, what are the working-women to do about it? Masons make four dollars a day, and work eight hours; and clerks make two dollars a day, and work twelve hours; and professional men make nothing, and are twenty hours a day about it. What then? "Make labor honorable," says the lecturer. How? I ask, as a disciple. In a general way, labor is honorable; in the divine economy, it is desirable; but in practical daily life we all wish to be rid of it as fast and as far as possible. Nor is it likely ever to be otherwise. No advance in civilization or enlightenment will ever make labor any thing but a burden. Indeed, we measure our civilization by the extent to which we shift the weight of labor from our own shoulders to the forces of Nature. An honest man is honored, but we all recognize the fact that brain-power is of a finer and higher order than muscle-power, and we never shall and we never can help paying greater homage to the one than to the other. Indeed, we shall long strive after the semblance of the one more strenuously than after the substance of the other. But, even granting that it is manly to be a mason, and effeminate to be a clerk, how does that heal the grievous hurt of the daughters of my people? If merchants persist in hiring boys instead of girls, what can the girls do? How are serving-women helped in the battle of life by being told that they ought to have the place which men will not give up, and which women can not secure?

And suppose the serving-women of New York might make

good lawyers if they were properly trained—how are they to be trained? They have no means to support themselves while learning a useful trade, says the lecturer. Very true. There are scores of boys in the same predicament. Sometimes they make a brave wrestle with fate, and overcome. Sometimes they go down in the conflict, and lie in unknown graves. Sometimes they never strive at all. It is the old unsolved and insoluble problem of evil. Hundreds and thousands of souls, men and women, never seem to have a fair chance in life. If only all human beings were wise and virtuous, the serving-women of New York might become chief justices. If wishes were horses, beggars might ride; but is it worth while to collect five thousand beggars in their best clothes in one room to tell them so at fifty cents a ticket?

We were given also a pathetic and eloquent invective against men in general, and Philadelphians in particular, on account of a certain young woman who was then lying in prison under charge of having slain her illegitimate infant. Her story was told with great solemnity and sternness, and the young person was invested with a sentiment, a tenderness, and an interest which we do not always take to women who have married their husbands and not murdered their children. The poor creature had been betrayed by hypocrisy in high places, and was perishing from cold and hunger; with woman's devotion, she refused to give the name of her seducer, lest she might bring to grief the wife whom he had subsequently married; the lawyer whom she had employed had grasped all her money and left her defenseless; the Philadelphians in general, we could but infer, were a sanguinary race, famished for a poor girl's blood: and would a jury of WOMEN, think you, have doomed this young girl to die?

Now, if this appeal, under the circumstances, meant any

thing definite, it meant that this woman did not receive full justice because she was judged by men; while, if she had been tried by a jury of women, she would have been more fairly—that is, more leniently—treated.

Is it possible that any woman can believe that female criminals would receive—I do not say more justice, for that is quite possible—but more lenity at the hands of women than at those of men? This is a subject which hardly admits of discussion, and on which discussion is fruitless. But it seems to me that women who are guilty—especially of this class of crimes—have need to pray with peculiar fervor, From all women judges and women juries, good Lord, deliver us!

It hardly needed subsequent developments to show that the case was chiefly a made-up one. Philadelphia is a respectable American city; and, notwithstanding the unspeakable and indelible infamy which broods over the administration of justice in New York, and which puts to shame our boast of the typical American gentleman, it is impossible to believe that any American community of men, with no political pressure upon them, could do to death a helpless, innocent young woman. Notwithstanding the hard-heartedness of masculine Philadelphia, and the thrilling tones of the speaker, and the tears of her audience, I confess that I held a stolid, stoical belief that the prisoner was perfectly safe, even in the dungeons of Philadelphia. So one was not surprised when affidavits from her own hand robbed the unhappy girl of all the romance and all the delicacy with which she had been invested, and of all the sympathy which her alleged oppression had worked, and, without making her personally any less an object of profound pity, took her case entirely out of the region of national eloquence and invective, and left it where it first lay, in the hands of local justice and benevolence.

Undoubtedly our laws are defective, and their administration imperfect, but it is not by such processes that they are likely to be improved. A good cause suffers more from being defended with false statements than from going undefended, or even unespoused.

I can not refrain from adding, in passing, that the old, unwritten, but inevitable social law which makes woman, though the least offender, bear the heaviest penalty for crimes against personal purity, seems to me less harmful to woman than that sentiment which makes the criminal a martyr, suffering from the persecutions of a hard-hearted, pharisaic, because virtuous world. There goes John Bunyan, but for the grace of God, in every thief and murderer; but if, on that account, theft and murder are to be made poetic and pathetic, not to say saintly, it will be likely to increase the number of those whom not even the grace of God can keep John Bunyans. I know that the destruction of the poor is their poverty, but I do not believe that in this country women are ever reduced to the alternative of starvation or shame. If the alternative ever faces them, they have reduced themselves to it.

While I am writing this appears a letter in the public prints saying,

"No woman will embrace a life of shame unless she is driven to it, as can be easily proved in ninety-nine cases out of every hundred. . . . .

"Perhaps some will ask, 'How do you know all this?' I answer, from a personal knowledge of city life in all its various phases; and I could cite hundreds of cases that have come under my notice during the past twenty years; but I will mention only one as an instance, which is of late occurrence, which is true in every particular.

"Not long ago, a gentleman of education, who had formerly been a teacher of languages, came to this city with his family—his wife being an accomplished lady, and moving in the best society of our sister cities. The husband and father sought employment, and found, after a month's search, a situation, which he filled with satisfaction to his employers till about the 1st of February, when he was discharged because business was dull. Since then he has searched for employment in vain. For some time his little family have seen much suffering, some days starvation actually staring them in the face. In such circumstances, with little ones crying for bread, is it a wonder that the wife and mother, who is a good-looking lady, should go on to the street,

"'And sell her soul to whoever would buy,
Dealing in shame for a morsel of bread'

to keep her little ones from starving? She tried to get a situation as teacher of music, but failed, and was finally offered a situation to play the piano in a Broadway concert saloon at twenty dollars a week, but declined, as it was too public. I learn that she will enter upon a life of shame, or else end her sufferings in death, before she will longer see her loved ones suffer. This is a true picture of many cases which daily take place in this city of boasted charity and religion."

And every case is deserving of the severest condemnation and abhorrence. Here are two able-bodied adults, in a country where the unskilled laborer, twenty miles from a city, can earn two dollars a day and rent a tenement for twenty dollars a year, and where a woman in a city, in a vocation not indeed reputable, but not vicious, can earn twenty dollars a week, counting themselves reduced to the alternative of starvation or shame! A woman refuses twenty dollars a week, not because the work or its tendencies are bad, but because the situation is too public, and considers herself forced into wickedness. She prefers private vice to public virtue. I, for one, am quite willing that such persons should starve. The children, indeed, are objects of pity and charity; but if the parents choose to end their sufferings in death rather then in a country farm-house, it is difficult to see why society should interpose any objection.

The writer makes special asseverations of truth. No

doubt his story is true, and true in the hundreds of cases he does not mention. No doubt "in ninety-nine cases out of every hundred" a life of shame comes because people would rather die both the first and second deaths than work. Virtue may proffer toil, plain clothes, hard hands, but she proffers also certain and sufficient food and shelter. Vice holds out apparent ease and shabby splendor; and women, hereditarily weak, weakened farther by unfavorable circumstances, lapse to vice rather than work for virtue. But a will enervated if not annihilated, a moral sense blunted if not destroyed, will never be strengthened and sharpened to effective activity by being enveloped in never so picturesque a cloud of melodramatic sentiment, while we do grievous harm to the weakness which is still innocent when we admit that vice can be any thing but the lowest depth of vulgarity and the last degree of profaneness.

A woman has the same right to be a lecturer that she has to be a laundress. I will confess that all my prejudices and all my instincts were against it. But when, for the first time, I saw an audience gathered to listen to a woman, the right and reason of the thing rose up so strongly that instinct and prejudice were forced to give way. Here is a company of respectable, well-behaved men and women, come together for no material good, but for mental improvement or amusement. Woman's sphere, the most conservative admit, is pre-eminently the sphere of influence; and surely a woman is far more femininely occupied when she stands, well-dressed, erect, graceful, dignified, and self-possessed, before a respectable assemblage, and speaks to them

"High thoughts, and honorable words,
And courtliness, and the desire of fame,
And love of truth,"

than she is in a shabby gown, with the skirt upturned around the waist; sleeves pinned above hard, red elbows; thin hair, untastefully bunched upon the back of her head; coarse shoes, and no collar; bending over her wash-tub or her cooking-stove ;. flying from broom to boiler; all womanly softness and beauty worn out of face and figure; all womanly leisure and repose chased away by the hard requirements of life, and only a glimpse of the woman shining now and then through the dreary crust of the drudge. Indeed, the vocation of lecturer may come peculiarly within woman's sphere, for her work is work upon mind, soul, heart. It is hers especially to teach, to entertain, to soften, to refine, and the more persons who can be brought under her influence the better.

But we also—we the public, we society, we the audience, the unregenerate, hard-hearted, money-making, justice-demanding world—have the same right to require good lectures that we have to require good laundries. And because women have always been washer-women, and failure in that line attracts no especial notice ; while women have not long or largely been lecturers, and failure there is noticeable and widespread in its consequences, it would seem as if there were an imperative need that women should be good lecturers if they lecture at all. I acknowledge that this is a factitious need, a requirement created by the peculiar combination of circumstances, not by the inherent nature of things. For example : the lecture to which I have referred was indeed inconsequent, rhetorical, and for the purposes for which it was professedly designed worthless ; but in point of substance, in point of logic, and rhetoric, and mental worth, it was every whit as good as Mr. Actor's, and Mr. Actor is the most popular lecturer in the country. He makes people cry, though it is hard to see why. He makes them laugh, and it is very easy to see why. For the rest, he is always on the side of temperance and morality ; but if you look at his lecture for argument, or intellectual power, or any thing but acting and anecdote, you look in vain; and he receives I do not know how many hundred dollars a night, and is engaged for I do not know how many hundred nights in a year. But the lady, also, is on the side of temperance and morality; she is, too, on the side of suffering women, which is even more definite and praiseworthy. Why should she not also, if she can, secure her hundreds of dollars for hundreds of nights? Why shall a man make his fortune with a single talent, in spite of deficiencies, while a woman must keep hers in a napkin, unless she has the other nine to go with it?

Why, indeed? Far be it from me to say that she should. So far as the Conservatives are concerned, she should not. If an opponent of the woman movement were to make this affirmation, he should immediately be put down with a strong hand. For any thing he has to say, a woman has the same right to play the fool that a man has. He should no more demand from her sweetness and light than from a man. Indeed, we will not let our opponent off so lightly. We will hoist the remorseless but now wretched ruffian with his own petard; and when he says that women are not intended by Nature for public speakers—since he attended the last woman's convention in his own town, where a good many women spoke, and he could count on his fingers all who could be fairly reckoned as good public speakers—up he goes without mercy. His own words condemn him. After generations of dumbness, with no training, no traditions, and scarcely any education, women at length mount the rostrum, and in a single assembly, in a small city, an iron-clad doctor of divinity needs all his fingers in estimating the number of good speakers! He would have to call in no further assistance than his thumbs could afford if he were in an assembly of men. Ten good speakers in a Sunday-school convention or a conference of churches is a thing undreamed of in lay philosophy. It would be difficult for an advocate of female oratory to produce a stronger argument in its favor than this opponent brings forward—all factiously, indeed, so that he shall have no credit for it.

But speaking not as an opponent, speaking from a profound sympathy with the sentiment that underlies the "woman movement," and with a profound contempt for the insight and intelligence which see in it only an itching for notoriety on the part of a few discontented women, it is a great deal worse for a woman to give a poor lecture than it is for a man. The fruits of his failure he gathers alone; but if a woman fails, it is not simply laid to the account of her individual weakness—it is the character of her class. Her speech is sound and fury, signifying nothing; therefore the woman's rights movement is a reform against nature.

Nothing is gained for the cause when you fall back on the fact that this, that, and the other female lecturer draws large audiences; that she is popular; that, good or bad, people go to hear her. "Men," said a great-hearted gentleman to a great-hearted and strong-minded woman, who was bewailing her disappointment on hearing a much-applauded lectur*ess*—"men don't judge her so severely as you. She is fine-looking—at least by gas-light; and they don't mind if there isn't so much sense and substance. *I* liked her, and I would go again."

But the point we are all up in arms about is not whether women are pretty, and graceful, and attractive. They have always been, and always been acknowledged that. Not even a pulpit or a platform can make beauty unlovely, or grace uncouth; but certainly the pulpit and platform are not necessary to female loveliness. Women are not breaking out in public for the sake of showing how fair they be! It is presumably because they have something to say so important, so irrepressible, that the old channels of communication are insufficient, and it is worth while to break through all the prejudices and customs that hedge them in, and say their say in cavalier fashion; or they do it for the simple and honest purpose of getting a living. So far as that is their motive, I do not quarrel with them. But when a woman comes before you inspired with a grand purpose, demanding great opportunities, advocating a great cause, and employs a reasoning and a rhetoric that are good for nothing but to furnish fallacies and infelicities to the logic-class in a girls' school, the woman cause has not gained—it has lost. No woman has gained any thing for that cause so long as allowance has to be made for her as a woman. Except so far as she works for a living, she does not justify herself for taking hold of man's work unless she does the work better than men. I am not in the least degree exalted or exhilarated by hearing a woman preach unless she preaches so powerfully that I forget she is a woman. If we are to have prosing and platitudes, what care I to which sex the platitudinarian belongs? There is no legal disability that I know of. Nothing hinders a woman from lecturing or preaching except lack of audiences. Men have preached us deaf and dumb, or bitter and bellicose, with their inanities and their superficialities, their pettinesses and their passions also petty. Is it worth while to have brought out mitrailleuse and Chassepôt, and to have rent the heavens with their roaring, for the sake of showing that women can be as stupid as men, if they only have the chance?

In saying that the female preacher should make her audience forget that she is a woman, it is not necessary to demand that she should be like a man. A woman can scarcely be more distasteful than when she imitates the other sex. Our conservative friends are very right in fearing that women will be extremely disagreeable if the new movement makes them into a sort of man, and there are weak-minded women enough engaged in it to make their fears not wholly groundless. Women who are without genius, without judgment, without sweet sound sense or instinctive delicacy, but not without ability in certain directions, attach themselves to the woman's rights cause as naturally as every one that was in distress, and every one that was in debt, and every one that was discontented, gathered themselves unto David in the Cave of Adullam. These women are not necessarily noisy, though sometimes they are noisy; but they are pertinacious and pushing, virtuous, but altogether abominable. If they become ministers, they lean on their elbows, and press down the leaves of their sermons, and read the hymns badly, and begin one exercise before another is over, just as male ministers do; and you withdraw, confirmed in your opinion that you don't want to hear a woman preach. If they go into business, they raise a clamor about it; they are interviewed; their ways, means, and motives are chronicled; they frequent the haunts of men, and get to be coarsely mentioned. They take up the dress reform, and devise a hybrid costume, which combines all that is ugly in male attire, and rejects all that is graceful in the Bloomer suit, and turns a woman into a nondescript object which ti becomes all civilized humanity to avoid, and secures no benefit that is not just as well secured without the sacrifice of a single line of beauty. If such things were the consequence of woman's enfranchisement, better that women never were enfranchised. Better a woman should be unhealthily than unbecomingly dressed. Better she should be a useless fireside figure-head than a noisy nuisance. Better a feminine than a masculine fool. But the choice is not so limited.

I have seen and heard a woman preach sermons with an unction which any clergyman might emulate, to an audience whose attention any clergyman might envy. Her addresses were not called sermons, and her listeners were not called a congregation. The most conservative find nothing objectionable in a woman's being at the head of a female seminary, and a school of young girls is a perfectly orthodox sphere; but the interest of no congregation is harder to secure, the position of no minister is more commanding. This lady would read a chapter from the Bible, select her text, and for half or three quarters of an hour secure the rapt attention, the entire sympathy of her audience. With clear, impressive voice, with speaking, conquering eyes, with mobile mouth and eloquent hands, with decisive and incisive manner, with illustration keen, apt, and vivid, in language homely, terse, touching, pathetic, poetic, amusing, she elucidated truth; she enforced duty; she aroused impulse; she stirred conscience; she incited effort; she touched heart, till her congregation sat before her excited, thrilled, magnetized. Like a man! Good heavens! There are no men. Man is a lost art beside such a woman. Let her go into the public pulpit, and preach as she preaches in her own, and you would no more be reminded of a man minister than you would of a mastodon. She is never more intensely, more *differentially*, so to speak, and I will say more winsomely a woman than in doing this very manly work. Therefore the work is not necessarily manly.

I have heard another woman speak in public, and, what is worse, preside over public meetings, and, what is worse still, if any thing can be worse, these meetings were woman's rights conventions. It is impossible to conceive any thing more profoundly obnoxious to a conservative and orthodox mind, like—well, if the egotism may be pardoned—like my own. Yet this woman, with all her social sins upon her head, by the mere charm of her sweet, simple personality, by the force of her pure womanliness, melted away antagonistic prejudice, and won all hearts to do her reverence. She walked in the manly ways with womanly gait. She threaded the devious paths of parliamentary law with an unconscious, innocent confidence; and when sometimes she hesitated, she appealed to superior knowledge and experience, not only without shame, but with a natural grace more pleasing than knowledge itself. The success of woman's rights will alienate the sexes, will they? This woman had not the beauty which attracts the eye. She was but comely and wholesome; but under the spell of her musical, modulated, varying voice, her simple, appealing, child-like, yet motherly manner, her sound sense and her fervid conviction, every fool who came to scoff remained to approve and admire. I was amused to see hard-headed lawyers, who had only advanced from contemptuous indifference to breathing out threatenings and slaughter upon strong-minded women, involuntarily rush to the rescue when she hesitated upon some involved parliamentary point. They were not, perhaps, converted to the cause, but they were, at least for the time, converted to her. And I observed, too—for I turned all eyes and counted nothing trivial—I observed that her husband artfully and heroically concealed the shame which must have torn his heart, stood by her like a man, and shawled her, and cloaked her, and cared for her, unostentatiously, indeed, but as naturally and "protectingly" as if she had done nothing all her life but suckle fools and chronicle small beer. And what man has done man may do.

It is such women as these in the pulpit and on the platform, and only such, who are really advancing the welfare of women. They show by well-doing what woman can well do. They command the respect, if they do not compel the conviction of their opponents. And it is this which is the measure of fitness. The flattery of a clique, the suffrage of a mutual admiration society, the laughter and applause of galleries, do not hinder an address to the people from being false in logic, foolish in sentiment, a grief to the judicious, a snare to the unwary. When the charm of the woman sets off comprehensiveness, acuteness, broad and just thought, right feeling rightly tempered, wisdom and benevolence combined, a woman is never more in her sphere than when she is addressing an assembly of men and women. But when her beauty or her grace, her prettiness or her ugliness, has underneath it only the echo of thoughts, the shadow of ideas which she can neither comprehend nor reproduce; when she has only vain and vapid words without knowledge; crude and impracticable measures to suggest; a culture whose only redeeming point is that it is shallow, the spectacle is simply pitiable. Over against her, sitting respectfully among her listeners, are men of life-long study and experience, of severe and responsible thought—men whose theories have every day to be put to the touchstone of actual trial, and to whom her random talk passes for the vain and idle, though well-meant babbling that it is. They are courteous and deferent; but their considerate and restrained compliments are a greater insult to the female understanding than any censure could be. How can they honor the female intellect when it presents to them such ground and lofty tumbling as its ideal of agility and activity? How can they believe in the gravity, the equipoise, the social worth of a woman's mind, when the first thing they are obliged to do for this representative woman is to put aside all thought of mental gravity and equipoise, and fall back upon the world-old flatteries and fooleries of personal compliment, or pass beyond into a half bitter and half ludicrous disgust?

VII.
DISABILITIES.

It is sometimes amusing to see the great gulf fixed between general assertions and particular facts in some of our statements regarding women. Neither side monopolizes the inconsequence. Perhaps that religious and respectable ecclesiastical newspaper, edited by doctors of divinity, and conducted with irreproachable masculine logic, may be considered as leading off the dance of *non sequiturs* when it gravely says:

"Having so persistently and skillfully engineered the woman's rights movement that it has passed beyond the region where it encountered only indifference or scorn, to that where it meets with earnest and conscientious opposition, the advocates of the reform can afford to pay a decent respect to the opinions of their opponents, and should, therefore, put away childish babbling, and speak as becomes men and women engaged in one of the most revolutionary reforms of the century."

Can even a D.D. tell us why? If this childish babbling has so skillfully and persistently advanced the cause, why should it be discontinued? Having won in one fierce battle, shall the revolutionists now throw away the sword they fought with, and betake themselves to some other weapon selected by their adversaries? Rather, one would say, if they have babbled so brilliantly thus far, they can not do better than babble on to final victory.

But we woman's rights men also sometimes roam rather wildly amid cause and consequence. "The stimulus of politics, in their reaction upon the mind," says one paper, enforcing female suffrage, "is immense. The American girl never felt it till the late war. Give her the ballot, and the mass of her powers will so increase .... that only we, whose mothers, and sisters, and wives have been the best man's eyes ever looked upon, can imagine what woman will become."

But these good mothers, sisters, and wives grew to what they were without the ballot, so that the inference we draw is directly the opposite of what we were expected to draw. We say immediately, no matter what the ballot may be good for, it is certainly not essential to the excellence of American girls, since they grow in grace without it. We may need wars to stir them to activity. We do not need suffrage.

"Without the ballot," says the same paper, "women can never permanently share in this vitalizing experience" [of political campaigns]. Yet another column, arguing for another purpose, indeed, says:

"The Whig party elected Harrison and Tyler *by introducing woman for the first time into their great political assemblies.* ... *The presence of woman* was the talisman of Whig success. The abolition question gained the ear of the people only when it enlisted the aid of woman. The Liberty party in Ohio obtained its first animating impulse from the thrilling eloquence of Abby Kelley. ... The presence of women in Republican meetings, and their absence from those of Democrats, were facts conspicuous from the very outset. ... Informally the influence of woman was always prominent. Who can estimate the influence of Harriet Beecher Stowe's 'Uncle Tom's Cabin' upon the politics of the nation? The conscience and enthusiasm of woman elected Lincoln, and sustained the Republicans through the war. The hunker State of Connecticut was carried at the critical moment by the eloquent addresses of Anna Dickinson."

Really, people who have believed in a sequence of thought

must begin to rub their eyes and ask themselves if they are awake. American girls must have the ballot to make them worth while, because American girls have grown into the best of women without it. American women must have the ballot to stir up their interest in politics, for they have vivified parties, aroused principles, carried states, elected presidents, maintained wars without it. Under which king, Bezonian? If these are the facts we bring forward to show that women need the ballot, what kind of facts should we produce to show that they do not need it? What can you do with a syllogism that turns somersaults in the middle? The premise is as sound as a nut. The conclusion may or may not be true; but the hidden Major Premise looks very little like a fighting soldier when we unearth him. "All persons," says that silent gentleman, forced to stand and deliver—"all persons who for thirty years, chiefly of peace, have been showing intense interest in and exerting a marked effect upon politics without the vote, need the vote in order to take an interest in politics in times of peace." I greatly fear that Archbishop Whately would not find his hearty contempt for the female intellect materially diminished if this method of reasoning be the device of the female brain.

Again: "Give woman the ballot," says one column of the reform organ, "and their motto will be, Equal pay for equal work; and the first question they will ask the would-be nominee for school commissioner will be, 'Will you faithfully carry out our motto?'"

But another column of the same paper says:

"Working-women are wanted in Colorado. Reliable reports say that a thousand could find immediate employment there, and at high wages. A competent girl commands better wages there than a male laborer."

And also:

"Masculine ministers must be looking out for their lucre

as well as their laurels. We learn that some women are paid $25 a Sunday for supplying the same pulpits where doctors of divinity are compelled to put up with only $15."

How is this? Are we agitating to bring down the pay of the Colorado girls to the level of the male laborers? In the good time coming, shall not the Rev. Mrs. Smith be allowed to receive twenty-five dollars a Sunday because the Rev. Mr. Brown was paid only fifteen? And how is it that we need the ballot to secure equal pay for equal work, when without the ballot we have already secured unequal pay in the woman's favor?

"Going to New York," says the biographer of a woman's rights woman, "with her brother and his newly-wedded wife, her soul was agonized with the thought that for single women there was no place in the universe. The world had choice of employments, varied interests, independence, and honors only for men.

"Arriving in New York, she spent some time with a married sister, trying to satisfy the unrest of her nature by assisting in the family sewing and the care of the children."

Not feeling sufficiently absorbed, she went to the editor of a paper and applied for a situation as reporter. The unrest of her nature would, no doubt, have been effectually and permanently disposed of had she succeeded in becoming the reporter of a city daily newspaper. But its proprietor laughed at the idea, and she went home and wrote a letter about it, which letter so pleased another editor that he published it forthwith. Thereupon she continued to write, was soon put in a responsible position upon a newspaper, and shortly after was offered by another paper double the salary she had at first received.

Considering now that this woman, according to her biographer, had been twice engaged to be married, had taken the whole charge of her brother's motherless children, had assisted in the family sewing and the care of her sister's children, became a writer for a daily newspaper, was married, and kept house, and made shirts, has been fashion-editor of two magazines and editor of one, has for years furnished a monthly bulletin of fashion for some twenty newspapers throughout the country, has been a regular contributor to one review and to one weekly journal, an occasional contributor to almost every prominent paper or magazine that has been published in New York for the last ten years, is an exemplary mother, occupies several important offices, and is still a young woman—how are we to construe the statement that the world has

1st. Choice of Employment,
2d. Varied Interests,
3d. Independence and Honors

only for men?

In what Pickwickian sense are we to understand the assertion that for single women there is no place in the universe? How many men have chosen a greater number of employments, or have had more and more varied interests, than this still young woman?

The same paper tells us that Miss Blank has been appointed teacher of English composition at Blank College. Miss Blank is a graduate of a certain academy, " and is the young lady whose remarkable success as a proof-reader was mentioned, etc. At the Celebrated Press in Utopia she secured the highest reputation in that difficult vocation. On such points she is already a high authority."

Men and brethren, especially women, do you not see, vote or no vote, slave or free, just as soon as a woman is good for any thing, every body wants her? Society runs wild after an able woman, and seems sometimes to think that because she is good for one thing she is good for any and every thing. As soon as she shows that she can turn her hand featly to one act, scores of hands reach out to clutch her. Why did not the college let Miss B. alone if she was doing well at the press? There are plenty of women who would have snatched at the professorship. Because she was doing well. If she had been doing ill, they would have let her alone severely enough. No one wants the person whom no one else wants. It is true the world over, in science, and politics, and property, as well as in religion: To him that hath shall be given, and from him that hath not shall be taken away even that which he seemeth to have. It sounds harsh, spoken of human, sensitive beings, but it is as inevitable as a law of nature. It *is* a law of nature. Man can no more help it than he can help the blowing of the wind. To him that hath power shall be given power. Ability begets influence. The sagacity that acquires wealth increases wealth. He who grasps life feebly, he who hangs on to his position imploringly, and does not occupy it commandingly — he will be continually jostled, and is likely to be dislodged.

The pursuit and the profit of an occupation are matters pertaining to the individual as well as to the sex. They are affected by sex in that women have not been trained to aggressive personal effort as men have been, and therefore do not so readily determine their work. They have not been educated to believe that they must take hold of something, and therefore they do not so easily see or so quickly grasp what offers. But there are multitudes of young men who ponder over their future, question what they shall do, try what they do not like, and are baffled, repulsed, and rejected. There are scores who do not know precisely what they want to do, and would embrace any one of a dozen different offers. No doubt many of them walk up and down in agony, think there is no place for them in the universe, and try to satisfy the unrest of their souls in dry-goods stores.

But they mostly settle after a while into some sort of a nook, and make the best of it. A woman can do precisely the same thing. Why not? The woman whom I have mentioned did it, only better. She refused to content herself with what did not satisfy her, and kept on until she found something that did; and she found, also, that so many voices called her that it was hard to choose which she should obey.

These are but illustrations of a fact which can not be too often or too impressively repeated, that in this country a woman need no more be without occupation than a man. She need not be without healthy and remunerative occupation. In the higher latitudes her pay is equal to that of a man. In many latitudes, if she has a man's sense, she gets a man's emolument. Trade makes little inquiry concerning success. If a shop-girl receives less wages than a shop-boy, why does she not go into business herself? I suppose a large proportion of our rich merchants walked into town with the traditional shilling in their pockets. There are women also who have succeeded brilliantly in trade. The largest, most popular, and most successful dry-goods store in a certain American city was founded and is owned and managed by women. They make no fuss about it. They are not bartering on high moral ground; they are not in the papers with plans and projects, and I fear they give very little thought to the starving women of New York. They simply buy and sell, and get gain, and invest in real estate. I suspect they are in favor of woman suffrage, but their actions speak very loudly in showing how well women may prosper without it.

What does a man do when his pay is not enough? If he is a commonplace man, one of a multitude, he joins a strike, which he has a perfect right to do. If he is an ignorant man, with crude notions of liberty and tyranny, of right and wrong, he not only strikes work himself, but attempts by force to prevent his neighbor from working, and thus makes himself a criminal and dangerous to society. But if he is a man of mettle he only works the harder, and makes himself so necessary to his employer that he becomes master of the situation. When a man gets the service that he wants, a few dollars more or less are a trivial matter to him. It is exactly so with a woman. What mother of a household would hesitate between two dollars and a half to an ordinary housemaid, and three dollars to one who would do the work as she wants it done? What young lady would hesitate between paying ten dollars for an ill-fitting dress, and fifteen for a well-fitting one?

I am informed that a first-class workwoman even in New York earns fifteen dollars a week at a sewing machine. It is not wealth; but many a man who has spent thousands of dollars on his apprenticeship earns less than that in the pulpit. I know a forewoman in a sewing establishment who has a salary of fifteen hundred dollars a year, and I know a township in which not five men have seen a yearly income of fifteen hundred dollars in all their lives.

Why do not sewing-women establish sewing-houses, and become proprietors, instead of being at the mercy of brutal employers? Suppose a hard-working mother of a family wants to buy a winter outfit of under and outer clothing for herself and three little girls, plain but strong, and at a cost no greater than if she bought the cloth and hired the dressmaker and seamstress to make them at home. How many houses are there to which she could go? Men do this every where. The making of male apparel has passed almost entirely out of the family hands into those of the shopmen; but women have scarcely begun to organize their supplies. Every woman has to go through the process for herself, and with as much proportional disadvantage as if she should shear her own sheep and weave her own cloth. But women can establish sewing-shops. Why talk of disability, when you see a woman begin on nothing, make bonnets, gradually but steadily enlarge her borders, open a fancy store, engage apprentices, rebuild her house, open a boarding-house, make her own purchases, superintend her business, send her sons to college and her daughters to academies, maintain vigorous health, and entertain decided convictions as to the cause and consequences of the French and Prussian War?

Women are employed in telegraph offices, and receive fifteen and twenty dollars a week. It is said that they understand the details as well as men, that they manipulate more deftly, and are more faithful at their posts. I do not know the wages of male operators; but, if the female operators surpass them in skill and service, they are in the right way to win not only their own case, but the case of all women. Every woman who legitimately succeeds in a legitimate business helps all women. And when I go to one telegraph office ten minutes after the hour of opening, and find it closed; and to another, and find a woman crusty, indifferent, and negligent, treating me as if it were a favor to permit me the use of the telegraph, my annoyance is not confined to my personal inconvenience, but I think how surely these women are creating a prejudice against all other women.

Here is a girl who happened not to be born poor. Her father is rich enough to live in Fifth Avenue, but he does not live there. He gives her all the advantages of city education which she chooses. Eight months in the year she spends in home duties, charities, parties, concerts, operas, theatre, her own music, and the like; but in the other four months she lives her own true life. She has found a pure country town, undiscovered yet by the tourists, and there she goes, with a bloomer dress, and lives on a farm and works like a farm-hand—up in the morning with the men helping take care of the animals, then to the fields to work with them, driving the oxen and pitching the hay. She has a very definite idea of perfect earthly happiness. It is to raise animals on a stock-farm; and, if she were thrown on her own resources, no doubt she would do it. No starving over the needle or stooping behind the counter for her. And yet she is no Amazon, but a pure, womanly girl, without a grain of coarseness, a true lover of nature.

I know two girls born to ease and wealth. In their early youth they were rich, careless, free. They walked, and drove, and rode, and hunted, and boated, and drank great draughts of happiness and health. Presently trouble came. Affairs were involved. The stalwart father became a confirmed and helpless invalid. Did they sit down and wring their hands? Did they go moaning all their days, begging men to give them a little sewing, a little copying, a little teaching? Not they. They began, in a small way, in a country town, to keep a "dry-goods and grocery store." They were prompt. They gave fair measure and right change. They kept what people wanted; and if any thing was called for which they had not, they put it down on their list of future purchases. They had the cleanest and nicest grocery for miles around. They hired a clerk, and bought a horse, and built a house, and are at this moment independent property-holders, as well as piquant and agreeable women.

The newspapers tell us that the head of one of the larger New York tea-dealing firms is a woman. Previous to the outbreak of our Civil War she was extensively engaged in utilizing (?) the leaves of the great blackberry and raspberry crops of Georgia and Alabama. By a generous and judicious admixture of imported tea, these blackberry leaves were worked up into all the proper varieties of the black and green teas of commerce. After the war had turned her field of fortune into the field of battle, her basis of operations was changed, and the costly green teas were manipulated from the less costly black teas ; but there is no record that her trickery was any less genuine, skillful, or lucrative than that of men.

Through the same newspapers we learn of another woman who, after her husband's death, took sole charge of his business. A grist-mill, a saw-mill, six hundred acres of land in homestead, besides other tracts, and four daughters, came under her single supervision. She accepted the trust, accomplished the work, and conducted every thing to success and prosperity.

The appointment of a woman to the post-office of a Southern city was hailed by the newspapers of that city with execration. She wisely let the newspapers alone, and expended all her energies on the post-office. She introduced needed reforms, so far as possible, and paved the way for those which could not be immediately effected. She was prompt, polite, faithful, and the papers that reviled her were forced to admit her excellence.

Even the schools, to which the young women flock, are not made of cast-iron. I have known a young woman so highly valued that the committee of the school, having already raised her salary to the highest legal standard, offered her a third more out of their own pockets to secure her continued stay, and offered in vain. The rush to the schools is so great that the pay is permanently and generally low, yet a good teacher is hard to find. Sixty and a hundred teachers apply for a single situation in a single school, yet in that same school the principal says despairingly to the parents, who all want their children in Miss A.'s class, that he would have Miss A. cut up into twenty pieces if he could, so that she might teach them all. In the heart of New England, in a highly cultivated community, an attempt was made to substitute female for male principals in the higher grades of schools. A salary was proposed nearly, if not quite as large as the average salary of the clergymen in the vicinity; and the committee, who had been for years conversant and connected with schools, knew of only one woman within a radius of thirty miles whom they were willing to intrust with the experiment. I have heard a woman complaining of injustice, of the partiality shown to men, and affirming that she could not live on her salary, when that salary was four hundred dollars a year, when she had received only the most slight and common instruction from the most common schools—an experience that could in no sense of the word be called education—and had attained a culture sufficiently indicated by the fact that she found offense in being spoken of as a female teacher instead of a lady teacher! Now I admit that it is very exasperating to have a man in the next room, no better, and no better educated than you, doing the same work that you do, and getting twice as much pay. It is still more exasperating to have him set over you, and getting three times as much pay. But where there is a glaring discrepancy not only between a woman's work and her wages, but between her duties and her fitness to perform them, it would be encouraging to see her efforts not wholly confined to the former; but I have heard her speak ten words for increase of pay where I have heard one for improvement in performance. Men may be no better than women, but women are not half as good as they ought to be. When you have secured to uneducated female teachers the same salary which uneducated male teachers receive, when you have paid for a woman's shabby work the same wages which you pay for a man's shabby work, have you really elevated society? You have, indeed, brought about an equality, but it has not been by a leveling-up process.

Poor work is the fatal disability, not poor pay. Good

work may be a slow, but it is a sovereign remedy. Yet women will not administer it. They have not the ingenuity to devise, the courage to commence, the perseverance to carry out responsible undertakings. They have not the patience, the sense, the wisdom to work faithfully under some other person's responsibility. It is easier for them to moil on in the old ruts, to live from hand to mouth, to be serfs to heartless employers, to complain of partiality, and cry out against injustice, than it is to strike silently into untried paths, to bend circumstances, and defy injustice, and compel respect, and control fate.

All, alike the advocates and opponents of woman suffrage, agree that the avenues of employment should be open to women; but if women have not the ability to open them for themselves, have they the ability to walk in them after they are opened? The barriers are such that her feet can not pass beyond them whose hand can not remove them. Stupid men plod, and bright men invent. They make a business. They devise a supply, and create a demand. Women can do the same, if they have the head for it. If they have not, perhaps the next best thing is to pass a law that head shall be counted out in the general judgment.

It is not so much opportunity that women need as qualities. They do not succeed in business for the same reason that men do not succeed—because they are timid, tame, unadventurous, ineffective. They have not energy, enterprise, persistence, spirit, daring. They are not far-seeing, ready in plan, fertile in resources. Nothing else fails them for success. It is not that they are poor, for the ranks of our "merchant princes" are replenished from just such poverty as theirs. It is not political disability. Men with political ability have failed in just such careers, and women with political disability have succeeded. If this day men and women should change places—the successful men and the unsuccessful women—I doubt not that in five years every thing would be just as it is now. The thirty thousand starving women would have gone into the stores and offices; would have lived comfortably, dressed tastefully, never have acquired a half understanding of their business, nor a whole understanding of what understanding business means, until the whole thing had slipped through their hands. The thirty thousand men who had taken their places would at the start have looked around them, seized the first opening for making money, or made an opening if none appeared, thrown away the needle, combined forces, and in five years be bullying the poor sewing-women just the same as ever. And the poor sewing-women would stand and take it just as meekly as ever.

"This gully must be filled by Saturday night," said the overseer on the Pacific Railroad.

"Impossible," was the reply. "There is nothing to fill it with."

"It must be filled with five thousand Irishmen, if there is nothing else; and it must be filled by Saturday night."

And it was filled.

"This river must be bridged," said the general, on his march to the sea.

"There is not wood enough in the village to build a bridge," replied his officer.

"Take the village!"

The bridge was built.

This is what all need for success, will—will that takes no account of obstacles except to overcome them. What is the use of talking to women about wider opportunities, when opportunities are dying every day for want of being used? What is the use of lamenting lack of employments, when women are still feebly fumbling around in a jungle of employments? Why talk about poor pay, when it is almost by sufferance that women get any pay at all? Women in trade are nothing but men. If they are weak, helpless, complaining men, we may as well acknowledge the fact; but, weak or strong, they are men, and must be dealt with as men.

I have two letters, received at the same time, and written on the same subject, which so unconsciously but so admirably illustrate the difference between the masculine and the feminine treatment of a question, and which also throw so much light, indirectly, upon our theme, that I propose to make some extracts from each. The first is a woman's letter, the second a man's. With both I take private liberties in respect of spelling, punctuation, and superfluities, but I add nothing.

"I am well aware that any work properly done will command a living price paid to any woman, and that an unskilled worker who sends out poor work must not expect first-class prices. But that is not (in my mind) the point which women argue. It is not that other women can command higher prices. It is the universal partiality shown to men. The cry of the working-women of the land is, 'I can do a man's work, and I ought to be paid a man's salary.' Yes, they ought to be; but are not mankind agreed that women are the best ones to instruct the young? If so, then why do not men (for they make and always have made the laws) make laws to protect teachers of schools? Why do they lessen the salaries of lady teachers so that they may increase a salary of some man—the man having refused to accept the salary of a woman?

"It has been argued by many that men should be paid more than their sisters, for the reason that men have so many expenses to bear for women.

"One instance is, when a gentleman takes a lady to ride with him, he pays for the horses, refreshments, etc. The lady has nothing to do with that. Why should she? The gentleman took her for his own pleasure quite as much as he did for hers. If the lady happened to be one who earned her own living, she would willingly pay the man, if he wished it. *If it happened*, I say. You know that we who depend upon our own exertions for support are not very often invited to ride, eat ices, etc., by gentlemen of society. Ah! no. They reserve their invitations for the butterflies of society. But we do not ask to have it otherwise. Everyday toil unfits one for the frivolities of fashion.

"If women who are at ease do not believe that the host of noble women suffer who support themselves, just let them try it, and see your former friends turn their backs upon you. Then, and not till then, will you know.

* * * * * *

"Don't you expect as much pay for your MS. as any man would for the same amount of labor? Don't your paper, pens, ink, and board cost as much as if you were a man? Are you willing to work for less?

"Let us, then, join hand in hand, and stand shoulder to shoulder, and try to elevate our less fortunate sisters," etc.

Now for the man's letter :

"I have always supposed, and still think, that if there is a demand or a market for any thing, and there is money in it, that demand is sure to be met, that market supplied. Now, in your article, you give us to understand that there is a great demand for skilled workers, and advise poor working-women to become skillful in some trade, and then they are sure to do well. This, I think, is not so. There is no demand for skilled workers; and if you look carefully among the various mechanical trades in our midst, you will find it the almost invariable rule, the better the workman the poorer the man. Take my own business, for example—*Gas-piping*. I can find you in the city of —— lots of first-rate workmen. They are all of them poor; and I can't call to mind a single man that has got rich in the business (and I know many that have) that can pipe a house decently. Why, the man that has done the best business in the city the last ten years in gas-fixtures never made one that I would take for a gift to put in my house. I have worked at the business ten years, and am accounted a skillful workman. Can I get a cent a foot more for piping than the veriest botch? Not at all. In fact, he rather has the advantage of me, for most people seem to think poor work is the cheapest, anyhow. At any rate, they won't pay any more for good work.

. . . . . .

"The true idea, it seems to me, is not to know how to work well, but how to buy and sell well; and the man or woman who knows how to dispose of their wares in the market is sure to get rich. There are many notable examples of this. I will give you one or two. There is Mr. A., one of the governor's council now, I believe. Well, he has got rich at the carpenter's trade. He knows just about as much how to do a job of carpentering as an old setting hen; but he knows how to hire men that do know how to work, and he knows how to manipulate boards of aldermen and common council so as to get fat contracts, in which he so manages that the bill for extras will be larger than the original contracts. He knows how to carry his wares to market, and he is made president of this, that, and the other; and Mr. B. C., in that wonderful production of his, the oration at the last annual dinner, points to him with pride as an example of what mechanics can accomplish. That oration, by the way, was a big thing. In it he spoke of the readiness of wealthy people to help mechanics. That's so. Help them get rid of their money. . . .

"That is the reason why boys shun mechanical trades. We read long homilies in the papers on the advantages of having a trade, but both parents and children instinctively know better. They see that the great prizes of life don't lie in that direction. The great traders rule the world.

". . . To sum up, the world don't want skilled work; it wants cheap work. The creators of wealth don't get any of it. Those that trade in that wealth are the favored ones."

Leaving out of sight the question of correctness, who does not see that the woman's letter is sentimental, the man's letter brawny? The one is piteous, wavering, longing, feeble, the other is sturdy, bitter, scornful, and direct. The one admits every thing, and wanders off into side issues and devastated ways; the other plumps down upon facts at the outset, and denies them.

"Why is the woman's salary lessened that the man's may be increased," asks the woman—"the man having refused to accept the woman's salary?"—and does not see that one breath asks and answers the question? It is *because* men refuse a woman's salary that they get men's salary. It is because women accept a low salary that they do not get a high one. The world will never pay any more for work than it is obliged to pay. This never looks so wrong as in schools, and I do not say that there is no injustice in it. But I do say that the remedy is not in expostulation, but in action. If a woman writer gets the same pay as a man, it is not because she reasons with her publisher about her board bill and stationery, but because, if his price does not suit her, she takes her wares to the publisher over the way. Unless she can do this, and until she can do this, she is in precisely the condition of the teacher and the seamstress—she must take what is offered. Against this horrible necessity no law can be framed to protect her.

And is it not just the least in the world grotesque for a working-woman to face the great questions of equality and relations with an argument built on ice-cream? The oppressed and downtrodden, the noble, suffering, self-supporting host sends up a bitter cry, one of whose component parts is a well-defined wail that gentlemen do not take them to ride! Surely there ought to be a law passed for the protection of the bees against the butterflies; and as men make and always have made the laws, and as the same men take and always have taken the butterflies to ride, it is useless to hope for any reform or "refreshments" until the bees have a seat in council. Women have heavier burdens than these, but it will be hard to make the world believe it so long as they bring these forward as burdens.

One may be pardoned for thinking that the women who earn their own living find, at least, a moderate degree of compensation in contemning the women who do not. The former are "a host of noble women," the latter are the "frivolities of fashion;" but why it is not arrogant and pharisaic for a woman to class herself among the nobility because she is poor, and her "sister" among the ignobility because she is rich, I fail to see. If a woman has no one to provide for her, she must provide for herself. It would be ignoble for her, in sound health, to go to the poor-house; but is there any thing especially noble in staying out of it? Is independence inherently any more glorious than dependence? Both have ample room for excellence, but both are in themselves neutral. It indicates no more merit in a woman that her husband has died, and left her to support as well as train her children, than if he had lived and supported them himself. She may be noble in doing it, but another woman, who never earned a penny in her life, may be just as noble. Literature has always been rather hard on butterflies, but I do not know where we find our warrant for supposing the butterfly any less perfect or pleasing in the eyes of its Maker than the bee.

We speak of the dignity of labor, but labor has no dignity. Dignity is in the workman, not in the work; in the motive and attitude, not in the task.

Circumstances are but the frame-work of character. Sweetness, modesty, dignity, charity, self-respect, and respect for others, are personal graces among rich or poor. No life is lovely without them; no life is mean with them.

The man's letter does not make out the man's case; but what a ring it has. The world, he says, does not want skilled labor; but does not gas-piping—which requires skill—pay better than hod-carrying, which does not? The poor gas-pipers get rich, but is it not by making people believe that their work is good? The old setting-hen of a carpenter does not thus characterize himself to his customers, I suppose. He is not skilled in carpentry, but he is an adept in the still more skillful labor of palming off good work for poor. All I design to do, however, is merely to call attention to the different way in which the man and the woman take hold of the same question. The woman must have more of the nerve and muscle of the man, must talk less of shoulders and sisters, and think less of ices and gentlemen, before her fingers will have grasp, her protest power.

VIII.
SERFDOM.

ARE women to be blamed for their inaptitude? Only partially, at most. One trouble is that they are where they do not belong. They can not see where business lies, because they were not born with business eyes. The few women succeed. They have an exceptional fondness and fitness for traffic, and they buy, and sell, and get gain as readily as men, and do not necessarily lose any grace for their worldly wisdom; but women in general have not capacity for business. It hurts them; it annoys them. They are ill at ease. \ They instinctively make every thing a matter of feeling.\ They constantly, if unconsciously, refer every thing to the standard of chivalry. They think trade ought to take off its hat as deferentially as courtesy. They are worn out doubly by the wear and tear of the struggle, and by the unnaturalness of such wear and tear. What says Miss Mitford—that brave and blameless lady, who upbore out of the ruin of the home which himself had wantonly destroyed a worthless and wicked father? "Women were not meant to earn the bread of a family. I am sure of that; there is a want of strength." No one has gained a better right than she to speak authoritatively on this point; and, remembering her long suffering, and the years of anxiety and anguish that followed the brilliant promise of her opening life, one restrains his inclination to cuff her when she says, "I write merely for remuneration; and I would rather scrub floors if I could get as much by that healthier, more respectable, and *more feminine* employment."

(But there must have been some defect in a woman who

could pay court to such a man as Dr. Mitford. A daughter must honor her father, whatever be his character. She must do her filial duty, however gross, selfish, and ungrateful he be; but to give to such a man the homage of her heart makes heart's homage of little worth.)

All that can be done for women is to help them do as well as possible what they never can do well, but what it is absolutely necessary they should do somehow. It is improbable that women will ever become, to any large extent, tillers of the soil; but the Horticultural School established in Boston most wisely offers to them an opportunity for thorough education in the theory and practice of horticulture. It aims to choose that part of agriculture most suited to women, and to substitute trained, skillful, well-directed labor for untrained, clumsy, and spasmodic effort. We may admit that women can never equal men in trade, or commerce, or industry; but, because many women are born to self-support, and because all women may be reduced to self-support, he who founds a college to teach women the various branches of science, art, and industry confers a real benefit. A woman thoroughly trained to the occupation of type-setting or hair-dressing may or may not be inferior to the thoroughly-trained male printer or barber, but she has a great advantage over the untrained woman. That she is less deft than a man is no reason why she should not be as deft as a woman can be; and I fancy her best is far beyond the masculine average. So the objections raised to these schemes—that they tend to take women away from their homes—is not only futile, but fatuous. Women are out of their homes already. It is not a question whether their life shall be domestic, or mercantile and mechanical. It is whether they shall be intelligently and lucratively mechanical, or awkwardly, unprofitably, and fatally so. Were it otherwise, did the choice lie between self-support and man-support—coming, of course, naturally, and, therefore, honorably—there would be but one answer. And here is where I branch off from the woman's rights reform. If I understand it, the leaders teach the absolute worth and desirableness of manual labor to woman. They say (I quote from one of their prominent journals), "Women should earn their living. This is the first spring to action. Girls should be reared, like boys, to depend upon themselves for support. Self-support . . . . creates a self-respect which nothing else can confer. No true happiness is found in dependence. No true life is consistent with it."

Thus it puts men and women on the same plane. It counts pecuniary independence equally incumbent on, and pecuniary dependence equally degrading to, both sexes. It demands entrance for woman into all departments of labor, not as the remedy of an evil, but as the fulfillment of a mission. I do not know how strongly enough to express my dissent. I think the necessity of earning her own living is a woman's misfortune. She who must support herself in order to respect herself is an inferior sort of woman. Indeed, so far as regards any conception of her part in the economy of life, she is no woman at all. Probably her instinct overbears her intellect, and she is nineteen twentieths more a woman than she would make herself out to be, but her theory is wholly defective, and grievously below the real standard.

Pecuniary dependence, degrading to men, is not only not undignified, but is the only thoroughly dignified condition for women. In a renovated and millennial society all women will be supported by men—will have no more to do with bringing in money than the lilies of the field.

It is the misfortune of our age to be as yet far removed from that day; but to imagine it, and then call it degrading, is altogether intolerable. Says a woman's paper:

"The intervening years (between girlhood and marriage) are replete with dependence—conventional, honorable, but still grinding dependence ; chained to one house, to one round of duties, one constant claim of service. If claimed in love, it is well. [This seems to be inconsistent with a subsequent assertion.] If claimed as payment for benefit received, it is a fraud upon her time, her thought, and purpose in life. With no will save her father's, and no benefits save of his conferring, and no privilege save of his indulgence, she and her mother are serfs—loving and beloved, petted and indulged, caressed and flattered, it may be, but serfs notwithstanding.

"When the girl prefers to risk all and help herself, desiring a little means of her own earning, it is regarded as a direct reproach to her father. It is regarded as a still greater reproach to the husband when the wife aims at self-dependence. 'Can't that man support his wife?' is the everywhere-urged question."

Surely this is wild writing. An artist might as well sketch the outline of heaven and label it hell. What meaning have words to the mind that calls a "loving and beloved, petted and indulged, caressed and flattered" wife or daughter a serf? The cause must be hard pushed for grievance which finds such a state of things a grievance.

And the remedy is as grotesque as the grief is imaginary:

"Suffrage will be to her what concealed weapons are to the traveler—a provision for defense which, if unused, still secure respect and an unmolested transit.

"The presence of three or four citizens in the house, with a citizen's power of redress and a citizen's power to change poor laws, is a very different thing from the presence of several abject, timid, dissatisfied women, whom it is a pleasure to abuse because they can't help themselves."

To me, I must confess all this seems a mere travesty, and a ludicrous travesty, of real social conditions. We will admit that, technically, legally, the husband and father has the right of eminent domain. He is a citizen, wife and daughter or not. Actually, also, if he is a wrong-headed or bad-hearted man, he may be an intolerable tyrant. There are men so persistent of will, so feeble or *twisted* in intellect, that never so superior a wife can only *manage* them—can never thoroughly subdue or renew them—Scanlans who conquer by their very weakness. But there are also female Scanlans, and no law can be framed to touch them. Civil codes may reach a state of absolute perfection, doing equal and entire justice to man and woman, and a husband will still be able to hector his wife to death, and the wife her husband; and as between the two, one is inclined to think she does it best. A woman has rather more power to make a home steadily and unmitigatedly uncomfortable than has a man. But this writer is not speaking of petty tyrants. He expressly depicts a husband and father, able, willing, and longing to support and to cherish; loving and expressing love in all love's ways. To call wifehood to such a man serfdom is to denominate at random. If there is any serfdom about it, it is far more on the husband's side than on the wife's. There is no slavery so abject as the slavery of a man to the woman he loves. Abject, for it goes behind his will and possesses the whole man. And the more a man he is, the more strong, and bright, and free, the more thorough is his enthrallment. Woe to such a one if he falls into the hands of a weak, a frivolous, or an unworthy owner. Joy to him if his proprietor be a large-natured woman, for then his completest thrall is his most exalted and divine freedom.

In every known sense of the word, a woman owns the man who loves her more than he owns her. Her love is perhaps as great, but it is not so absorbing. She sees the situation, where he only sees her. She is as strong as all his strength, because his strength is hers. With whatever of power, or wisdom, or renown he is endowed, she also becomes possessed, and no enlargement of his borders diminishes one iota of his dependence upon her for the ability to enjoy them. If there is any difference, the supreme control, the court of last resort, is hers.

As for the loving and beloved, the petted and caressed daughter, the case is even harder for the happy father. A beloved wife is a constitutional monarch, after all, but a good daughter is apt to be an absolute despot. Indeed, she often carries things with so high a hand that the more experienced mother and less captivated wife has not infrequently to interfere to mitigate the rigor of paternal servitude. A mother will often wisely discriminate against her daughter's wishes, where a father will make an immediate and unconditional surrender.

"Father," says Susy to that gentleman, on his return home after some weeks of absence, "you are going to the theatre to-night."

"Why, no, Susy, I think not. I never was at a theatre in my life."

"But you are going to-night. Fanny and I mean to take you. I have bought the tickets. Your education has been too long neglected, and you must see the world."

And, so sure as evening comes, the respected citizen and Church-member is boldly and bodily taken possession of by the saucy chits, and marched off to the theatre—clanking his chains, it must be confessed, as if he loved them. Loving and beloved, petted and caressed, indulged and flattered he may be, but the veriest serf notwithstanding.

"With no will save her father's." If parents were called upon for evidence, I suspect they would testify to a different state of things. It must be a humdrum sort of family of which the father would not depose and say that there are as many wills in it as there are daughters.

"Grinding dependence." The girl who submits to such

a thing in her father's house is an inferior girl, and the constitutional amendment that is to avail her must come from heaven, not from Congress. The world is all before her where to choose. If her father does not wish her to be dependent on him, or if he taunts her with her dependence, she can leave him and make her own way in life; and she always should. A girl who will stand insult from any quarter is simply mean-spirited. If she would rather stay at home and grind than strike out for herself and grow, how can law or Gospel help it? You can not put *pluck* into people. There are women, and men too, for that matter, who seem to lack not only the aggressive, but the resisting element. They are born to be cowed. There is no snap in them. They never stand up to any thing. And if a man, coarse, somewhat tyrannical, and a little brutal, has them in his house for wife or daughters, he is tolerably sure to impose upon them. He will generally give all that they will take, and can any law be framed that will prevent it?

But where a father loves and cherishes his daughters, feeling that they are a part of himself, and that their happiness is his honor, no place in the world is for them so suitable and fit as their father's house, and no way of getting a living is so suitable as with their father's money. If they are gifted in any direction, let them exercise their gifts. If money follows such exercise, it is no disgrace. If the cultivation or the desired and desirable exercise of their power call them away from home, let them go; and if, as they attain maturity and self-poise, the absence is prolonged, still the home-circle is but stretched under wider skies—it is not broken. If they have no special gifts, there is still the common field of home and society, which will bear ages of tillage without danger of running to too much richness. Such dependence is the natural order of things, and is not degrading, but ennobling. Like the quality of mercy, it blesseth him that gives and her that takes, and is even more blessed in the giving than in the receiving. I suppose the care, provision, and support of a family is just as much a means of grace to the care-taker as to the care-receiver. For the consolidation of his own power; for continuity of purpose and vitality of heart; in one word, for the perfect development of his manhood, a man needs wife and child to cherish. Nothing else so constantly calls forth his tenderness, his chivalry, his unselfishness. Surely it can not be degrading for a woman to receive what it ennobles a man to give. Surely God never would have made the instrument of a man's salvation the tool of a woman's destruction.

Sometimes, even where the father feels as all fathers should—where his happiness would be in gratifying every wish of his daughters, in winning for them a home that should satisfy at once their wants, their tastes, and their hearts—he is yet unable to do it. He can not command the income that will enable them to live as he and they would wish. Dutiful and affectionate daughters will then be glad to help their father by helping themselves; or, where the father is able to provide and does provide abundantly, a girl may still desire to incur expenses or bestow charities which she feels that her father hardly ought to be asked to meet, and she takes keen pleasure in some money-earning scheme of her own—a scheme, too, in which she often enlists her father's sympathy and assistance. A thousand such incidents diversify and enliven, without deteriorating the dependence of daughter and wife; but all the same and always I maintain that the dependence of a loving daughter upon a loving father is the ideal condition of things, and her ideal home is in his house. It is only in such or similar relations that woman can do her real work. If she must go out and earn her living for herself, it is so much time and vitality taken from her higher and appropriated to her lower uses. Whatever work she does from inward prompting, from an irresistible love of it, detracts in no wise from her womanliness, for the one is as natural as the other; but doing work simply to earn a living is unnatural, and not to be desired to make her wise.

Let me not be understood to defend a state of things occasionally seen, but disgraceful to all concerned—a father occupied only in earning money, a wife and daughters occupied only in spending it. The father is immersed in business, works early and late, takes little holiday; the wife and daughters wear fine clothes, fare sumptuously, and live in idleness. His life is all drudgery, theirs all recreation. His aim is to keep as much money out of their clutch as possible, theirs is to clutch all they can; or, if he is a notch lower down financially, his struggle is to meet their ever-clamorous call. It is a case of self-denial, without dignity, on the one side, and of repulsive selfishness on the other—the mere travesty of a family whose sham splendor is the least of its shams. Let us hope such families are few; but there are far too many who verge toward it—too many who find pleasure in finery wrung from toil, rather than in the sympathy and affection of the toiler; who care not how dreary may be the life, or how ungratified the taste and unsatisfied the heart of the father, so they can pursue their round of useless and senseless frivolity. Nor, on the other hand, let these women be confounded with those saints and martyrs who are connected with miserly and self-willed men—women whose lives are a constant effort to fetch water out of a rock; high-spirited women, who know that there is money enough, who know how to spend money judiciously, yet who, to insure even a scant supply, are forced to expend upon their crabbed bondholders an amount of ingenuity and persistence that, properly applied, would have tunneled the Hoosac Mountain years ago. Their life seems to be a prolonged Battle of the Wilderness; but they look at their young in the rear, set their teeth, and square themselves for the fight. And they generally come off conquerors. They educate their children, introduce them to and keep them in good society, and, hardest of all, varnish their old dragon himself with a thin coating of humanity, and hold him up to a shuffling, shambling ambling alongside themselves. Sometimes Heaven is kind, and he dies. Then a sweet peace suffuses their lives, and their faces shine with a lustre not to be hidden by all the crape wherein they swathe themselves withal.

Nor let me, by any possibility, be supposed to cherish or defend that class of women whose existence in this country one could never credit except on unimpeachable testimony; women so radically different from the genius of the place and the age, so entirely aside from the line of our national development, both in its strength and its weakness, that I am not sure but we ought to cherish them as a sort of *memento mori*—a needed reminder that human nature is the same in all ages and countries; and that, though we pride ourselves on our independence and energy, there is a latent indolence or passivity in the blood which occasionally shows itself, and which may at any time burst out—perhaps it would be more appropriate to say creep out—and reduce us to the unresisting, undignified subordination of the "effete despotisms" of the Old World.

I mean women who, by death or disability, are deprived of their natural guardians; who have to choose between taking care of themselves and being taken care of by persons on whom they have no claim, and who choose the latter. The natural guardians of a woman are her father and her husband. They, of their own free will and choice, assumed her life, and it is their shame if they do not, or their misfortune if they can not, provide for her. But nobody else is her natural guardian. Upon no one else has she an unspoken claim. Into no other home than theirs has she an undisputed right to enter, and no other doors is it impossible justly to close against her.

A father dies leaving his family penniless. It is a wrong thing to do, but men will sometimes do it. We should all think it selfish and unmanly for the sons to go on their way and leave the daughters to go on theirs, unhelped. It is happily a sight we seldom do see. I often wonder at the bravery, fidelity, and delicacy with which boys assume a burden devolved upon them, often through what was neither more nor less than the improvidence or incapacity of their fathers. They "fight the bitter fight" for two, or three, or a dozen, without taking on airs, simply because it is the thing to do, and never imagine themselves heroic. But just as disgraceful as it would be for boys to neglect their sisters is it for sisters supinely to permit themselves to be a burden upon their brothers. A sister has no such claim upon her brother as it is ever safe to presume on. She can not, after arriving at maturity, be honorably supported by him unless at his expressed and perfectly untrammeled desire. Even then the connection may not be free from embarrassment. I can hardly conceive of a case in which independence would not be preferable. For a time the common support may not be onerous, and the common home may be happy. But by-and-by the brother forms new attachments, and his marriage puts a new face on matters. He must either maintain two establishments, which he may be very far from able to do, or he must have wife and sister in the same, and very few houses were ever built large enough for such an arrangement. *Men, and their wives, sisters, and mothers, may all be saints, but when the code of laws regarding married women is perfected, it will be a state-prison offense for a man ever to propose to his wife *in esse* or *in posse* to live in the family with his female relatives. | If his wife propose it, or they invite and she accept, that is her own affair; but for a man to arrange it, and call that providing for his wife, is a part of the naïve and touching blindness which distinguishes men in their conduct of delicate domestic affairs. | A girl must then be in some sense cast off by her brother, or she must be a superfluous member of his household, and uncertain at any time whether she may not be a burdensome and undesired one. The time may come when she will be needed and summoned, but how much better for her to be self-sustaining from the beginning and *be* summoned! This does not necessarily involve isolation or even separation from her brother, but it does involve a partnership whose benefit shall be mutual, and in whose existence both shall have a power of choice.

There are women who will rest, or at least exist, upon weaker ties than these; who will depend for support upon the merest shadow of a claim; who, strange as it may seem, appear to think that it is more unladylike to work for money than it is to endure an obligation. They fondly imagine themselves to be decayed gentlefolk, and that their narrow, straitened, useless life allies them to the English nobility. So they deny themselves society, amusement, travel, all largeness of life; they shut themselves in dingy rooms ever growing dingier; live in dressing-sacks from which they emerge only on rare state occasions; devote all their powers to evolving elegant garments out of shabby ones, and very likely succeed; expend in the struggle to live respectably on the allowance furnished by some grudging relative an amount of time, industry, ingenuity, and perseverance which, properly directed, would secure them an ample income, and find their one consolation in the reflection that they are ladies, reduced and impoverished like the ladies in English novels, but ladies still. But a lady would rather dig ditches, and die in the last one, than live on charity. A gentlewoman is decayed beyond all tradition of past grandeur and all hope of future resuscitation before she can levy contributions on reluctant connections, or become the recipient of unwilling bounty. No occupation is so menial as beggary, and no beggary is so mean as indirect beggary.

Sometimes these women may be found clinging together, and sometimes they attach themselves singly to other households, and occupy an undefined, but always unhandsome position. Few sights are more pitiable. "Anxious and aimless," bitter but repressed, without natural play of the faculties or freedom of choice, dependent upon the will and perhaps the caprice of men who do not love them, and who partially despise them, with their good qualities depreciated and their faults magnified, their greatest virtue an enforced patience, and the tenderest feeling they excite a half-contemptuous pity, they tread their dreary way from a youth without spirit to an old age without respect.

To be obliged to support herself is a woman's misfortune.

To shift the obligation from her own shoulders to those of another is her fault.

The best place for a woman is in the home that wants her.

The worst place is in the home that does not want her.

IX.
SERVILE OCCUPATIONS.

WHAT shall a girl do in her father's house? Oh! if girls had but open eyes to see the unreaped harvests, the unsown fields that stretch around them!

Looking only in one direction, we must see that our social life is largely lacking in the higher and finer elements, which women, and perhaps women alone, can supply. Men are absorbed in affairs. They have often little cultivation; and even their shrewdness, their hard sense, their practical sagacity they are too apt to leave behind them in field, and shop, and counting-room. Their time is limited, their theory of society meagre, their standard of womanhood low, and the women whom they meet are not concerned or adapted to raise it. I have seen the whole tone of conversation, even in a brilliant company, persistently dragged down by one aggressively ignorant and vulgar woman. If such a thing can be done in a green tree, what can not be done in a dry? If light can be extinguished by an unfavorable atmosphere, how much more can it be prevented? Not many women are aggressively ignorant or aggressively vulgar, but unconscious insipidity is by no means uncommon. There is a great army of women in city and country whose only individuality is a flavor of goodness. They are of power only in the mass. Of themselves they give no inspiration and hold no opinions. They are simply susceptible to influences. Their views on most things are nothing worth. In company they have an amiable desire to entertain you, and a traditional belief that you are to be entertained by conversation; so, when you have by good luck fallen into the company of the traveler just returned from Syria, and he is deep in his description of the last hieroglyphical discovery on Mount Sinai, this good and amiable woman at your elbow strikes out with her friendly, self-satisfied voice, and asks you if you do not feel sorry that round hats are giving way to bonnets! If she were a child you would say "Hush!" But she is a woman—yes, and a lady; so you reply politely, and of course discursively, and are just as effectually cut off from Mount Sinai as if you had received a telegram from home that your family are down, one and all, with cholera. Yet the lady did it out of pure goodness. Because you were not talking, she thought you were being bored. Mount Sinai had no attractions for her, and she had not discrimination enough to see that it had any for you. That a woman could be interested in hieroglyph would have seemed to her something altogether literary, unnatural, blue.

Even in those classes where the women are petted and supported, and the men preoccupied with business, are the materials for social entertainment as rich and abundant among women as among men, and the selections as sedulously and carefully made? Am I wrong in thinking that the complexion, the tone of our social assemblies is chiefly given by men? A dinner is successful according as the male guests are bright or dull; scarcely according to the female guests. Which is the oftenest invited for pure agreeableness, a man or a woman? Which is the more common, to bid a man to your banquet because he is his wife's husband, or a woman because she is her husband's wife?

But this ought not to be. Women ought to be good talkers. It is their eminent domain. There is much banter afloat on the subject, and one might easily suppose that our women were given to talk; but nothing is further from the truth. Their fault in society is that they do not talk. They are timid—not socially, but intellectually. They are afraid to imbibe, or to cherish, or to enunciate ideas. They mistrust their own capacities and acquirements, and have mistrusted them so long and so sincerely that the mistrust presently becomes final and fatal. They have too much sense to be silly, and too little power to be self-forgetful, so they take a secondary place when they ought to be in the van. It is not oppression on the one part, nor superiority on the other, but the natural effect of a long line of causes. Women not only fear men, but they fear each other. They fear themselves, they fear hobgoblins; and, perhaps, to their dying day, never find out that their next neighbor was just as afraid of them as they were of her, and that it was always a question of hair's-breadth which should flee first.

Here, then, is one thing for girls to do in their father's houses. Does it seem slight? Is it so easy that girls can give themselves to it, and yet find time hang heavy on their hands? On the contrary, it is so complicated and so important a matter, it is an opportunity so vast and munificent, that every woman of leisure in the country might find in it ample career, and yet leave a large work undone. No department of life offers a wider field for influence than the department of society; and here women are by nature rulers, and not subordinates. But to rule, and not to deteriorate, they ought to be women indeed, strong-minded and strong-hearted; women of nerve and beauty, of ideas and opinions, of reasons and facts; women who can influence, and command, and control; who can rebuke and encourage; who shall sway men by that which is highest in both; who can discern and elicit the hidden power, and be hospitable to the modest thought; who can repress without wounding, befriend without patronizing, and refine without enervating; who can resist silently, perhaps, but steadfastly, the onset of popular fallacy, turn quietly aside from a false standard, and

H

frame and fashion not so much by direct effort as by indirect influence. Such a woman need not say, " Be noble, be generous, be true ;" but, by reason of some subtile quality in herself, some unseen but persuasive and pervasive power, some insinuating grace and graciousness, no man brings to her any thing but his best.

Do you say such a woman is born, not made? Rather all women are born to be thus made. But the work needs care, and wisdom, and mental training, observing eyes and just reasoning, wide benevolence, and an infinite, delicate sympathy. It furnishes scope for every faculty which a woman possesses, and it demands imperatively her especial prerogative—tact. It is a work which, if not done by women, will not be done at all. Man has a perpetual tendency to disintegration. Woman is the cohesive element of society. It is not in man that walketh to direct his steps. It is in woman to direct them for him. In the best of men there is always a trait and trace of the savage. It is, indeed, necessary to constitute the best sort of man. If this savage is well held in hand by a woman, or by the feminine force of society, he is a serviceable addition to our social life, if not in a sense its substratum ; but, left to himself, he is always ready to spring upon the man to his undoing.

The mysterious attraction which every where draws men to women is a sacred trust committed to women by the Creator. It is not only a power irresistible, but a possession inalienable. By no misuse or disuse can it be forfeited. In listening to some of the arguments against woman suffrage, one might suppose that there was danger lest the sexes should become disaffected toward each other; lest women should be able so to array themselves in masculine armor as to alienate the regard of men. That will never be. The Minnesota farmers were far nearer the real state of the case in their comical Fourth of July " sentiment :"

"'The woman of the coming time?'
Shall man to vote app'int her?
Well, yes or no; your bottom dime
He'll do as *she's* a min' ter!
We know she 'will,' or else she 'won't;'
'Twill be the same as now;
And if she does, or if she don't,
God bless her anyhow!"

It is not beauty, nor wit, nor goodness, for the attraction exists independent of all these. It is simply womanhood. Man pays deference to woman instinctively, involuntarily, not because she is beautiful, or truthful, or wise, or foolish, or proper, but because she is woman, and he can not help it. If she descends, he will lower to her level; if she rises, he will rise to her height. This is the real danger—not that she *will* drive him from her, but in that she *can not* drive him from her. She can not help being his blessing or his bane. She can not make herself into a being whom he will not love. If she is insipid, ignorant, masculine, coarse, then he will love insipidity, ignorance, masculineness, coarseness, and be himself deteriorated. So much the more ought woman, by virtue of this mysterious and inalienable power, to rise to the height of its wise and worthy exercise. Instead of making it merely the minister of her own indolence and vanity, it should be made to minister all human grace and succor. Instead of regarding it as a reason why she may dispense with prudence and wisdom, it is the reason of all reasons why she should concentrate within herself every resource of prudence and wisdom. "I am glad women are *not* learned," says a little fool; "I leave that to the men;" and imagines she has said something womanly and winning; and because her feathers, and flowers, and flutters somewhat hide her inanity, and she has her feeble following among the males of her own kind, and the outward courtesy of men, she is perhaps never undeceived. But, whatever may be said of the undesirableness of learning for women, a woman never lost any thing by being intelligent. Cultivation, information, intellect always tell. More than this, their absence is fatal. Folly will not prevent beauty from being attractive and admirable; but whoever has other ends in view than the gratification of her personal vanity must have something besides beauty. Loveliness palls, and goodness loses flavor; and she who would do any thing for a man but pull him down, must add to her virtues sense. Women ought to be so ready in resource, so well furnished, and well balanced, and high toned, as to be the conscience, the judgment, the moral umpire of society. They ought so to live and so to think that men shall respect their opinions and solicit their counsel. Men in the thick of the fight may sometimes find their views obscured; women in a tranquil atmosphere should always be clear-sighted.

But, before this is done, women must be able to discriminate between the points on which they are competent and those on which they are incompetent to pronounce opinion. How many of these petted and caressed serfs, to whom the father says, "You have a good room, enough to eat, and plenty of nice clothes to wear; you are very unreasonable to crave more"—how many of these girls have a connected and communicable knowledge of the world's history? How many of them know where in the chain of logic to locate our great Rebellion or the last great European war? How many of them know the struggles, the advances, the retrogressions of mankind in its upward or onward progress; the developments of character or tendency of race, the trials and the modifications of different forms of governments, the checks and the impulses in result of which we stand in our place to-day? But why is it any more exalting or ennobling to go into a telegraph office, or a boot and shoe store, and "tend" all day, than it is to pursue such investigations? We say in America that we have no cultivated class like the cultivated class of England, because we have no hereditary wealth. Every one here must first "get his living," and take what of art, or science, or literature he can at odd hours. But we look forward to the time when we shall have a cultivated class. We pay great honor now to those sons of rich men who, instead of going into business to increase the wealth which their fathers accumulated, or going into dissipation to scatter it, betake themselves to learning, illustrate their country, honor their name, and show the true blessing, the highest, or one of the highest uses of money. They do not perhaps immortalize themselves by great discoveries; perhaps they add nothing to the common stock of knowledge, but they are invaluable to those who do. They form a circle gratefully receptive of and stimulative to all greatness; and, without noise or parade, by their refinement, their calmness, their judgment, their critical power, their discriminating observation, and freedom from personal ambition, they become not only the ornamental, but one of the most useful and potential forces of a society which has sore need of them.

I doubt not that where young men of these possibilities are to be numbered by units, young women are to be numbered by hundreds. It is the rule in our country for young men to go into some money-making business, whether their fathers be rich or not. It is the rule for young women whose fathers are rich, and for many whose fathers are far from rich, not to earn money. Here we have at once the material for a cultivated society. We have the very condition necessary for intellectual advancement—that is, material comfort. And, indeed, this is no trifling consideration. Believe me, girls, a good room, enough to eat, and plenty of nice clothes to wear, "without the soiling one white hand" to procure them, is not a bad thing. The women who must spend all their time in earning these can not turn aside to cultivate the amenities of literature. Upon you—you, to whom all these good gifts come without money and without price—upon you devolves the duty of serving your country, and repaying to society tenfold what it has given you, by becoming repositories of knowledge and of taste, shining lights of social life, women whom the wisest men shall seek, whom the weakest shall not shun, and whom only the wicked shall fear, but whom they shall fear exceedingly.

It is but a conjecture, yet I offer the conjecture that if the father finds his three or four daughters as conversant as himself with the history and philosophy of politics, holding opinions as decided and as well founded and fortified, talking French poetry with his French visitor, and German metaphysics with the German visitor, each in his own tongue, suggesting difficulties to the astronomer, and adding curiosities to the museum of the professor—it is but a conjecture, yet I conjecture that this father would by these manifestations be as soon deterred from abusing his daughters as he would by the consciousness that he had three or four citizens walking around the house with a ballot in their hands!

To the petted, caressed, and indulged serfs may there not be suggested the possibility of some good work to be wrought upon the bloated aristocrat, the remorseless and relentless tyrant who thus pets, and caresses, and lodges, and dresses them?

He is a human being even if he is their father, and, as a human being, perhaps not wholly hardened to gracious influences. It is not much to be the father compared with what it is to be the mother. Still it is something; and where the father does the best he knows how, and learns better as fast as he can, it is a good deal. The father who is now standing prisoner at the bar seems to be one of the first of his class. He does all the material duty of a father in providing for the material comfort of his child, and he goes a long way in the performance of all other duty by loving, caressing, and indulging her. Is it really a worthier, a nobler thing for his daughter to go into a type-setting establishment, and handle bits of metal all day, than for her to stay in his house, to brighten his home, comfort his heart, kindle his sympathy, medicine his weariness, freshen his ideas, dispel his despondency, pour youth into his age, and keep him mellow, and receptive, and alert? I think work on mind is more dignified, more womanly, and, for a woman, more economical than work on matter, even if that mind be your own father's. If there be also a mother; if, besides, there are three or four brothers and sisters, with an occasional aunt or uncle, how can any bright, wide-awake, well-educated girl be at a loss for employment? With a family affectionate, well disposed, and well conditioned; with a society intelligent, free, and accessible; with the world of literature, art, and science thrown open to every explorer; with a future as great in promise as severe in requirement, be sure it is not opportunity that fails, but ability to see and seize it.

When a man who has inherited an abundant fortune lives narrowly, dresses meanly, and shuns the interests, the amenities, the responsibilities of life, we do not call him a great man, but a small man, a miserable man, a miser. If a young man, in good health, of good education, refined associations, and ample means, should, at the age of twenty years, choose to become a miner, or a coal-heaver, or a hod-carrier, we should not call it nobleness or independence. We should merely think that it showed a low taste. He is not earning his living, because he has his living without earning it. A living is the first, least, and lowest object of desire. It is the common aim to secure that, and then build upon it the beauties, graces, and sweetness of living. So it seems to me that a woman who turns away from the living which her father provides, and gives her time and strength to providing one for herself, is wasting the advantages to which she was born, and falls below the standard of divine—that is, of natural—requirement. Instead of beginning her ascent from the half-way house where she finds herself, she goes to the foot of the mountain and climbs up. If the question is between idleness and dress-making, by all means let a girl leave her comfortable home and apprentice herself to a dress-maker, but let her not demand admiration for her grandeur of character in so doing. It is better to be a dress-maker than to be an idler, but it requires a far higher order of mind and heart to do the social work that awaits the woman of leisure than to make gowns. It is better to do the lower work than none at all, but it is not better than to do the higher work. If a girl goes into a shoe factory to run a sewing-machine, it is chiefly a matter of hours, pieces, routine. If she lives the best life at home, she must observe, infer, compare, forbear—she must, in short, enlist every faculty of mind and heart, and this is far more complex than routine work. If she must enter the factory because her father is poor or churlish, that is another question; but if she goes because she chooses it, she simply confesses thereby her incapacity for a more exacting career, and ranks herself beneath many a poor girl who toils because she must —toils under protest, and loves high all the while she lives low.

I do not think these cases are common in life. The girls one usually meets in society are, happily, quite ready to take the good the gods provide them. Petted and caressed daughters, whose comforts are provided and whose tastes are gratified, will sometimes become artists, writers, teachers, sisters of charity, but I never knew one who was possessed with the desire of earning her own living. There may be such women, but probably the closest scrutiny would discover that, almost without exception, women earn money from necessity, not choice. They do it to piece out the scanty income of husband or father. They do it because he is niggardly, tyrannical, and insulting, and any menial service to a stranger is better than dependence on such kinfolk. They do it from love, or from disdain for help or defense, but never of pure liking and free choice. The honored and beloved wife, the beloved and cherished daughter, not only never ought, but never does, feel discomfort in dependence. She has no desire to renounce serfdom or to break chains, for there is no serfdom to renounce, no chain to break. Probably she seldom thinks of it at all; but if she does think of it, she thinks only how much happier is her lot, who is nourished through the ministry of love, than her neighbor's, whose life is only a thankless round of buying and selling. Girls born to wealth are ready enough to be idle, ready enough to be ignorant, and more ready still to be frivolous. Unhappy girls break away from narrow homes—from selfish, domineering fathers; from wayworn, heart-weary mothers; from coarse, hated, and hopeless surroundings—to fight feebly or bravely, but single-handed, the hard battle. The one needs to be roused and incited to higher aims, to better thinking, to wiser and wider living; the other as sorely needs to be recognized, instructed, encouraged; but neither the one nor the other is enamored of pure self-support. Without assuming to have made the slightest investigation, I count it not hazardous to assert that of all the respectable young working-women in the country, the most excellent and intelligent, nine out of ten would relinquish with joy their money independence in the prospect of becoming the "loving and beloved" wife of a man who was able to maintain them, while the caressed and petted daughters who would rush into self-support as a refuge from their caressing and despotic fathers is a class of the community seldom met, except in the columns of certain earnest and benevolent newspapers.

Far distant be the day that shall make it otherwise. Far distant be the day that shall send girls out from their father's roof to make their own way in life, as boys make theirs. Immeasurably further that day that reckons it no reproach to the husband for the wife to feel her dependence upon him an unpleasant thing. Badly as women do man's work, men do woman's work still worse; for it is a far more complicated, intangible, and indefinite thing. Women themselves do it not too well, largely because our imperfect civilization has as yet kept them bound so closely to the rougher toil of man. But if women, having been so long dragged into that arena as straggling, struggling prisoners, shall now organize their forces, and voluntarily march in with intent to stay there as their fitting and final place—why, water will run up hill and fire will flame downward. Under certain stress of influence, water will run up hill, and a fierce breath will fan the flame awry; but Nature is never permanently disturbed, and, in spite of all human hydraulics and pyrotechnics,

> "Rivers to the ocean run,
> Nor stay in all their course;
> Fire, ascending, seeks the sun;
> Both speed them to their source."

NOTE.—It is but fair to say that, since the above was printed, an energetic young lady writes to me, "*I* am one of the many women whom I could show you who are 'possessed with the desire of earning their own living.' I would not be dependent on my father (there are few fathers his equals . . . .) if he were a millionaire to-morrow. Solely from the 'desire of earning my own living,' I would go into a factory if I could not get my own shoes, and hats, and books in any other way. I never supported myself to 'piece out the scanty income' of my father, or 'because he was niggardly, tyrannical, insulting' (as well might an angel in heaven be !), or 'from love or from disdain for help or defense,' but from 'pure liking and free choice.' There's no man alive on whom I would be dependent till my last sickness knocked me helpless. If I had married it would be just the same. In fact, it seems to me *more* unnatural to be dependent on one's husband than one's father."

To which I would simply add the suggestion that when these principles are carried out in practice to their legitimate conclusion, we shall not wait long for our last sickness, but be knocked helpless *in limine*, and I, for one, should not much care.

X.
HOME TRAINING.

IF there is any person who has a keener sense than the present writer of the faults of men in their own families— their selfishness, their brutality, their downright dishonesty —that person is to be pitied. Yet is there not something touching in the situation? A man works all day with brain or hand, or both, year in and year out, forecasting, planning, anxious; and not his ships on the sea or his shops on the land, but some tender, fragile wife, some little chit of a child, it is who holds all his happiness in her feeble hands. He exiles himself from home eleven months in the year, six days in the week, shutting himself in dreary chambers, living in dismal boarding-houses, not that his children may be fed and taught, but that life may be gay and blithe to them; that they may have the dainties and luxuries which he could not otherwise afford them, and for which he himself has no especial taste. His enjoyment is not in kid gloves and fresh ties, but in his children's enjoyment of them. Often, when he is peevish, tyrannical,. and inconsiderate, it seems more the result of the false teachings and wrong surroundings of generations than any spontaneous outburst of original sin in himself. The selfishness is more superficial, if it is at the same time more obvious and disagreeable, than the unselfishness. Deep down out of sight is a root of pure affection, a capacity for self-abnegation; but nobody ever thought a man had any thing to do with such things as self-abnegation. His mother believed it was her prerogative, and never taught him the virtues of daily and hourly consideration for others; and as for the father—fathers have been rowing in the same boat for generations. So the man, kind at heart, and meaning only good to his fellows, goes helplessly on, making himself odious by small tyrannies and unrepressed impatience, simply because self-sacrifice and self-repression have never been drilled into him. If wife or child be sick, he will move heaven and earth to heal them. Then he denies himself instinctively; does not know that it is denial. Sleepless nights and anxious days, lavish expenditure and the tenderest and most unwearying care, count for nothing to save the lives or restore the health of those whose tastes and feelings he has ruthlessly trampled on a thousand times, and will trample on again as soon as they are strong enough to bear it. Here is good missionary ground for an enterprising Christian young woman to occupy, and not the less so that the heathen pays all her expenses, and does not know that he is her field of operations.

If the daughters of a house are "abject, timid, dissatisfied women, whom it is a pleasure to abuse because they can't help themselves," it is simply because they are not bright. They are what is called in vulgar phrase " under par." They are the very persons who ought not to vote—not because they are women, but because they are idiots. A grown-up woman who will stay at home and let her father abuse her is an object of pity, and should be sent to South Boston to receive the protection of the law, rather than to Beacon Hill to make it.

A thousand times less even can the ballot do for a woman, a thousand times less is a woman fit for the ballot, who is not her husband's equal at home. Nothing but character can give her this position, and nothing but her own weakness—weakness of will or of wit—can take it away. True, a man's peevishness, perverseness, and pertinacity will often make headway against immense superiority of nature in a woman — indeed, because of this superiority. The great heart yields where a petty heart would resist, and there is silence instead of sputtering. How this is done was never better told than in Miss Mulock's "Brave Lady," a book wonderful for the minuteness, the awful fidelity with which it transcribes the experience of a grand woman crucified by marriage to a mean man. But even there—so sure is superiority to conquer in that most difficult of races, the long run—Miss Mulock, all conservative and duty-bound as she is, a writer who not unfrequently exasperates one by a conventional true-womanliness, a sweet submission, and deference to marital and masculine superiority that is simply fatuous in a woman of her power, and is to be forgiven only to her English training—even Miss Mulock is obliged to release her heroine from the logical necessity of leaving her husband by discovering in him a heart-disease after the last trunk is packed. To be sure, the stumbling-block may seem but visionary. If Heaven has sent a heart-disease to a worse than worthless husband, the utmost that can be required of a wife is that she should not jump at him from behind the door. That, however, is an indifferent matter. The point established, so far as Miss Mulock can establish it, is that a woman who is superior to her husband, and we may infer also one who is his equal, must live with him on a footing of equality, or she can not live with him at all. Laws far more oppressive than our own did not hide Josephine's ability from Mr. Oldham, nor could divine sovereignty have revealed it to Edward Scanlan except as he already saw it through a glass, darkly.

Few men, it is to be hoped, are so hypocritical and imbecile as Edward Scanlan. Those few should be dealt with summarily. Many even of the irritating domestic despots have integrity and ability. What they lack is right training. Now, if a man of real worth happen to have these audacious plantation manners, shall his wife give in to them? Yes, if she has no respect for herself and no regard for his character. But if she values her own growth in grace, if she believes her husband capable of becoming a polished cornerstone in the temple of the Lord, let her set about polishing him at once. If he thinks that she lives upon his bounty, let her not try to earn money in by-ways, that she may avoid calling upon his bounty, but let her be instant in season and out of season to uproot and overthrow his notion that he is bestowing bounty. A woman takes a man for her husband of her own free will, and she has no right to give up his soul to weeds and wilderness because the soil is hard to cultivate. Until she has proved beyond question that he is a hopeless desert, she should not desert him. But to do neither the one nor the other—to see his selfishness, and to pamper him in it; to suffer from his false opinions of their relations, and yet to confirm him in them; to endeavor to compete with him in buying and selling, instead of showing him how far more vital, how infinitely more intricate is her work than all his buying and selling—this implies a recklessness of moral and conjugal obligations not pleasing to contemplate. If she can not convert him she may control him. If she can not renew, she can at least repress. If she can not open his heart, she can close his lips. If she can not bring him to walk with her happily in the right path, she ought to prevent him from taking any comfort in the wrong.

The trouble is that women too often hold the same erroneous opinions as their husbands. They, too, fancy—or at least admit—that pecuniary dependence involves inferiority of position. Because their husbands earn the money, and themselves spend it; because their husbands claim to be the real owners of property, and class the wife as a recipient of favor, they let it go so, think it is so, act as if it were so. Thus men walk blindly, led by blind leaders.

Just as well might the rough and rocky foundation claim to be superior to the marble temple that rises upon it stately and beautiful. The foundation supports the temple; the temple does not support the foundation. The foundation is not dependent upon the temple; the temple is dependent on the foundation. Therefore the temple is the inferior and subordinate structure!

The queen is dependent upon her subjects. The work she does for them is almost as intangible as the ideal woman's work, but nobody considers the queen degraded thereby. It is because she is queen that all her realm pays tribute to her. Would her position be exalted, or would she do more for her kingdom by apprenticing herself to a linen-draper? She might, indeed, earn her wage, but she would have to give up being queen.

If there is really no need of queens, let the queen turn linen-draper. If there is really no better work for women, let them become hewers of wood and drawers of water, and thus obtain equality with men. Let the marble dome grub in the earth alongside the granite foundation, and witch the world with noble architecture.

The demand on the part of female writers and speakers that women shall earn their own living, the assertion that they must earn their own living in order to retain their self-respect, ought not to surprise one, and is, indeed, rather an encouraging token. Any thing is better than for a wife to remain unprotesting in the degraded and dishonoring position assigned her in too many families. If the only way out of it were through ditch-digging, she would much better dig ditches than stay in her place content. No doubt ditch-digging is easier work than converting many of these hard-headed husbands to right ideas of their own place in the world after they have gone on for years imagining themselves the sole rightful, and making themselves the sole real, authority in the family. But if women would only begin right! Nature seems to have been aware that man in his ordinary estate is not malleable, and when she is about to bring him into "the Woman's Kingdom" she has recourse to special means of grace; she causes him to undergo a preparatory process of softening and sweetening, which the unregenerate call being "in love," and which relegates him to the woman's care, pliable, yielding, and, indeed, amazingly susceptible to her wise and gracious influence. This is the tide in the affairs of women which, taken at the flood, leads on to fortune. Omitted, all the voyage of their lives is likely to be bound in shallows and in miseries. This is the time for a woman, not to assert her equality, not to announce her sovereignty—for that might imply a possible opposite opinion—but to assume it. The time during which her authority is unquestioned should be sedulously employed in making it unquestionable. It is at the beginning that wrong action can be hindered. It is the rising of a wrong spirit that should be repressed. A woman is the mistress in her own house; and if her authority be disputed, or, worse still, despised, the world had better stop revolving than she yield to the insubordination. But if she has gone on for years giving way before it, she may nearly as well hope to turn the stars from their courses as the man from his ways, though it never can be too late to try to mend. The very first outcropping of a disposition on the part of the husband to look upon their property or their income as any more his than hers should be indirectly, if possible, but resolutely and really, put down. When a woman is married to a man, the idea is that they are made one. If they are one, she, at the very least, becomes endowed with all his worldly goods. If they are two, they have not scripturally been married at all. But would not this involve control of business, justify, or at least permit, extravagance on the part of the wife, and place the husband completely at her mercy? Yes, if the problem of life is to be wrought out by arithmetic. Yes, if a social principle or a rule of ethics be as exact, as exhaustive, and as immitigable as the multiplication table. I do not know how to express the rightful ownership of a woman in her husband's property without using language which should allow a disastrous interference with his business, neither can I express strongly enough my opinion that a man should manage his business himself without using language which should involve an exclusion of his wife from the control of their property. And, unfortunately, language is no more unmanageable than facts. Men will conduct their affairs on principles so unsound that ruin and disgrace must follow, while their wives see, understand, and deplore the causes which bring ruin, and vainly strive to apply the checks that would prevent it, or the remedies that would restore prosperity. Yet the general fact remains that the man is the rightful natural manager in business, and the woman the rightful natural manager at home. And in actual trial there is not only no trouble involved in this arrangement, but there always must be trouble without it. Economy, improvement, harmony, and happiness are impossible under any other *régime*. A wife is never more unbecomingly occupied than in meddling with her husband's business, and a man is never more despicable than when he is bothering around in the house. The phrase is not elegant, I know, but it is elegant enough for the thing phrased. There is no reason why a man should not control his business himself, except that he is unfit for it; and, if he is unfit for it, his wife should not have married him, in the first place. If a man has not confidence enough in a woman to intrust his house to her care, he should not have asked her to be his wife at all. If either has made a poor choice, he must simply make the best of it. This classification of responsibility means neither isolation nor autocracy on any subject whatever. The wife whose position is precisely what it ought to be is the one who makes her husband's comfort, convenience, and pleasure the first principle of housekeeping. The man who is most successful in conducting his business is the very one who is likely to talk it over every now and then with his wife. The wife who has only to go to the bureau-drawer or to send to the bank for money, with a clear understanding of the resource whence bank and bureau draw their supply, and of the plans and requirements of the future, is the very wife who will make that money go the farthest and bring the most. In the ideal family there is constant, instinctive, conscious, and unconscious consultation. The husband and wife are in all each other's thoughts. Authority never appears, for it is never appealed to. The husband and wife simply go on from day to day leading the life which is natural, doing the things that are considerate, helpful, restful, heartening, that make business interesting as well as lucrative, and home stimulant as well as happy. And when you see these homes—homes free from the ostentation of love, but full of its richness—little worlds of busy thought, and activity, and opinion, not devoid of perplexity, not exempt from trouble, but always nurturing a character free, and fresh, and strong, and wholesome—it seems as if this is the only kind of home that ever could be.

Alas! that it is not. Alas! that its rarity is largely because women will not come to their own—to that which would be theirs for the coming, and which no ballot could ever give or take away. Looking at those unhappy men whose wives and mothers have permitted them to grow up crabbed, morose, unreasonable, domineering, illiberal, one might speak like David in haste, and say, If a man is not good by nature he can not be good by grace. Yet I suspect there is no creature more amenable to training, as there is certainly none more dependent upon training, than man. The irreclaimable are few. By far the greater number might, by firm, gentle, wise treatment, be made as good and agreeable in the common as they are in the casual relations of life; might be made as reasonable at home as they are polite abroad; and if by no patience and no possibility can gentle treatment make them good, then, as I have already hinted, let heroic treatment make them submissive. Here nothing avails but a courage that amounts to recklessness. This women seldom have till the last gun is fired. They are more afraid of public speech than private suffering. They will toil and moil, coax, storm, overreach, contrive, argue, tease, shame, scold, but keep on; and the husband does not mind the teasing and scolding, and does not know of the overreaching and contriving, and really cares for nothing at all so long as the wife keeps on. The only thing he would care for she does not do. She does not plant herself fair and square, without words, but with an unalterable resolution, on her reserved rights. A farmer will go out in the morning with three or four hired men, and leave his wife, without any servant, to do all the work, which she does not complain of, but also to bring in wood and water, which she does complain of. Now if, instead of complaining, and bringing wood, and making up for lost time by extra hurrying, she would leave her cooking-stove at the precise point where wood or water gave out, and spend the rest of the morning in pleasant reading, welcome her husband when he comes home hungry to dinner with that cheerful smile that we read so much about in the newspapers, and say pleasantly, "Charley, dear, you did not leave me any wood. I will be setting the table while you are building the fire again, and we will have dinner all ready in two hours," how much more likely would Charley be to fill the wood-box next day before he drove his team afield! A masterly inactivity is more effective than scolding. If a wife is denied access to or power over the common income, and, instead of striving to keep up appearances on a niggardly and grudged allowance, which, after all, may be the result of pure inexperience, would swiftly, deftly, and emphatically bring dress, table, husband, every thing down to the allowance, wearing only calico gowns, and pinning a towel around the children's necks—putting the deficiencies, that is, where her husband could perceive them—I think he would speedily relinquish his solitary grandeur, and pray madam to become chairman of a committee of appropriations. Once a man gave his wife five dollars to buy a little lad's first outfit. She stretched it as far as it could be stretched, cut up her own cambric gowns, and for the rest assumed indifference, and made, after all, a brave display. The five dollars was perhaps enough to buy one little slip. Suppose, now, she had bought the little slip, and said to her husband, "It is to be hoped, my dear, that our son will bring a hardy constitution with him, as there is nothing awaiting him in *this* world but one muslin frock"—which will probably astonish the nurse, and make lively talk among the neighbors—" but, if you like it, I have no objection, and no doubt there will be a contribution taken up for him in church before winter sets in!"

There are undoubtedly cases in which defective law causes suffering in families, but we are utterly beguiled by words if we suppose that, in the every-day family life, because the husband votes and the wife does not, the husband has therefore any real power over the wife; that because the father is a citizen, and the daughters are not, he takes opportunity to abuse them. If he domineers over them now, he will domineer them into voting his way. If they have not spirit enough and wit enough to hold their own against him now, they will surely follow him, a timid, abject, and dissatisfied procession, to the polls. And good enough for them, and good enough for all women who are so foolish and weak as to let men tyrannize over them, when nature and grace alike call upon women to tyrannize over men!

XI.
FEMALE SAGACITY IN POLITICS.

THE ballot is the head and front of the "Woman Movement." Work and wages, education, property rights, all are subordinate to or comprehended in the one demand for female suffrage. It is not claimed that the suffrage will immediately redress every wrong, but it is claimed that wrongs will not and can not be righted without it. The demand for the suffrage is based, first, on woman's natural right to it; secondly, on the ground that it is effective, and, indeed, necessary for the purification of politics and the uplifting of society; and, thirdly, that woman needs it for her own protection against unjust laws.

The question of natural right is an abstract one, and may be argued forever without changing one's preconceived opinion. Some persons even deny that there exists such a thing as natural right to vote; but if it do exist, it is difficult to see why a woman does not possess it in precisely the same measure as a man. Certainly no argument has ever been presented by the opponents of female suffrage that seems to me to have a particle of weight. But the matter appears to be of slender practical importance. When women have acquired the power to vote, their right to do so will pass out of discussion; and so long as they are not able to do so, the right is of little use.

As to the second point, the improvement of politics, are we equally at the mercy of pure reason? Must we simply say that women are better than men, and, therefore, when women become officially connected with politics, it follows as the night the day that politics will become clarified? Must we, that is, walk by faith alone till the rising sun of woman's enfranchisement shall turn faith into sight?

We are not here left wholly without witness. The character and effect of participation in politics by women are not wholly matters of conjecture. Women have now for many years directly concerned themselves in politics, and the champions of female suffrage boast of victories already won—years ago, through the influence of women, under the marshaling of men; later, by the direct efforts of women, organized by their own leaders upon their own principles. When, therefore, we are called upon to say whether the desired improvement in society will be furthered by placing men and women in the same position—not as men and women, but as citizens, with identical duties and identical responsibilities, or, rather, for this is not an adequate statement of the case, whether society will be advanced by woman's securing or by man's assigning her what have been considered his own peculiar duties and responsibilities in addition to those which she already has in common with him and those which are peculiarly hers, and which she can not delegate to him, then it is fair and fitting to look not only at what women may be expected to do when they have gained full political rights, but at what they actually have done in the use of political weapons and the exhibition of political wisdom.

I have watched with unflagging interest, with such intelligence as was vouchsafed me, and from what vantage ground I could command, every phase of the movement that came within the sphere of my observation. That movement has advanced from weak and despised beginnings to a point where it is discussed with seriousness, recognized by parties, deferred to by leaders, and acknowledged in some quarters as a not very remote future possibility.

From this careful observation of its course thus far, I can not see that any thing in its treatment of difficult questions, or in its conduct of delicate affairs—in the ends which it proposes, the methods which it selects to accomplish those ends, or the manner in which it pursues those methods—gives us the smallest prospect of an introduction to a higher grade of political life than that which we are already occupying under the dynasty of man. I fail to see that it is more comprehensive in vision, more inexhaustible in research, more radical in thought, more scientific in method, more conscientious in action; that in discussion it is more sober, candid, just, and courteous; that it displays more information and less inflammation, more of philosophy and less of personality; that it is more accurate in presentation, and more conscientious against misrepresentation; that it is more judicious in the selection of agents; that it appeals to higher motives, or teaches a wiser mode, or points to a wider field of activity. It appears to me, on the contrary, that the woman's party copies with singular fidelity the old ways of the old parties, which ought never to have been entered at all. Women, so far as they are already in politics, are doing right over again, and often with a peculiar feminine facility, the very things which have been done by men, and which ought never to be done at all, while I have not been able to discern the introduction by them of a single improvement or sign of improvement in political thought or action. Universal purity, freedom, and happiness are indeed noble ends for any party, but no party in the country confesses or professes any other ends. When we look at the means by which the woman's party proposes to reach the desired results, we find that they are either general, and, therefore, practically worthless, or specific, but empirical, and often worse than worthless, or they are the same means which men have been employing and are continuing to employ. This has nothing whatever to do with the right of woman to the ballot. A man is not forbidden to cast his vote because he casts it for the wrong person or the wrong measure; no more should a woman be. But when the vote of women is urged upon the nation as its means of grace and hope of glory, it is requisite and necessary to infer somewhat from such preliminary grace and glory as have been displayed. If the dawn is darkness, why shall we suppose that at evening time it shall be light?

Nor do these statements, if admitted to be true, involve the inferiority of woman to man. It does not imply inferiority to fail where he has not succeeded. It simply indicates that at present she is not politically his superior. It dismisses again to the domain of abstract reasoning the idea that government and society are to be uplifted by the direct professional participation of woman in politics, and leaves it with presumptive evidence against it.

"If women were allowed to vote, hold office, and make laws, they would be the means of purifying politics and elevating the standard of morality among our officers and representatives; and we should, therefore, have better laws, and criminals would not be so often permitted to escape their just punishment."

So says a female suffrage newspaper; and I ask for a sign, unbelieving Jew that I am, and read on eagerly through a column or more describing the defects and declaiming upon the disasters of our present laws, till I come to the conclusion of the whole matter in the final paragraph:

"When women are permitted to vote, they will not be long in changing the unjust and tyrannical laws which men have made for them, and we may confidently expect that they will soon find some way to prevent intemperance and the sale of poisonous liquors, to shut up gaming-houses, and will prove that the arm of the law can be made powerful enough to overthrow even the social evil itself. . . . And our legislative halls will not so often behold such disgraceful scenes as at present, and our representatives will be obliged to be more dignified and more alive to the duties which they are sent to perform."

Certainly the absolute and speedy prevention of the three great vices of society is worth forming a new party for. No one will deny that the rapid success of women in bringing about a millennium which men have been trying and failing to bring for centuries would be a victory brilliant enough to justify all their eagerness to share in the fray.

But when we ask the plan of the campaign, we find nothing but glittering and sounding generalities. All these desirable things are to be done, and done soon, but the only way in which they are to be done is—*some way!* Appetites, habits which have hitherto baffled legislation, despised affection, defied religion, are to be speedily overthrown, and prevented from further encroachments, in some way. The incredulous must be pardoned if they withhold their faith until that way is more definitely marked out.

Another organ of the same party is sufficiently specific, and affirms:

" It will be understood that we are a unit to help elect in every town the man who is our friend; to help defeat in every town the man who is indifferent. Soon no man who is *not* our friend will stand a chance of nomination. George William Curtis says, ' Behind every demand for the enlargement of the suffrage hitherto there was always a threat.' It will be so in the present case. *Our* threat must be an active, determined organization, in dead earnest to dig a political grave for every man who opposes the enfranchisement of the women of Massachusetts."

The party, it seems, will follow the simple standard of that fine old English gentleman who classifies his acquaintance by one rule : " D—d scoundrel, sir ; he is opposed to me !" or, "First-rate fellow, Smith ; he is my friend !" It does not question a man's principles or character. It is enough that he be "our friend." However stainless and able he may have proved himself, however well he may have wrought for his country in the service of truth, freedom, and honor, he shall give way to any charlatan who may choose to ride into office on the hobby of woman suffrage, and who is perfectly indifferent on what he rides, so he rides in.

And is there not shown, in the construction put upon Mr. Curtis's words, an entire failure to comprehend their real scope? What sort of threat is it that has lain hitherto behind every demand for the enlargement of the suffrage? In recovering from our late civil war we were sore pressed. On the one side was the danger of putting the ballot into the hands of an ignorant and inexperienced class, out of whom intelligence, integrity, straightforwardness, independence had been well-nigh crushed by generations of slavery. On the other side were the ranks just conquered in rebellion, whose monopoly of the vote would be likely to betray the newly-won states into the hands from which they had been so hardly wrested. The danger from disloyalty seemed more imminent than the danger from ignorance, and emancipated slaves were intrusted with the suffrage. Disaster to the nation was the threat which lay behind the demand for negro suffrage—a demand made not so much by the negroes themselves as by the nation which incurred the risk. The threats which have induced England to enlarge her suffrage have in like manner concerned the public safety. A strong and resolute populace has made its wishes felt. Armed mobs have alarmed the custodians of the nation. Tumult, and violence, and quiet, fierce determination, and despair born of suffering, have menaced the whole fabric of society, till old power recognized new power, and granted it self-direction in self-defense—relinquished a part of its prerogative to retain its continued existence.

But *our* threat has nothing to do with national danger or national honor. No pillar of society seems about to give way, no foundation-stone rocks in its place. *Our* threat is a political grave for our opponents. *Our* threat is loss of place to some office-holder or disappointment to some office-seeker!

What is this but an appeal to the lowest personal ambition of the lowest political hacks? How will such an argument be likely to purify politics and put better men in authority? Are these considerations calculated to induce men to seek the truth, and let all the ends they aim at be their country's? What sort of politician would probably be evolved from the man who would form his opinion and shape his action under the influence of such a threat? Must not the result be that, while any real thinker, high-minded and clear-sighted, would stand unmoved, or moved possibly into an antagonistic position, the demagogue, ambitious and unscrupulous, would hasten to lay hold of so easy a help over hard places, and use it vigorously for his own aggrandizement? Are politics to be purified by a mode of operation which have a tendency to exclude the men of careful and conscientious thought and exact speech, and attract those whose opinions arise from consequences rather than evidence, and who are ready to become all things to all men if by any means they may gain office for themselves?

After all, is there not a touch of grotesqueness in the situation? A cause in search of a danger wherewith to re-enforce its ranks must be reduced to its lowest terms when to past national peril of the gravest moment it parallels the ambition of the virtuous citizen to be sent to general court or to be made a city alderman. Even a non-election to the governorship or a defeat for Congress is hardly to be compared to the rehabilitation of slavery or a forced return to anarchy.

There is perhaps no question of public interest on which the woman's vote promises more direct improvement than the question of the prohibition or regulation of the sale of liquor. It is a point that has been debated for years, has been legislated upon with appalling frequency, and seems yet further from settlement than when the Maine Liquor Law was supposed to have exorcised the evil spirit forever. Let women vote, we are assured, and the matter will be speedily and permanently arranged. This would be a boon indeed; for a perpetual settlement—that is, a real settlement—can be only upon the right foundation; otherwise there is no settlement at all, but temporary adjustment, renewed upheaval, and constant unrest. Have men been bungling over it with ignorant heads and unskillful hands all these years? "*Place aux dames!*"

"I am convinced," says the Woman's Organ, "that if woman's intuition and emotional force were free to speak through the ballot, this greatest crime of the age [the liquor traffic], which is doing more than all other crimes and causes combined to make woman's heart and home desolate, might, in its commercial sense, be banished within ten years."

I confess I do not precisely understand what is meant by banishing this crime in its commercial sense; but the notion that a woman's vote can do in ten years what her voice has failed to do in ten thousand years seems to me to banish any suspicion of common sense. Undoubtedly, if you appeal to the woman whose heart and home have been made desolate by a drunken husband, her woman's intuition would speak with great emotional force, and say that the simple and absolute prevention of drunkenness was the entire suppression of the liquor traffic. Without wine or spirit it is impossible to be drunk. Forbid wine and spirit to be sold or made, and in a moment, in the twinkling of an eye, drunkenness is swept from the face of the earth.

Nothing can be plainer—not a mathematical axiom, not the multiplication table itself; and the only wonder is that we should have waited so long, and suffered so much in mind, body, and estate, before discovering or applying a remedy so simple and so accessible. In all the prognostications of good to arise from woman's vote on temperance, I have seen no hint of any other mode of action. Women set their face like a flint against intemperance, and they will suppress it by sheer force. They forecast no plans to destroy a love of liquor, or to increase self-control and self-respect, but they will simply make it impossible for their husbands and fathers to buy liquor.

When a suffering woman passionately advocates the burning down of the grocery which supplies her husband with the bad rum that is destroying him; when a company of energetic women, out of patience with the inefficiency of the laws, and with the self-indulgence and self-destruction of their husbands, go in a body to the dram-shop and empty its contents into the gutters, one is not shocked. Human nature is not infinitely elastic, and breaks if put upon too great a stretch. But when a body of women, who are demanding active participation in political management for the purpose of securing wise laws—when they propose to incorporate this vigilance committeeship into our civil code on the strength of their intuitions, one is tempted to be impatient. Has history, then, no lessons which women are bound to respect? I have yet to see the first evidence that any woman who has pronounced judgment in this matter has ever taken count of any thing in it except the object to be gained, and her "noble purpose" to gain it. One would never suspect from the prohibitory arguments used that there exists a vast and complex human organism, delicate but unconquerable, upon whose mysterious and unchangeable laws must be based all measures for its benefit, or they will come to naught. One would never suspect that for centuries human wisdom and human benevolence had been studying that organism, investigating those laws, and, though still far from a complete knowledge, had arrived at some conclusions which can not be overthrown. Nothing of this—not even a reference, not even a recognition that such a state of things exists—can I find in the arguments of the woman party. It is true that many men are equally innocent in regard to it, but women are coming into politics to supply the deficiencies of men. What if they only increase the bulk by adding to them their own? If a cause is beset with danger because it lies on the exact boundary-line between individual liberty and public safety, and because the evil that threatens on one side is immediate and obvious, while the evil that threatens on the other is remote, unseen, far-reaching, are we any thing helped by never so great re-enforcements of pure but unthinking partisans, who see only the obvious and never the hidden danger, only the individual suffering and never the individual inviolability; who have not familiarized themselves with past experiment and past effort, but throw themselves into battle for what was long ago lost just as enthusiastically as if the fight were but this day begun? Intuition has undeniably its own field to work in, and a woman can find ample use for all that Heaven has bestowed upon her; but to run a political party upon it seems the very height of intellectual indolence, amounting almost to crime. Have not women under the old *régime* been sufficiently pampered with this pap? Have not women from time immemorial been taught that brain-work was too severe for their "delicate organization;" that study and thought were for men; that they could jump at all the knowledge that was necessary for them, that necessity being reduced to its minimum; and been taught it with a result to be met in the hosts of illiterate, incapable women whose frivolities and follies furnish a text for every newspaper in the land, and (more disastrous still) will enstamp themselves with unerring distinctness on the generations to which they give birth? For those who desire and design to keep women away from political action and influence, it is well enough to enfeeble and deteriorate them with the notion that intuition is sufficient; but it is startling, indeed, when those who are urging them on preach the same doctrine. No man would commit the building of his house to intuition or even to a keen moral sense. Shall we then commit to it the building of this great national temple, under whose roof-tree alone can life, and fortune, and sacred honor find sanctuary? Masculine ignorance lies in wait on every hand to destroy it. What shall we say when womanly intuition comes to the re-enforcement of masculine ignorance?

The relations of labor and capital are becoming of vital public interest. They concern the happiness, the very existence of thousands of homes. It is not strange that the question has laid hold of politics, or that it has attempted to lay hold of legislation. The woman party has taken it up with an earnestness and a unanimity second only to those with which it makes its first requisition upon the suffrage. Its battle-cry on labor is as direct and simple as its battle-cry on liquor. All those complications which for years have baffled alike the political economist and the practical philanthropist disappear before the talismanic formula, Equal wages for equal work. Nobody is disturbed by any question as to what constitutes equality of work, or whether quality or equality be the more important. Nobody troubles himself or herself by any irrelevant conjectures about demand and supply. All is as plain as the sun in the sky. Give to woman the ballot, and no longer shall the grammar-school-master have thirteen hundred dollars a year, while the grammar-school-mistress has five hundred dollars; but the lion and the lamb shall have the self-same salary. Give to woman the ballot (I have never heard this said; but, of course, it naturally follows, and is as certainly meant)—give to woman the ballot, and no longer shall Bridget receive her three dollars a week, while Patrick has two dollars a day; but Bridget and Patrick alike shall be paid their fifty dollars a month. How the ballot is to accomplish this we are not yet informed. No one has definitely mapped out this Promised Land; but we are fervidly assured it is there, albeit just beyond our secular vision. One female writer, rebuking the hard-heartedness of those who coldly point out waiting work to suffering women, gives us her more excellent way. I quote from memory her indignant assurance, that when a woman, poor and unoccupied, came to her with her sad story, "I did not point her to my kitchen. I threw my arms around her neck and wept with her." But whether this mode of relief is permanent and efficacious, whether it is susceptible of incorporation into our civil code, or of wide introduction into our political system, may admit of doubt. In spite of special cases, there is at present small reason to believe that the time will ever come when laborers in general will combine and cry rather than "strike," and capitalists will hug instead of resisting.

But hugging or haggling is a point of local and temporary interest. The real gist of the debate touches a darker depth than this. There is a dangerous element in the discussion to which women are but adding strength.

Masculine ignorance, plastic in the hands of partisan ambition, breathes covert or open threats of violence; in a free country does not disdain to use force against its fellows, and does not see that it is arousing for the laborer his most formidable foe. It implores the interference of legislation, not discerning that the immediate good it craves would, even if obtained, be a thousand times overbalanced by the evil of bringing legislation into the field. And at this crisis, when it needs all the resources of culture and patriotism to steady affairs ; at this crisis, when it is almost a crime for an educated person to couple legislation and labor ; at this crisis our emotional woman comes rushing into the fray, and demands the ballot for the purpose of procuring equal wages for equal work. That no one explains how the ballot is to adjust matters signifies nothing. The fatality lies in appealing to the ballot for adjustment. It is the resource of ignorance and narrowness. It is the resource of women.

There are many other matters of national and international concern which the leaders of the woman party have touched lightly, if at all. These are the only two prominent political questions on which their future action is plainly foreshadowed. It was not, indeed, indispensable that they should do so much. They might have fought the battle out on general principles, if they had so chosen. If a man or a woman has a right to act, he shall not be forced to say how he will act before he exercises that right. But as the leaders of the woman party have of their own free will announced their intended course, we, the people most concerned, may pronounce judgment upon it. That their discussions and decisions have helped to swell the flood of ignorance, passion, and unreason which already menace us with a serious danger is but a small part of the evil. It is not so much that any special advocacy is unwise—it is that they advocate on a false ground. It is not so much that they may emotionally vote wrong—it is that they assume in entire good faith that womanly intuition and emotional force are an admirable basis on which to exercise the right of suffrage. They exhibit no perception of the fact that it is because women have counted their intuitions and their emotions as their sole capital that they are so weak, insipid, and uninfluential, as we too often find them. "When women of pure character and noble purpose," they say, "participate in practical political campaigns, a great step will be made toward enlisting public sympathy in behalf of the disfranchised sex." They seem not to discern that pure character and noble purpose, though indispensable, are insufficient, and fatally insufficient; that a pure and noble-purposed woman may do her cause and country as much harm as a bad man. Instead of endeavoring to strengthen woman on her weak side, they rather apotheosize her weakness as the true strength. She is not exhorted to bulwark her intuitions with reasons, to correct her emotions by judgment, but simply to crystallize both into laws. Indeed, one of the leaders, in addressing the members of a Republican Convention, whom she "supposed to be above the ordinary level of the Republican party and men of political sagacity," frankly avowed that she never liked to speak simply to political sagacity. The cause which she had to present was just, and that was enough. "Simply to political sagacity." Are women going into politics, then, with political insagacity for a weapon. and a watchword? It must be the one or the other. There is no middle ground. Is it enough that our cause is just? Rather, it is notoriously not enough. All things are lawful unto me, but all things are not expedient. Perhaps no great battle was ever won on the ground of simple justice. A system of laws is a system of checks, and balances, and averages, of the nicest and closest calculations. The engineering of a great party, the existence of a party, demands the utmost political sagacity—a sagacity which strikes every note of human nature, from the highest mental perception to the lowest emotional force. Paying all reverence, and most eagerly aspiring to this highest, most comprehensive quality of the statesman, the only one which embraces within itself all that is necessary to action, we shall be in no danger of reaching too near perfection. Human nature is pretty sure to fall short, even if its standard be high; but the party that sets out with contempt for it, the party that proposes to dispense with it, and vote the straight-out womanly-intuition-and-emotion ticket, must have exceptional luck, indeed, to conduct this great nation with safety and honor along its tortuous and intricate path.

XII.
PRESS-WORK.

THERE is one department of political action, not least in importance or opportunity, which is easily accessible to women, which they have already entered, and in which they occupy no inconsiderable or inconspicuous ground. I refer to the department of political writing—more definitely called political correspondence—more definitely known, perhaps, as Washington correspondence. In its capacity for use and abuse, in its opportunity for good and evil, it is difficult to imagine a more tempting field for the display of womanly wisdom, prudence, and purity in the way of reforming influence.

The power which centres in newspapers is appalling. It is as strong for evil in the hands of evil men, as it is for good in the hands of good men; and evil men have not been slow to find it out. It goes to the ends of the earth, and brings to the humblest hearthstone the latest discovery of science, the latest contribution of history, the latest combination of power. It tells to the workman resting under the trees at midday how the whole world fares, and intrenches on visible and tangible ground the brotherhood of man. It is ardent and eager. It rends the veil from hypocrisy, it voices the general conscience, it opens to thorough and wholesome discussion all plans and plots that concern society. But, unhappily, it is also reckless, revengeful, dishonest. It is careles of truth, and delicacy, and privacy. It pries and tattles. It corrupts the taste, and vulgarizes the manners. It makes and mars reputations for personal or partisan ends, or from the mere commercial value of scandal and "sensation." It uses its power for a menace, and its opportunity for a stab. It has even descended to minister to the vanity of the vainest, to the weakness of the weakest, and to degrade intelligence to drivel.

Let me give one or two examples—not to prove, but to illustrate. I shall take them not from such newspapers as strike their roots in wickedness and feed on iniquity. There are such, but they are generally well known; they are not quoted as authority, and their opinions have little weight. I select the newspaper which is, perhaps, in all the country, the most calm in advocacy, the most judicial in tone; which assumes and appears to be moderate, courteous, far-sighted, above the heat of the hour, and deaf to the clamor of party. Certainly no paper has been more forward to emphasize the importance of accuracy, to denounce violation of courtesy, looseness of statement, and disregard of individual rights. It has been steadfast in enunciating correct principles, and, if it be not high-minded, truthful, and honorable, it is Pecksniffian to the last degree. Yet in such a paper as this one may read the following paragraph:

"To the Editor of the ———:

"Sir,—A writer in your last week's issue . . . . . speaks by name of three leading railroad men, of whom Mr. A. B. C. is one, and characterizes them as 'avaricious, unscrupulous, often dishonest, and always unreliable.' As one who has had some opportunities of knowledge on the subject, I beg to say, in behalf of Mr. A. B. C., that there is nothing in the private character or public record of that gentleman to warrant a paper like the ——— in affixing to his name such damaging epithets."

Then comes the editorial statement:

"The charges are certainly such as should not be made

against any body unless supported by specifications, and we regret their appearance, which was due to an oversight."

I do not know how, in so small a space, a greater public and personal wrong could be perpetrated. An editor uses his paper to proclaim to all the inhabitants of the land that a certain man is habitually a liar, and occasionally a thief; and, being confronted with a denial of his statement, neither proves nor retracts it, but quietly "regrets" that he made it! More than this, the "regret" is so framed as to leave an impression on the mind of the reader that, after all, the charge may be true.

A man might just as well "regret" that he had slain his neighbor as that he had thus attempted to slay his good name. What shall he do? Stand in the pillory an hour every day for a month, with a rope around his neck, and proclaim to the assembled crowds, "I am the man who, with a full knowledge of the greatness of the crime, bore false witness against my neighbor." "False," because a man who asserts what he does not know to be true is radically as untruthful as he who asserts what he knows to be false. This first; then, having thus robbed a man of honor, he should immediately investigate the matter, at whatever personal inconvenience to himself, and either prove that the man was justly dishonored, or reinvest him with integrity in the most explicit manner.

The same paper says again:

"When we read from time to time in the papers that Mr. B. was associating with German scholars, and making speeches to Germans in the German language, and otherwise entering fully, freely, and with perfect familiarity with its ways and ideas, into German society, we felt he was trespassing a little too far on our patience, and we have been expecting for some time that he would come to grief. Accordingly, we are not surprised to find that the proposition, which, we believe, emanated from him originally, and which the President has embodied in a message to Congress, to send to the new German Empire a mission of equal rank with that of Paris and London, will, if carried out (as is probable), involve Mr. B.'s retirement by involving the suppression of the present Prussian mission. The new place, it seems, is wanted for Judge O.; and he ought to have it, because he will bring to its duties a thoroughly fresh and unbiased mind, owing to a thorough want of diplomatic experience, and a fair ignorance of the German tongue. He will thus enter on his duties without any entangling alliances or prejudices, from which Mr. B. can hardly be free."

Here the assertion is made in the most offensive manner —that is, by implication, and with a sneer—that Judge O. is unfit for the position which is supposed to be assigned him, by reason of inexperience and ignorance. Diplomatic inexperience in a foreign service organized—or, rather, unorganized—like ours means nothing whatever; but what shall we say of this autocrat of all the newspapers when we learn that Judge O. spoke the German language exclusively for the first fifteen years of his life, that he still addresses crowded German assemblies in their own language with an eloquence which arouses them to enthusiasm, and at the very moment when this paragraph is pointed out to him he holds in his hand a letter from a distinguished German scholar, consulting him about some delicate point of German philology!

Here the editor uses his paper and his commanding position to spread through the land a statement which he either knows to be false or does not know to be true, and draws from it an inference which the fullest establishment of the fact would but partially justify. The statement is somewhat prejudicial to the person concerning whom it is made, and the inference is extremely prejudicial to the government officers. It simply implies that they choose their servants for unfitness, and dismiss a man as soon as he is discovered to have peculiar qualifications for his place. The statement is untrue, and the inference falls to the ground. What, then, becomes of the editor, who, by the extent of his knowledge, the soundness of his views, the wholesomeness of his inculcations, and the grossness of his transgressions, gets himself to be esteemed almost a saint, and makes his own damnation sure?

I have referred to definite and demonstrable untruths, circulated by a leading newspaper as truths, to the great detriment of individuals. I will mention one or two examples of a more common, more general, but equally misleading mode of statement.

In the same paper occurs the following paragraph:

"We have no wish to depreciate Congress unduly. We have no doubt its desire to do right is generally underrated by the newspapers; but nobody claims for the great body of the members familiarity with financial history or political economy. There is nobody, too, who has ever attempted to master these subjects, or who knows any thing of the lives of the great explorers of these fields of political science, who is not aware that proficiency in them is only to be bought by years of laborious study and constant observation of all their phenomena at home and abroad. Now, as Mr. K. pointed out the other day as the result of his own sad experience, members can not, in the present condition of the civil service, give even the smallest amount of serious attention to the great economical problems now before the country. All the time they spend out of their seats is devoted to interviews with the worthless class who are hunting for offices, or to correspondence with constituents on the subject of "claims." They are, consequently, as helpless in the presence of tariff speculators as a band of untutored savages in the presence of a body of skilled riflemen armed with repeaters. And yet the revaluation of the property and business of every man in the community is committed every winter regularly to this body."

This is an assertion which can not be proved unless we appoint a board of examiners to question Congressmen on financial history and political economy, and thus ascertain the exact depth of their ignorance. But, granting it to be true, it would seem that a community which year after year intrusts its business to men who are not "familiar" with the business, to begin with, who are in a situation where they can not give "even the smallest amount of serious attention to it," are simply a constituency of fools, and are adequately represented by a delegation of savages.

But the same paper, noticing in another column a biography of a deceased member of Congress, gives as an illustration of the "carefulness and laborious industry with which Mr. Choate laid the foundations of his fame and usefulness" "the fact that when at the age of thirty he was elected to Congress, he made a memorandum of *facienda ad munus nuper impositum*, which begins as follows:

"'1. Personal qualities. Memory. Daily Food and Cowper *dum ambulo.* Voice ; manner, *exercitationes diurnæ.* 2. Current politics in papers—*cum notulis*, daily. Geography, etc. "Annual Register," past *Intelligencers.* 3. District: Essex South, population, occupations, modes of living, commerce—the treaties—and principles on which it depends. 4. Civil History of the United States in Pitkin and original sources. 5. Examination of pending questions: Tariff, Public Lands, Indians, Nullification. 6. American and British eloquence—writing practice.'"

Then follow, says the editor, "more than twenty pages of the closest writing, with abbreviated and condensed statements of results drawn from many volumes, newspapers, messages, and speeches, with propositions and arguments for and against, methodically arranged under topics, with minute divisions and subdivisions; as, for example, a discussion under the head of 'The Tariff,' beginning with an analysis of Hamilton's report, made in 1790, followed by a history of internal improvements, a statement of their cost, a discussion of the constitutional power of making them, and a history of the legislation affecting them. A good deal of worse rhetoric than Choate's would be required to overlay such preparation as that."

This second paragraph is not a complete refutation of the first. Doubtless constituents and claims have increased since the days of Mr. Choate, who was probably not forced to spend absolutely *all* his time with worthless office-hunters and clamorous constituents, and who, therefore, might have given a very small amount of serious attention to economical problems while he was in Congress. But, having accepted the principle that proficiency in these things is only to be bought by *years* of laborious study, and *constant* observation of *all* their phenomena at home and *abroad*, it is a little confusing to hear the next moment that a busy lawyer could do any thing worthy of account between the time of his election to and his appearance in Congress, and that, too, without leaving his own district! I would suggest, also, that this systematic, industrious, and elaborate preparation was not known to the world till many years after Mr. Choate's death, and that he was, perhaps, the last man of whom such laborious preparation would have been suspected. May not, therefore, future biographies show that some of the well-meaning but helpless " savages" now in Congress are not quite so "untutored" as is conjectured? I am very sure that any member elect, male or female, who shall enter Congress with the expectation of finding a body of men well meaning and innocent, but ignorant and helpless in the presence of tariff or any other speculators, will be far more likely to come to grief than he who prepares himself to encounter such politicians as Mr. Choate's training would help to form.

But his brother editors fare still worse than Congress at the hands of this gentleman. Congress, for aught we see, does the best it knows how. Of certain book-notices he says:

"They are well-written, too; and though, of course, the publishers pay for them, and they are not in any good sense critical, nor to be relied upon by any one who would learn the exact value of the book noticed, still they can be read. And even they may be profitably read, if the reader will remind himself now and then that they are paid for, and are eulogistic and not critical. This, however, is saying no more against them than may be said against the so-called critical notices which appear in nine out of every ten newspapers in the country. Most American criticism is dishonest criticism; and the matter is not at its worst, either, when the dishonesty is the result of our national good-nature or of ignorance, for hardly a book issues from the American press concerning which editors do not for money say things which they know to be false, and which they intend shall deceive."

I can not say whether or not this is true. I have never seen it contradicted. But, if nine out of ten newspapers can be hired by publishers to deceive their readers, there is surely a very loud call for the purification of the press as well as the purification of politics.

So much for the world and the flesh. Hear now what a doctor of divinity says in the columns of a religious newspaper:

"And now, standing by his grave, I desire, in the most public and unreserved manner, to retract an unwarrantable criticism upon the personal character of Mr. Dickens made by me in the first number of the *New Englander*. The rather crude estimate there made of his literary ability and his then published works (it was almost thirty years ago) may stand for better or worse, according to the test of time. But, roused by the popular indignation at his 'American Notes,' and misled by some expressions in that work, and by exaggerated rumors touching his personal habits, I was betrayed into the representation that he drank to excess. I do not now believe that such a charge was then warranted, nor that it has been warranted by any thing in his subsequent life. And I have come also to recognize in him a deeper soul of truth and goodness, and a nobler, purer sympathy with what is highest and best, than I then gave him credit for.

"I might well believe that nobody of late years has read that article, and that nobody who read it at the time remembers or cares about it now; but when the news of his death came, recalling how much of enjoyment and quickening I owed to Mr. Dickens, I took down the volume and read it with a tingling regret. It is of no account to him, and of very little to any body else; but when the invisible stone-cutter shall mark the next name to be registered for the grave, I should be unwilling to pass out of the world with the feeling that I had done any man an injustice, however unwittingly, for which I had not made the fullest atonement and reparation. 'And so,' as Tiny Tim said, 'God bless us all.'"

I have no tenderness for Mr. Dickens. I do not believe in his deep soul of truth and goodness, or in his noble and pure sympathy with what is highest and best. "I desire, in the most public and unreserved manner," to declare that a regiment of little Nells and Tiny Tims can not redeem the man who publicly dishonors the mother of his many children. Mr. Dickens, holding the pen of a ready writer, told his story glibly to the world. Mrs. Dickens, suffering the deepest wound a woman can know, has remained steadfastly silent. The wife's silence is full of dignity; the husband's speech bristles with disgrace. He feels no shame in saying that he lived with a woman as his wife, exacting from her all the duties and enforcing all the sufferings of a wife, until he had consumed the vigor of her youth, and then turned her away, and announces to the world that she was unfit for him! He feels no shame in saying virtually that, while this woman was living in his house as his wife, another woman was also in his house, holding in regard both to himself and his children a position which belonged to the legal wife and mother. England is beating her obstinate head against marriage with a deceased wife's sister, but here it is a living wife's sister superseding the living wife. It was Mr. Dickens himself who made this public property. By his last will and testament he even stretched his dead hand out of the grave to injure his discarded wife; and neither in this world, nor the next, nor the world after the next, shall a man escape the cordial hatred of at least one heart for such coarse and shameless selfishness.

But our doctor of divinity is moved by none of these things. Thirty years ago people were very angry with Mr. Dickens; and, on the strength of some ambiguous expressions and exaggerated rumors, this clergyman spread abroad the printed report that he was a drunkard. Now people are very fond of Mr. Dickens; and the clergyman says he is not a drunkard, and never was, and thinks he has performed the whole duty of man. For thirty years I have to fight against the assertion made by the religious press that I am addicted to a beastly vice, and, having fought it successfully, and won my way, the religious press stands by my grave and says I never was guilty, and thinks it has made the fullest atonement and reparation, let alone magnanimity.

I do not know much about original sin or total depravity, the Trinity, atonement, or justification by faith. I believe them all; but when it comes to understanding them as you understand the multiplication table, or a friend's letter, I am free to confess that I do not really understand one word of it. But I do perfectly understand that the man who recklessly, revengefully, publicly, for any purpose whatever, bears false witness against his neighbor, is originally sinful, totally depraved, and will never be justified by any faith; that a legislative assembly ignorant of its business, and unable to give the smallest amount of serious attention to it, is the sign of a country ripe for revolution, and can scarcely be saved by a newspaper press nine tenths of which is in the market for sale to the highest bidder.

Now then, again, *Place aux dames!*

The columns of the newspapers are as widely and as fully open to woman as to man. Neither publisher nor editor cares for the sex of a writer. The possession of the ballot could not give to woman any greater freedom to print her opinions on politics, religion, manners, or morals, and the extent of such influence is immeasurable. It can not be otherwise than that her defective education and her limited experience should be seen here, and we have no right to expect the breadth of thought or vigor of style which come only from long training. But we may expect to see that "refining, ennobling element wanted in politics, that woman's finer nature, intuitive perception, and aptness for moral truth can alone supply;" that "innate refinement" which is to "give to ambition a more elevated object than mere love of power." There is no reason why the greater conscientiousness, accuracy, modesty, peaceableness, unselfishness —the charity which thinketh no evil, the sensitiveness which forbids to ascribe bad motives, the instinctive sagacity which impels wise choice, qualities which have long been conceded to women, and which are to purify and elevate politics— there is no reason why all these should not have free course to run and be glorified in the columns of the political or social newspaper.

I take up a copy of that which is spoken of as the most lively, vigorous, and able of the woman papers, and find it offering itself as a "great organ of popular thought and principle, whose columns [shall] be open to the fullest and freest expression of the writer's knowledge and conviction upon any and all subjects, persons, and estates."

Here surely is a plan of operations comprehensive enough to meet illimitable ambition. Violation of individual rights, carelessness of privacy and delicacy, have been great and growing sins of the press; but the world has always considered that

"Sins for want of legislation
Are not quite like sins by law."

It was reserved for a woman's newspaper to come out with the public announcement that individuals have no rights which newspapers are bound to respect. Hypocrisy is the tribute which vice pays to virtue; but in the red glare of such a new light as this one is disposed to call hypocrisy it self a virtue. Certainly righteousness has made but a sorry gain when the villain pulls off his mask, not to reform, but to practice vice openly. Men are constantly breaking down the barriers which religion, and honor, and instinct have erected; but women ignore honor and instinct, and deny that there should be any barrier at all. Whatever any person happens to know or chooses to infer about any other person, he shall be at perfect liberty to send abroad in the newspapers. How hatred, envy, malice, and all uncharitableness could give itself looser rein than this, how a code more unprincipled could be promulgated, or a license more reckless be established, it is difficult to imagine. That the paper is not indulging in glittering and sounding generalities, but knows what it says, and says what it means, is proved by its following up this announcement with two columns of personal abuse of a private gentleman in regard to his personal and private affairs—abuse whose vulgarity is not lost in its atrocity, abuse alike of his benevolence and his business, abuse that deals in motive as freely and confidently as in fact, and abuse that does not so much as shadow any authority beyond "as we learn," "as we hear," "we have heard from what should be good authority," "it is said."

Such a transaction as this would, I believe, among men, condemn its perpetrator to infamy. No man of honor would lay down such a law or write such an article. No respectable newspaper in the hands of respectable men would print

K

it. That a woman's newspaper does it without misgiving argues a hardness of heart or a blindness of mind that promises ill in the way of purifying or elevating society.

Again, in the same paper occurs the following paragraph:

"The other day I overheard a gentleman say to one of the women clerks in the Treasury Department, 'I saw you at the Convention. How did you like it?' 'Very well indeed. We had some smart women there, hadn't we?' 'You say *we* had some smart women there. You don't mean to say that you are a "woman's righter" too, do you?' 'Show me the thoughtful working-woman that is not.' 'Why, there's Mrs. ———, she came from the working-classes.' 'Yes; but she does not belong to the working-classes now, and seems to forget that she ever did. Just let her have a family to support, as I and hundreds of others have, and she'll quickly change her tune.' This is the spirit that animates them all."

For the name which I have put in blank the paragraph gives the name in full—a name that should never cease to awaken grateful emotions in this country, but the name of a woman who is known to be actively opposed to female suffrage. In this paragraph the idea is presented that this woman was once a poor girl, belonging to the "working-classes," but had since risen to prosperity and renown, and that, in her desire to forget, and make others forget the low estate from which she sprung, she was opposing the cause of the class to which she once belonged. In a country like ours few charges could be more obnoxious or opprobrious, and I may say more ingenious than this. If true, it argues a vanity, a vulgarity, a baseness of mind which ought to neutralize one's influence; but if false, it is embarrassing to disprove. No lady would like to come forward and deny that she ever belonged to the laboring class, as if such belonging were disgraceful, were a slander to be repelled; apart from the fact that no lady would like to come forward at all, and apart from another fact, that nobody could define exactly what is meant in this country by the laboring class. Probably the lady in question never saw this paragraph; but it happens that she is one of the few who are reared from their birth in affluence and luxury—the daughter of a family of high social position, of distinguished public service, representing generations of culture, and enjoying a national fame. This woman writer, therefore, has published against another woman, her political opponent, an offensive personal slander, either knowing it to be false, or not knowing it to be true—in either case equally slanderous, and in neither case founded on stronger authority or further investigation than an "overheard."

Thus does woman's finer nature, intuitive perception, and aptness for moral truth supply the element wanting in masculine politics and masculine newspapers. That they do not produce ideal serenity or suavity in female deliberations must be inferred from the published complaint of one of the most prominent leaders. "What," says she, "with the inveterate hatred and persistent malice of my sisters, and the contemptible self-importance and overweening self-sufficiency of my brothers, have I had to cheer me in the course I have marked out?" "Art thou in health, my brother?" asked a wily male politician; but all the same he smote his brother in the fifth rib, and he died. Evidently the courtesies and tendernesses of kinship shall not prevent the happy family from speaking its mind; but it is not easy to see how political manners are to be improved by adding the persistent malice of our sisters to the contemptible self-importance of our brothers.

Is it the innate refinement of women which produces such a criticism as the following in one of the most moderate and high-minded of the woman papers upon a series of articles opposing female suffrage?

"They might be supposed such as some superannuated old maid of disappointed hopes, and of blasted aspirations might easily be imagined to indulge in, with a view of avenging herself on her more favored sisters."

Will the asperities of political discussion be softened, and the passions of political excitement soothed, when these refining and ennobling side-issues are brought to bear upon the settlement of claims and the adjustment of duties; when the advocate of a high tariff shall have to defend herself not only against charges of undue desire to protect her own coal-lands, but of matrimonial designs upon the bachelor protectionist from Arcadia? And with what a naïve unconsciousness does the writer reveal her own opinion that, after all, the state of thraldom to a man is one for hope and aspiration, and that the favored sisters are those who are under its direct yoke!

A third woman's paper closes a column devoted to the "twaddle" of an opponent with a lofty conception of motive and an intuitive perception of moral truth which woman's finer nature can alone supply.

"Between the lines of ———'s writings I think we can read, 'It would be well to find something to write smartly about. Now *I* receive all the recognition *I* want, or, rather, *used* to receive. If these woman's rights women are to be every where recognized as doing a good work, I shall cut a sorry figure with the quips and squibs I have written—or, rather, no figure at all. Well, a smart person, such as I am, ought to be saying something; and the men, many of them, and the fashionable women, most of them, and a good many of the papers—these, if I say smart things about women, disparage them, etc., etc., will give me all the recognition I want.'"

Woman newspapers, passing judgment on each other, refine upon the coarse, old-fashioned, masculine methods of controversy by admonishing their opponents in the following gentle, "innate" manner :

"We know of nothing more contemptible than for the proprietors of a paper to descend to vent their spleen upon a contemporary by going among newsmen, and endeavoring to prevail upon them to discard it from their list of papers kept for sale by misrepresentations. But to such shifts does a journal professing to be an advocate of woman's suffrage resort to preserve its life against the encroachments of the ———. Vain endeavor! The ——— has sustained shocks compared to which the present exhibition of impotent rage is as a mole-hill to a mountain.

"Neighbor! you are a very good paper so far as you go, and we gladly recommend you to those readers whose mental stomachs can not yet digest strong food, or which have become dyspeptic from injudicious aliment; but your limits are by far too contracted by bigotry, intolerance, prejudice, and pharisaical godliness to suit minds which have burst the bonds of custom and practice, and boldly struck out for truth, and which accord to every body what they claim for themselves. It may also do you a service to remind you that every body do not believe your simple assertions, unsupported by any fact. Ponder this well, and do not die unrepentant."

And again:

"Without presuming to lecture any body, we may be allowed to say . . . . that the ——— and other papers of its class should have a little more regard for common honesty, and not forget, in their personal malice, to be consistent; for there are some people who even read the ——— that are not so stupid as to be blind to it. . . . . It informed·us, not long since, that the determining of this case should be with 'pure hands.' Verily a Daniel would come to judgment! Let it be from this time forth understood throughout the length and breadth of this land that the editors of the ——— are those perfect ones whom the Lord hath appointed and sent to Boston to judge the earth; and let no rash woman lift her voice for any right she may think herself possessed of until she shall have journeyed to Boston, been tried, found pure, and thus labeled by these holy and wise (?) judges, who are more troubled about what they surmise women may have been than about what they are."

It is not necessary, as it is certainly not agreeable, to multiply quotations. Those which I have given are not exceptional in tone. Of the three suffrage newspapers published by women, one is generally temperate and not undignified; the second is not inaptly represented by these extracts; and the third descends so low that the paragraphs I have given represent it on the heights. I have seen, I admit, only two or three numbers of that paper, but a single one of those contained three articles each of which should be enough for the condemnation of any man's newspaper in which it should appear, and to banish from honorable business and social circles any man who should confess himself to be its author. The articles are not quotable either in letter or spirit; they have nothing whatever to do with female suffrage, or free love, or any other disputed point. It is simply a foul taste creating and embracing an opportunity for indulgence. If any one choose to ascertain for himself how far this judgment be correct, he can consult the paper—which it is not necessary more particularly to specify—of March 18, 1871.

There may be differences of opinion regarding modes of warfare. Since writing the above, I have, I confess, been astonished to see one of the three articles to which I have referred, and that, perhaps, the worst of the three—an article which to me appeared thoroughly filthy and otherwise indecent—transferred bodily from the woman paper in which it originally appeared to the columns of an eminently conservative weekly paper, published by men in an equally conservative city, and constantly opposed to the cause of woman's rights. This paper quietly prints the article, without apparently seeing in it any thing objectionable except its source. That, with a carefulness or carelessness little honorable, it conceals, but the article itself it copies as desirable reading for its own subscribers. Just the same, however, this style of political and journalistic discussion seems to me to be equally wanting in feminine grace and masculine strength; as deficient in native delicacy as in literary finish; seems to be blunt and brutal rather than fine and womanly; seems to be a tussle with bludgeons and cleavers rather than a meeting of noble minds and a comparison of elevated views.

But the proprietors and editors of these papers—the authors of these discussions and criticisms, are women, acknowledged leaders of the movement, standing in the forefront of battle, and giving the word of command. Through such channels must come the refinement and nobility which women are to contribute to politics, and there is no visible reason why the first installments of that contribution should not already have appeared. That all female politicians, or all woman's rights newspapers, or all parts of any one newspaper, are coarse and indelicate, no one will aver; but whoever examines the matter will find that coarseness, inaccuracy, ill feeling, and ill manners are just as prominent and, occupy proportionally as large a space in the political counsels and political papers of women as in those of the corresponding class of men, and that the effect thus far of women's active participation in politics has not been an infusion of modesty and refinement, of moral elevation and spiritual sanctity, of sweetness and light.

The department of newspaper writing known as reporting and correspondence has of late years fallen more and more into the hands of women. In the hands of men it had greatly deteriorated. From being an honest and honorable collector of items which have a legitimate if local and temporary interest, the reporter has come to be one who does not disdain to hide under a table for the purpose of overhearing and reporting the conversation of the dinner-guests in the next room. It has come to be possible for a man bearing a name of historic renown, that would of itself disarm suspicion, to visit a private house on the footing of a gentleman, and then send to his newspaper a minute description and criticism of his hostess by name, and a pretended and detailed report of the conversation. There are others, who would not descend into these lower depths, who yet do not think it unbecoming the estate of those who were made a little lower than the angels to employ their vigorous intellect and their sinewy strength in informing a breathless audience that Mrs. A., the elegant lady of the Grand Mogul, was assisting to receive, and looked charming in a splendid black gros-grain silk, with court train, heavily trimmed with folds of green velvet; that Mrs. Ex-Sultan B. looked queenly in a lemon-colored moire-antique silk; that Mrs. C. looked charming in a white silk, long train; that Mrs. D. was, if last, not least in beauty and tasteful arrangement of toilet, in a lavender silk, court train; that Mrs. E. received her friends as usual yesterday, and the dressing of the hostess was superb—just what good taste and unlimited wealth would dictate—and a fine collation spread for those who desired to partake; that Mrs. F. was "at home" in elegant style, and her dress was of fine texture and of elegant make, and her toilet tastefully and elaborately made, and the good things of life were offered to those who desired to partake; that Mrs. G. presented to her many friends a fine entertainment, and they were well provided with the good things of life to eat and drink, and her attire was elegant, and her toilet tastily and beautifully arranged; that Mrs. H. welcomed her numerous friends, and the dressing of the hostess was magnificent, and an elegant repast was spread for those who desired to partake.

There was a time within the memory of men still living when the standard of social morals was such that a man was summarily dismissed from society for having sent to the public prints a description of the ladies at a ball, though he used only initials for names. Now the reporter presents himself, with note-book and pencil, as openly and serenely as if he were the mainspring of our institutions, and, having taken a bird's-eye view of the situation in the parlors, and swept in a rapid list of the cards from the servants, he departs to work up his court trains and high corsages at leisure, or to make further observations in the next house; and all with that quiet assumption of legitimacy and that absolute ignoring of outlawry that would be amusing if its results were only a little less annoying. If remonstrated with, he remarks, with wide-eyed innocence, that he has his living to get! though, to be sure, the highwayman might make the same plea. Or he carries the war into Africa by turning upon you and affirming that the ladies like it; that he should give offense if he did not report their dresses; that he has been sent for, previous to a party, and furnished by the host with minute descriptions of dress and decorations, that no item of self-glorification should go unrecorded!

What a field is here for the refining and ennobling influence of woman! Are there women who enjoy the vulgarity of publicity; who love to see their homes invaded, their hospitality recorded, their dresses unfolded to the curious gaze? So much the more should right-minded women win them away from so false a standard by a scrupulous reverence for the privacy thus lightly esteemed, by an intelligent and discriminating observation, and by a graceful and attractive presentation of that which is worthy and enduring. Whether, moreover, such women do or do not exist, it is certain that there is a large class of women in our chief cities, and particularly in our chief city, to whom this style of letter-writing is a source of annoyance and disgust; who desire from correspondents nothing so much as the mercy of their silence. A female writer has, therefore, not only an opportunity to ennoble numbers of her sex by the dignity of example, but she may also be sure of a large and strong following among a long-suffering but sufficiently respectable class.

No man has gone so low in the depths of epistolary degradation that a woman has not gone lower. Men correspondents are inane, but they are generally good natured. They flounder about amid point lace and moire antique with masculine intrepidity, and, it must be added, with masculine insensibility. They turn your cherry velvet into pink silk, but without any conscience of sin. They put you in a maroon gown without a moment's warning, and derange all your harmonies with the most amiable intentions; for their crescendo is as gushing and guileless as their diminuendo. Your last season's rumpled and faded finery comes out as "superb dressing." Your modest house is a "spacious mansion." Your sedate horses turn into prancing steeds under this magic wand; and you yourself—a quiet, domestic, and not over-self-confident person—hardly recognize your portrait in the "votary of fashion" or "queen of society" into which you have suffered a sea-change. If your correspondent has unwittingly robbed Peter, he has lavishly paid Paul. If his insipidity has flavor, it is a flavor of sweetness. He irritates and exasperates you; but he does it gently, as if he loved you. He must get his living out of you, but, beyond that, he would rather please than displease.

It was a woman's name that was appended to a letter which mentioned certain estimable ladies only to ridicule their physical peculiarities—ladies who were, in a sense, guests of the nation, and to whom, therefore, civility was peculiarly due. It was a woman who employed her pen and her position to ridicule the person and dress of another writer, a gifted and excellent woman, with a coarseness, a bitterness, a malignity which it would not be speaking too strongly to call infernal. It was a woman who thrust herself into the presence of a widowed mother and her grown-up son, to whom this nation owes nothing but respect and deference, if only for the name they bear, and boldly and baldly questioned the young man as to his mother's pecuniary resources and marriage possibilities. It was a woman who pried into the *trousseau* of a beautiful and modest young lady, and on the wings of mighty winds sent flying all abroad a complete list of her wardrobe, regardless alike of common decency and of the feelings and reputation of the person most concerned. It was a woman who occupied column after column of the newspaper with narrations of the past history of her still living female friends, never faltering before what are generally considered the most secret and even sacred facts, recounting with equal nonchalance the family struggles with poverty and the number of offers which a lady received before her final acceptance. And it is a woman who comes out in a conservative newspaper to defend these things on the ground of reason, and right, and common sense, and to denounce as mock modesty and affectation the reluctance which some women still retain to seeing their names or any facts of their personal history exposed to the public gaze.

I need not add to these specifications, nor can I any farther designate them without repeating and increasing the harm they must already have caused; but I do not hesitate to affirm, as the most painful and unexpected result of my own observation, that the grossest violations of courtesy, modesty, delicacy, and decency, attributable to correspondents, have been perpetrated by women.

It might happen that women should here and there be found who would not feel it derogatory to themselves or their profession to use their pens for the gratification of personal malice, personal revenge, or public curiosity, and yet that the general influence of this irruption of women upon the political press should be elevating. Here and there a "sister" may go to greater lengths than any "brother" without affecting the fact that in general sisters are more moderate, impartial, clear-sighted, comprehensive, and dispassionate than brothers.

As the pens of correspondents have fallen into the hands of women, has there been manifested a disposition to correct the tendency of correspondence toward deterioration into gossip? In spite of the indiscreet and unwomanly revelations made by some female writers, do we find the general result to be an increasing respect for individuality, a gradual disuse of personality, a deference to the claims of courtesy, to the divinity that doth hedge a man and a woman by virtue of their manhood and womanhood, and which is not forfeited by any amount of public service? Do we see an intelligent recognition and observance of the forms of society which, though sometimes apparently arbitrary and sometimes really irksome, do yet constitute the best available and the certainly indispensable protection of the individual against society, the reign of constitutional law as against anarchy, without which life becomes intolerable and fruitless? When we hear that a woman is attached to the staff of reporters, do we feel that now we shall creep out from under the dinner-table, disentangle our feet from court-trains, take it for granted that every body wears his best clothes in company, and enter the circle of real interests, of grave considerations, of close scrutiny, and careful comparisons, and keen analysis, and high aim, and just award? Do public officers, members of state or national Legislatures, and all who directly concern themselves in the ship of state, feel an assurance that, when women are on the witnessing stand, official acts and deliberations are subjected to a wiser scrutiny; that trivial or irrelevant facts will be left in the background, and only those which are pertinent brought forward; that falseness, chicanery, and sophistry will stand a

-greater chance of being detected, and sense, and honesty, and comprehensiveness a greater chance of being recognized; that personal liking and disliking will be laid aside, and motives and methods judged abstractly; that clap-trap will lose power, and quiet ability come to the front; that business shall be understood, and progress signified, and work not to be mistaken for idling, nor an itching for notoriety be mistaken for spirited patriotism?

It must be admitted that women will find it no easy task to outstrip the best class of male correspondents. It will not be denied that there are among the latter men of eminent ability and integrity, who can see and report with equal clearness; who understand that the part of a correspondent is not to nurse prejudice, nor indulge predilection, nor confirm opinion, nor even to enforce doctrine, but, as far as possible, to put his reader in possession of the situation; who are able to comprehend it because they are the peers of those who make it; men whose views are wont to be correct, whose judgment is based on their views, and, therefore, likely to be sound, and whose opinions and co-operation are therefore apt to be sought in shaping action; men who do not boast of their power or prowess, who apparently do not think of it, who are simple, direct, and unconscious in their business, and whose influence, springing from qualities rather than position, is as wholesome as it is widespread.

Am I wrong in believing that this class is not perceptibly increased by re-enforcements from the ranks of women? I do not deny that among female correspondents there are women of spotless character and brilliant parts; but, as things are, is it possible they should equal men in the possession of political influence and of political intelligence? The man is in constant contact with men, and face to face with events. If he is at the capital, he goes every where—

to committee-rooms, to the departments, to the newspaper offices—at all hours; wherever measures are under discussion, there is he, to judge for himself. He becomes as familiar with the working of the machinery as the machinist, and he follows the course of legislation with entire understanding. A woman takes observations from the galleries, where, with close attention, she can perhaps make out the words of one speaker in ten in the one house, and in the other vainly wishes she could hear ten speakers in one. That is, a fragment of such part of legislation as appears on the surface she sees, but of that large part which goes on out of sight she necessarily learns only by hearsay or from the male reporter. Nor is it easy to see how it can well be otherwise.

Even if she have a thorough understanding of parliamentary law, and if she be so constant and enthusiastic in her attendance upon legislative assemblies as to understand all the windings and turnings of bills and all the meanings of motions, she still labors under serious disadvantages. Unless she can forget she is a woman, and make every one else forget it too, and mingle as a man among men, it seems impossible that she should compete successfully with men. Women write eloquently and well upon patriotism, statesmanship, and the higher life, in the abstract; but when they come to definite measures, and make application of their principles, they are just as likely to blame and praise in the wrong place as are men, and just as likely to blame and praise in the wrong place as in the right one!

There are women who write better letters than men could do under the same circumstances, but the circumstances are an insuperable fact. No law hinders. Custom has nothing to do with it. It is simply that the woman is a writer and a lady, and can not bring herself—never thinks of bringing herself—to do what men do instinctively in the line of the same profession. And, if she did it, it would not be the same thing.

Scenic politics, then, is chiefly what is left to her of real politics, if, indeed, that be real politics. Certainly it is that part of politics which least needs cherishing. It is politics just dipping into personality—personality the least offensive, it is true, but politics the least improving, either to politician or constituent. Congress is public property, and I suppose we have a perfect right to gaze at its members from the galleries, and pen-photograph their sphinx-like faces, their haughty lips, their beetling brows, their opal eyes, and their majestic noses, for circulation in the rural districts. But has this kind of criticism a tendency to make or to keep public men upright? So far as it has any influence at all, is it not to call off attention from careful, conscientious, impartial work, and to make a man rather aspire to present a good appearance on the public stage? Already that tendency is sufficiently strong. A "spicy scene," a piquant repartee, will be telegraphed from one end of the country to the other, when careful research and solid argument, that really advance the case and would really inform the people, are buried past resurrection in the columns of the *Congressional Globe.* But women fall into this current, and float along with it rather than resist it. They do it not only in Congress, but they do it every where. If they are reporting the proceedings of their own conventions, they will give you the color of the feather in Phoebe Cozzen's hat, but Mrs. Howe's weightiest epigram they will leave you to learn from a chance comer or from a male reporter. If you remonstrate with them, they say the publishers want it. It is personality that is most in demand. Every fresh batch of eyes and noses, of ample cloaks and leonine hair, is in response to a fresh call. They are valued as letter-writers because they do this kind of thing so well. And it has even happened that a man has been asked at head-quarters whether he could not fashion his letters a little more like those of his wife—head-quarters not being aware that the lady in question was his wife.

Yes, but the worst crime of which we can accuse a *man* is yielding to temptation. Not the most wily and wicked politician that ever wrought evil wrought it except for the sake of procuring some good to himself. How are women to introduce incorruptibility into politics if at the first stroke of the publisher's wand they consent to descend? Why is it worse for a man to vote below his best than it is for a woman to write below her best? Why is it worse for a politician to "talk buncombe" than it is for a woman to write it? *It takes!* To be sure it does. The very worst letter to which I have referred—the one whose pen was dipped in venom to describe a comrade—was copied into other papers as a "charming" letter. But are women coming into political and public life to confirm or to combat trivial taste and low inclination; to render public service more effective, or to obtain a share of the spoils; to minister more skillfully to the love of gossip, or to substitute for it something worthy of both men and women?

In regard to social laws and individual rights, is the influence of women better than that of men? There are women who are scrupulous and honorable, but is the proportion larger than that of scrupulous and honorable men? The women who do sin sin with a high hand and a stretched-out arm apparently unattainable by men. A man recognizes rights and proprieties, and pays to them the small tribute of hiding under the table. He knows he has no business there—or, rather, he thinks he has business there, and means to prosecute it; but he advances no claim, presumes on no politeness, and deliberately, and I may say bravely, runs the risk of being turned out of doors.

But your female correspondent, on the occasion, for instance, of an afternoon reception at the President's, goes to the White House, enters the reception-room, stations herself at the end of the line of hostesses as if she were one of the receiving ladies, and stands there with paper and pencil ready to impale every unhappy fly who, unlike her prototype, is forced to come slowly flitting by. And the unhappy flies know it, and can not help it. It is like seeing your scaffold go up nail by nail before your chamber window. You could stand decapitation; but the process of preparation is the one straw too much. But a woman can not be turned out of doors. I say that the man under the table is less exasperating, and better bred, and not less "elevated" than the woman at her post of observation.

When you go to an evening party, and see a woman standing in the hall, holding her paper high up against the wall and writing vigorously, in the most conspicuous place and attitude, commanding with her guns all egress and ingress; when you see a woman at a ball bearing down upon you brandishing her note-book, and calling out in tones loud enough to be heard by all the by-standers, "Can't stop to talk now. I'm correspondent of the New Zealand *Honeycomb!*" when a woman accosts you in a public conveyance, and informs you that she is correspondent of this, that, and the other newspaper, and author of such and such books; when a woman constructs from her position a personal threat, one longs for the good old times when women were secluded and did not know the alphabet, and their husbands were allowed to use "moderate correction." Perhaps, when the novelty of appearing in print is worn off, women will cease to brandish their pens in our faces. They will feel that it is as ill bred to obtrude their authorship as it would be to obtrude their income, their wealthy relatives, their past career, or any other personal facts; that not only is this obtrusiveness unnecessary to good work, but is well-nigh incompatible with it. Certainly there are none to whom it is more offensive than to the better members of their own class. But, while the acclimating process is going on, those who feel that the lack of reticence or magnanimity in one woman is the loss of all women can but be penetrated with a lively regret and shame, not unmingled with dismay.

So far as the department of Washington correspondence offered woman a field for the display of intellectual acuteness and social wisdom, it has been largely neglected. Women have apparently restrained their ambition to doing deftly and as a regular business the inane work that men did clumsily and incidentally. For the laughter and applause of galleries they have been willing to make the judicious grieve. In dealing with politics, they have attempted well, though circumstances may have prevented a complete success; but, with few exceptions, in dealing with society they have not even attempted well. Dreary catalogues of dress and jewelry, eulogistic or depreciating descriptions of personal appearance, glittering and sounding generalities of wealth and splendor, are all that they seem to have aspired to. Given certain reception days, and certain public men and their wives—who in the eyes of these women are equally public—and unlimited command of silk and satin, and you have ample material for a Washington letter. No matter whether the man were at the reception or not. He might have been, and in the letter he is. It is generally safe to presume that the rural districts will never know that every thing did not happen precisely as reported. Very seldom occurs such a *contretemps* as last winter, when minute accounts of holiday festivities were brought to grief by the unexpected non-occurrence of the festivities; the interruption of which, however, was so late that the history of their happenings came out all the same as if they had actually happened!

Of the real significance of society—of that which makes our capital city brilliant, distinguished, or peculiar—you learn as little from the letters of most women as from those of men. And this is surprising. Here you would imagine women to be on their native heath. It may be because the best writers touch on society but lightly; but those who give themselves to it, so far as I have seen, give themselves entirely to the sensational and the silly. You might gather from them that Washington was a carnival of gayety, a whirl of frivolity and parade, a confusion of color and glitter, luxurious and voluptuous, if not selfish, heartless, and unprincipled. You would not gather that not only human nature, but human condition, is very much the same there as elsewhere; that Washington holds upright citizens, and careful mothers, and eager school-girls, and happy homes; that thrift, and economy, and good neighborhood, and good fellowship exist there; that the claims of God and man, religion and benevolence, are not forgotten; that friendliness, and chit-chat, and bright talk, and mental stimulus abound; that the glitter of party-giving and party-going is but a small part of the light that shines; and that, though one may, perhaps, more easily there than elsewhere, rush into foolish excitement and frivolous pastime, it is of his own frivolous and foolish will, since nowhere can he find more abundant material for varied and reasonable pleasure, or feel that, with his intellectual as with his personal wardrobe, his best is not too good for presentation.

The power of the press to delight and benefit, to annoy and injure, is practically determined only by the temper, breeding, and ability of those who write for it. No eulogy is so nauseous, no libel so gross, no gossip so scandalous, no item so frivolous that it can not somewhere find a ready market. For the tale-bearing, the black-mailing, the general sensationalism which mar the comeliness and diminish the value of journalism women are not to be blamed. They did not introduce them. Neither, it appears, for the redemption of journalism from these vital diseases are they to be credited. They have as yet shown no disposition to eradicate them.

XIII.
REPRESENTATIVE REFORM.

IF women had the suffrage, it is asserted that they would choose better men for officers than those now in service. "The very thing we want," says one lecturer, "is to bring into our politics some elevating influences. Do you believe, if women had the right to vote, you ever could put up such men as are put up for office?"

And the Woman Suffrage pledge, which ladies from all parts of the Union are invited to sign, confirms this view:

"And, believing that character is the best safeguard of national liberty, we pledge ourselves to make the personal purity and integrity of candidates for public office the first test of fitness."

Nothing in the history of the Woman Suffrage Party removes this from the class of points yet to be proven. It is so far mere hypothesis—with the presumption against it. My own opinion is that, when women vote, bad men will find no more difficulty in getting into office than they at present encounter, and bad women far less. How can a party which starts out with the professed intention "to help elect in every town the man who is our friend ; to help defeat in every town the man who is indifferent," so that " soon no man who is *not* our friend will stand a chance of nomination"— how *can* such a party make personal purity and integrity the first test of fitness? How often have we heard that women have good memories, and will never forget Governor A.— Governor A.'s offense being that he voted against some measure of the Woman Party. It is never alleged that Governor A. is impure or dishonest; that his vote was sold, or that it was given from any but conscientious and patriotic motives. It is simply that his vote was adverse to the party's wishes. I do not say that women, any more than men, should vote for their political opponents, but I do say that this assertion sounds more like a personal threat than like dispassionate discussion, is a style of argument not in vogue among the better class of unregenerate male politicians, and is not an improvement on their style.

"There is not in Washington a more corrupt lobbyist than Mrs. B.," said a gentleman in private life, not officially connected with politics, not unfriendly to Woman Suffrage, and a warm friend of Mrs. B., who was a lady of purity and integrity, unquestioned and unquestionable. There can be few women in this or any land brighter or better than she; but is it likely to be a wholesome thing for men to see woman taking, in ignorance and innocence, a course of political action which would for themselves be dishonest and disgraceful? And will not good women, even more than good men, be deceived by bad men? If women can blindly adopt measures radically wrong, may they not with equal blindness vote for equally objectionable men? No one can affirm that they will; but there is no ground for affirming that they will not. Good women, speaking from their moral consciousness, promise good officers; but in the candidates whom women have already elevated, and the political friends whom they have already adopted, it is difficult to see more discrimination or greater rigor of selection than are evinced by men.

"I hope," says an enthusiastic female lecturer, "I hope that I may live to see Theodosia in Congress." And she would then; doubtless, exclaim, with heartfelt sincerity, "Lord, now lettest thou thy servant depart in peace, for mine eyes have seen thy salvation." But to me it seems that the day which sees Theodosia in Congress will be visibly disastrous to the Woman Suffrage Party, or else invisibly disastrous to the best interests of the country, irrespective of party, for Theodosia has shown no one qualification of a legislator except the power to make a speech. That, indeed, is necessary. The man who is not only to frame a law, but to secure its adoption, must be able to speak clearly and forcibly on the field of battle. But, besides this, he must have something to say. Now Theodosia had never disclosed any comprehension of the requirements, the limitations, even the very fabric of government. With our foreign relations and the greater part of our domestic interests she had never troubled herself. That is, with by far the larger part of those matters which it is the business of Congress to adjust, she had evinced no familiarity whatever, as, indeed, there was no reason to demand that she should; but also, in the few political questions which she had touched, she had displayed powers of reasoning and practical sagacity far below the average of male politicians. Now it is one thing to make an address in a quiet hall to an audience assembled for the express purpose of hearing you, who are bound to be respectful and to make no reply; an audience composed in large part of men and women unable to speak in public themselves, unaccustomed to consecutive thought, and on whom fluency makes a far deeper impression than fallacy; and composed in small part of persons whom courtesy and propriety restrain as effectually as inability. It is quite another thing to be associated for months at a time, on terms of perfect equality—an equality which neither gives nor takes —with scores of men, each with his own purpose, and all meaning business. Most of these are the prominent and successful men of their own district. They are sent to Congress not to be courteous and attentive, but to represent certain interests, to secure certain measures. They not only have, or must act as if they had, a conviction that these measures are desirable; but their own personal and political future depends upon the success with which they advocate them. Theodosia has now to speak privately in committee-room and publicly in Congress to men just as eager and fluent as herself; men who have a keen scent for a false statement; who at the first point where her logic is weak will "beg to ask a single question;" who will, in one word, bring all their force to bear in combating her and in furthering their own plans. If Theodosia reveals on "Alabama" claims, land-grants, pig iron, national banks, whisky tax, and gunny-bags the same uncertainty in point of facts and the same unsteadiness in point of reasoning that she has revealed upon the platform, it seems to me that there will very speedily be nothing left of Theodosia. One sometimes sees in Congress a persistent member uttering dreary platitudes to empty benches, while a few members sit in their seats busily writing and reading; or one sees a full house apparently amusing itself by passing between tellers, or "taking the ayes and noes," sometimes by the hour together, and it seems like utter inefficiency and child's play. But try to slip through unobserved a bill for your private benefit, and the chances are ten to one that the apparently careless members will show a surprising understanding of what is going on. It is the fashion in many circles to speak slightingly and sneeringly of Congress, and, indeed, of all public service and public servants. Whether it is wise to send to Congress men who deserve slight and sneer; whether it is just, as well as wise, to send superior men and characterize them as inferior; and whether, in any case, it is likely to advance the dignity and value of public service and the best interests of the country to denounce and degrade its legislative assemblies, is a point that may admit of doubt. Perhaps this is considered the only way to induce in public servants a salutary humility. I should prefer to try the experiment of the Vicar of Wakefield, who wrote his wife's epitaph over the fireplace while she was yet in health, in order that, if she were not all that it portrayed, she might become so. This, however, is but a matter of individual taste and judgment. What is not a matter of taste is that there is no body of men or women in the country who take a man's measure more quickly or more accurately, no place where mere reputation counts for less, or where a man sooner finds his true level, or is more surely forced to earn his laurels before he wears them, than in the Congress of the United States. The standing of a man there appears to be in no wise determined by his standing outside. He may be great at home, and yet ground to powder at his first session. He may be little accounted of at home, and have weight with his fellow-members.

When Theodosia enters this body she enters it as a man. She must win her case by her own efforts—by knowledge of history, politics, finance, business, human nature, and parliamentary law ; by force of will, by strength of lung, by physical endurance. A "Washington correspondent" describes the House of Representatives on a certain occasion as "simply a mad-house, a bear-garden, a menagerie ;" and a woman paper, on the strength of such description, justly enough remarks that it does not "see how it would be possible for women to conduct public business in any worse manner than this." Let me entreat women not to found any expectations of reform on such statements. This correspondent was surely carried away either by traditions of past disorder or by the desire of making a sensation. The House on the occasion referred to was not in the least like a bear-garden, a mad-house, or a menagerie. There was nothing incoherent, indecorous, or unbecoming. There was intense eagerness, persistence, resolution. A dozen men were striving for the floor at once; there was quick consultation, modified action to meet emergencies, and, to the mere spectator, great confusion. But even the spectator might learn that there was a method in the madness—that, through all the apparent confusion, the course of business was going on as steadily and sturdily according to Constitution and amendment, in as strict subordination to law and logic, as if there had been the Reign of Silence.

A female writer in a woman paper says,

"If woman was allowed a participation in the privileges and honors of politics, gallantry, which Nature forces man to concede to her, would check this reckless ambition for power and supremacy, and oblige him to lay aside some of his self-sufficiency, here as elsewhere, out of mere civility; besides this, the propensity being deficient in the nature of woman, would flourish just the element wanted in politics to put to shame and do away with this corruption, while her innate refinement would give to ambition a more elevated object than mere love of power."

The meaning of this paragraph is somewhat shrouded in the words; but it seems to be that when a woman runs for governor or senator, men will yield their own claims and let her win, just as they now give up their seats to her in the crowded car or church.

I have some faith in the gallantry of my countrymen, though there have been times when gallantry, justice, and decency went down together. It is not two years since, in a court of justice, under the forms of law and by the officers of law, outrages were perpetrated upon women which should have made the ears of every one that heard it to tingle. It is not three years since blind rage and brutal ridicule from one end of this nation to the other were showered by men upon a woman, the latchets of whose shoes they were not worthy to unloose. And for what? For that which, at its very worst, was an indiscretion. If this woman had been herself guilty of the crime which she disclosed of another, she could not have been more severely censured. For that which no one alleged to be any thing worse than an error of judgment, and which has never been proved to be even that, a woman whose goodness is as sublime as her genius is brilliant, who has never touched pen to paper but for the furtherance of truth and humanity—a woman whose name is one of the brightest gems in her country's crown, and whose light is gone out to the end of the earth,—for such a cause, such a woman was reviled and maligned by men who may almost be said to have owed their political existence to her genius. They had not even national spirit enough to stand up for their own countrywoman against the assaults of the British; but, just as Hawthorne told us of Miss Bacon, "Our journalists at once republished some of the most brutal vituperations of the English press, thus pelting their poor countrywoman with stolen mud," so, in this case, our journalists each picked up his handful of mud and followed the English lead, like a faithful puppy yelping in the wake of a growling mastiff. Oh! then the old-time faith in American gallantry and American justice received a blow from which it will not speedily recover. You made it forever easier, my countrymen, to dispense with your approbation and to encounter your disapproval.

But when it comes to the point of expecting gallantry to stand aside, and let women win, I demur. Even if men might be counted on to this extent, would it be the best thing? If a man advocates a measure with false dates, and misplaced facts, and distorted history, and obtruded sentiment, is it not better for the country, and better even for himself, that he should be torn to pieces on the spot than that he should be salved and slavered with compliment? What we want in politics is real work, thorough work, honest work, not mere sham. The woman who has more useful knowledge, more political sagacity, more practical power than men may be a real accession to Legislatures, but any expectation of victory founded on the assumed courtesy of men seems to me at once futile, and, if not futile, fatal. It is sometimes alleged against Congress that every man is bent on his own cause, and no one thinks of the universal interest. But it is the best thing that can be said of Congress. The only way to take care of the universal interest is for each one to take care of his own. What is the country but the combination of all? The best way for Maine to look after the sugar of Louisiana or the wheat of Minnesota is to look after her own lumber. Pennsylvania fights tooth and nail for coal and iron. Let her fight. That is what she is in Congress for. Let Georgia fight tooth and nail for cotton. And when women go, let them also go prepared to fight tooth and nail. Let them not be deceived by any representation of the imbecility or the barbarity of Congress. Let them not expect an easy victory over savages or idiots; and let them, above all things, deprecate the magnetic captivation of an admiring auditory. They should be prepared to encounter a body of men not mentally below the average of any American community— and perhaps, on the whole, it would not be a tempestuous enthusiasm for deliberative assemblies that should rate them a little above—men who, in social life, do not, as a general thing, put their knives in their mouths, and with whom, if we are to enter heaven on the strength of good character and good works, one would as soon cast in his lot as with any other community, called by whatever name. But they should be prepared also to encounter men who, whatever may be their diversity of gifts and graces, are profoundly in earnest to accomplish their own objects, and to defeat objects that conflict with their own; men whose key-note is competition rather than courtesy; who in the heat of debate do not always defer to their foes, or even to their friends; who are often forcible even to bluntness, and who are not least sharp when they are most civil; men who, in perfect good humor, and quite within the bounds of propriety, are wont to address each other, and to carry their own over their comrades in a style to which women are not accustomed from men, and by which, if used toward themselves, they could hardly fail to be shocked. Women papers have a way of enhancing the merits of women by speaking of them as little-girl reporters, little-girl sculptors, little Greek professors; and, if his journalistic petting seems a good and pleasant thing, I do not know that it does any especial harm. But if these little girls are to be sent to Congress, and are to exercise any but a belittling influence upon politics, their little-girlhood can not be too speedily laid aside. They should divest themselves of every thing which shadows of diminutiveness and every thing that borders upon endearment, and stand only upon their knowledge, their sagacity, their practical legislative power.

XIV.
THE NECESSITY OF FEMALE SUFFRAGE.

THE third ground on which the ballot is demanded for woman is that she needs it for her own protection against man. Men, left to themselves, make laws for women which are unjust and oppressive. Women must have the law-making power in their own hands in order to secure fair play.

I deny this wholly. I deny it in full view of the fact that men have made laws unjust to women; that the only fear of personal injury felt by women is of bad men, and that a very large part of the suffering and sorrow of women comes from the selfishness or ignorance of the good men with whom they are connected. In the face of all this, I affirm that American women, as a class, do not need protection against American men, as a class; that, if they do need it, they will never get it, either from the ballot or from any other source; and that, on the whole, the law, as it stands, is more favorable to women than it would have been if women had made the law for themselves.

If we have come to the point that women must defend themselves against men, we may as well give up the battle at once. One man is stronger than one woman, and ten men are stronger than ten women, and the nineteen millions of men in this country will subdue, capture, and execute or expel the nineteen millions of women just as soon as they set about it. It is not even, like the suppression of the late Rebellion, a question of time. They could do it in half an hour any day. What is the use, then, of women's talking about protecting themselves against men?

The slaves of the South received the suffrage for their protection, but protection against whom? Against the power that gave them the suffrage? That is absurd. It is as if a woman should say to a man, "I believe you are a burglar, and mean to rob me. Give me a gun, that I may defend myself against you." If he means to rob her, it is idle to expect him to give her the gun. If he gives her the gun, it is proof that he is no burglar, and she does not need to defend herself against him.

But women do not propose to fight laws into existence. They propose to vote them. But voting power is based on fighting power. The rule of the majority is at bottom the rule of force. Sixty thousand voters yield to a hundred thousand voters not because they believe them to be wiser than themselves, but because they know them to be stronger. When they do not believe them to be stronger, they do not yield. They resist, and we have a rebellion. It is the knowledge that there is a physical force underneath the vote strong enough to uphold the vote that gives to the vote its power; so that the ballot is not simply the expression of desire, but the measure of strength. If the men of this country wish to oppress the women, will they be deterred from it by women's saying at the polls, or any where else, that they do not wish to be oppressed? The strength which women have to enforce their vote, compared with that which men have to smother it, is simply contemptible. Until women can march faster and further, and throw up earth-works more quickly, and stand longer in the trenches, and fight harder in the field than men, they must depend for justice upon the good will of men.

This would be a fearful sword hanging over women, a most unequal arrangement of forces, if there were not implanted in man a good will toward woman as deep as his life, as strong as his strength, as inalienable as himself.

This good will is often erratic in development, in some cases seems to be almost entirely suppressed, in savage tribes may be very feeble, in all tribes needs wise treatment, but increases and flourishes exactly in proportion as the higher nature of man is developed, and in civilized and Christianized countries may be counted on with entire certainty. This goes a great way toward equalizing matters. It gives to woman a greater hold upon man's strength than he has himself. His good will toward her is so great that he will work harder and endure more for her sake than for his own. Self-preservation is the first law of nature, but woman-preservation is the first law of civilization. The men on a sinking ship will save the women, and go down themselves, not because women are considered more valuable than men, not for any reason whatever but simply because men never think of doing any thing else. If the crew of a vessel should let the women perish, and themselves sail into port in safety, they would be mobbed at the first quay on which they landed. When Captain Herndon told his men that he proposed to save the women and go down with the ship, did they demur? I have heard that they responded with a sudden outburst of cheers, heart answering to heart with instinctive heroism. I do not know how that may be, but they manned the boats with a picked crew, they sent every woman away to life, and themselves, four hundred and twenty-seven men, went down to death.

And their countrywomen must protect themselves against their countrymen!

Individual men, under stress of temptation, or through ignorance, will do great wrong to individual women. Men combined in society, no doubt, often unwittingly injure women; but I do not believe that any body of men ever assembled in this country, or ever will assemble, with any purpose or wish to wrong or oppress the women of the country, or in any way to take advantage of their weakness or ignorance to their own furtherance, or with any other wish or purpose toward women than to protect and benefit them.

But look at the laws which men have made for women—the laws of marriage, the laws for property, the laws for the guardianship of children! I do look at them, and I see them steadily and even rapidly gathering about woman to secure her freedom and to protect her rights. From year to year, without retrogression, the march of improvement has gone on. In no other respect has the nation signalized its advance more clearly than in the ever-increasing liberality and wisdom of its laws regarding women. Unjust laws still mar our statute-books, but the performance of the past is full of promise for the future. There are states to-day in which the laws not only protect, but favor women, and every where is shown a disposition to redress wrong and secure right.

It is a great mistake to judge of the motive and scope of a law from its working in an individual case. I have no doubt that, as a general thing, law is the expression of the best thought and the best purpose of the age which enacted it. I have no doubt that, as a general thing, even those laws which to-day we consider disgraceful, were really, in their time, the working of reform; were an improvement on the customs which preceded their establishment. I dare say, if we could know all about it, we should see that the law permitting to the husband "*moderate* correction" of his wife was not to induce husbands to beat their wives, but to restrain them from beating them immoderately. The laws which seem to give husbands an undue control over the persons, property, or children of their wives were no doubt preceded by laws or customs which gave unlimited control. When we speak indignantly of "the laws which men have made for women," we may as well be indignant also over the laws which men have made for men. Has the law inflicted any greater outrage on woman than it has on the innocent man who is kept in jail as a witness while the criminal goes at large? A law can not rise much higher than the age and country which frame it. It must partake of the defects of that age. I do not know that there has ever been a time when the women of a nation were further advanced than the men in jurisprudence; and, unless such a time has been, we have small reason to suppose that women would have made better laws than men.

It is to be remembered that scarcely a law can be framed which may not bear hard on particular cases. It is impossible for finite beings to fit laws to every exigency. They can, at best, only approximate justice. They can only aim at the greatest good of the greatest number. Even where a law seems arbitrary and unjust, there is often another side which is less opprobrious. Looking at the laws for married women, we must remember that not only has the state to consider married women, but that husband, children, and society have rights which it is bound to respect. If any thing seems utterly wicked and cruel, it is robbing a mother of her children. To-day our hearts are wrung with the story of a mother thus robbed by a legal guardian on the occasion of her second marriage. To-morrow a father dies frenzied with grief because he can not snatch his children from his divorced wife; and his story is not a merry one. It seemed an unjust and degrading thing for a married woman not to be allowed to hold property independent of her husband, and one state after another changed its laws to enable her to do so; but testimony goes to show that the principal practical use made of the law, thus far, has been to enable the husband to put his property into the hands of his wife, and thus live on the enjoyment of it, and do business on the strength of it, without having it liable for his debts or subject to the risks of his business. In Connecticut a woman is actually thrown into jail because she refuses to give up her personal property to her husband, he and his two daughters by a former marriage being already supported on the proceeds of her real estate; and the women of Connecticut are therefore exhorted to arise, demand equal and just rights for both men and women, and banish forever from your statute-book laws which can be made the instrument of such injustice! But in New York a married woman holds, independent of her husband's control, thirty thousand dollars. This money she received from him when he was in good business and in full health. He became paralyzed; and she at once took a paramour and sailed to Europe, leaving her husband an annuity of three hundred dollars, and supporting her paramour out of the proceeds of the fortune which her husband had given her. Shall not, then, the men of New York arise and banish forever from their statute-books laws which can be made the instrument of such injustice? When fiction comes to the field, we are called upon to sympathize with a sick husband, who is unable to "tend store" where he is partner, but is able and willing to stay at home, keep house, "chop hash," and mind the children. The wife is healthy, able, and willing to become partner, and tend store in her husband's stead, and the other partner is desirous she should. She proposes to buy her husband out; but the laws do not permit a contract between husband and wife; so he makes her a present of all he is worth, and every thing goes smoothly, till it is suddenly discovered that a married woman can not be a partner, when every thing stops, the husband grows worse and worse, they can think of nothing to do but live on their principal, and "Shame on the Old Bay State for the laws its men have made!"

Leaving out of view the peculiar mental kink which enables them to devise a mode of escape from the impossibility of a contract between husband and wife by a gift to the wife of all her husband's property, but does not permit them to see any way of getting a living unless she can be a legal partner in the shop, how easy is it to give the story another twist! The sick man has presented all his property to his healthy wife. She goes into the store under the new law as partner. The new firm is unskillful or unfortunate, and principal and interest go down together; or she falls in love with the partner, who is likely to be more cheerful and engaging than the sick husband, chopping hash at home; and, as she is not liable for his support, notwithstanding he has given her all his money—for, while the laws have steadily enlarged the liberty of the wife, they have never, I believe, diminished her immunities—she turns him out of doors, where "damp door-step settles on his lungs," and he dies in the poor-house. I think a wife is just as likely to do this as a man is to put his wife in jail for not giving him her money. Or, we may imagine a sagacious and fortunate husband doing business up town, and suddenly finding himself penniless and his children beggared by an ambitious, extravagant, and incapable wife doing business down town.

These things are mentioned, not to prove that our laws, as they stand, are perfect, but to indicate that they may be unequal without being necessarily or intentionally unjust; to indicate, also, that there are on all these questions two sides. Society is to the last degree complicated and delicate. The relations of husband and wife are so peculiar, their interests are so identical, even though they do not maintain for each other a romantic affection, that I do not see how it is possible for the law to consider them two entirely distinct and independent individuals, like two men, without injuriously affecting the interests and claims of others. The Old Testament and the New agree in declaring that they twain shall be one flesh; and if the formula were written after the facts, to fit the case, it could not have been more concise or accurate. We can not legislate for that which is essentially one as if it were in all points two. Divine law is utterly regardless of our protests and insensible to our arguments, and holds just as strong when we ignore as when we obey it.

No law exists which can not be made the instrument of injustice. Under the best and wisest laws individuals may suffer. No law can be framed which shall completely shield man or woman from the consequences of ignorance, incapacity, or folly. You can place the control of property, the rights of contract, with husband or wife, or both, and it will still remain that, if a woman marry a brutal, coarse, selfish, or lazy man, she will suffer for it, in mind, body, and estate; if a man marry a frivolous, unprincipled, uneducated woman, she will drag him down. No change in laws can affect the fact that in marriage the character of the parties is of the first importance, and the settlement of their property is but subordinate. If they are wise and good, they are more likely to be happy than if they are foolish and selfish. If they are sick, they will suffer more than if they are well. All that law can do is to help people as far as possible against the consequences of folly, weakness, and wickedness, whether their own or another's. Notwithstanding all the clamor against it, this is what the law aims to do, and what in large measure it does. Our American law is, in the main, beneficent, and not oppressive. It steps in between a woman's self-surrender and self-devotion to the man she loves and the possible consequences of her act, and retains for her certain rights and makes for her certain claims which a woman would seldom think of doing for herself. When a girl is in love with a man, she does not dream of defending herself against him. She would gladly give him all her money, and only wish she had more to give. If there were no law at all on this subject, and the disposition of her property were left to each woman at her marriage, in nine cases out of ten she would relinquish the whole care and control of it to her husband, without any limitation whatever. But the law knows what she does not know. To the law her hero is no hero, but a fallible man, who may bring her to grief and poverty; so it hedges him about with restraints which, though often insufficient, are greater than she would ever impose. There is no need, as there is no use, in crying shame on the Old Bay State for the laws its men have made. Defective though they be, the Old Bay State nowhere, on the whole, makes a better figure than on its statute-books. Nowhere do its men appear more conscientious, more bent on justice, than in fashioning the laws regarding women. They have not reached perfection. They have not yet secured equity. Nor do I think equity is to be secured by equality. Women ought to have more than equality. They are heavily weighted in the race, and they ought to have advantage. The husband owes to his wife support. The wife does not owe it to her husband. The law ought to put its hand into the husband's pocket and take out enough for the wife's maintenance, whether he will or not; but I can not see any reason why it should put its hand into the wife's pocket at all. This, however, is only on the ground that women and men are not equal; that man has the facilities and woman the disabilities for business; that it is a man's part, and not a woman's, to earn money. If this is not so—if men and women are to be on the same plane—then I see not why the wife should not be responsible for the husband's support, as well as the husband for the wife's; why her property should not go to pay his debts as entirely, as inevitably as his goes to pay hers; why she should not be equally with himself liable for the support of the children; why, indeed, there should not be an entire readjustment of the laws of property and of obligations which shall involve a public investigation of family affairs compared with which the publication of the income tax would seem inoffensive and delightful. However this may be, impartial and exhaustive investigation and fair comparison will show that far more clamor is raised against the laws than the laws themselves give occasion for; that suffering arises far more from the weakness and wickedness of individuals than from laws; and that, where the laws are still insufficient for woman's protection, they are so not because men desire and design to injure women, but because they do not yet know what is for benefit and what for detriment; that they have thought far more deeply and broadly for women than women have for themselves; that they have taken far more pains to protect women than women have taken for their own protection; and that the earnestness, the vigor, and the success with which they have adopted and executed such plans of reform as have been presented to them is a sure sign that women have only to determine and designate what is for their advancement to secure it at the hands of men.

But why not secure it for themselves rather than ask men to secure it for them? Why retain women in a state of tutelage, not to say pupilage? Without detracting from the wisdom and good will of man, why not add to it the wisdom, self-knowledge, and self-interest of woman? Admitting that women alone would do no better than men alone, it may still remain that men and women together are worth more than either alone. If we agree that men do not know what women need and want until women tell them, why not ally them at the ballot-box, permit woman there to express her will, and thus do the work directly, rather than keep her away from the polls, and execute her will only by the roundabout method of man's agency?

Simply because man's agency seems a more direct and economical way than woman's personal action. Compared with the whole mass of law, that part of it which bears, or even which seems to bear, unjustly on woman is very small. A woman might as well turn farmer, and undertake the plowing and ditching herself, because she wants a tulip-bed, as undertake the whole field of politics because the part which relates to her needs fresh seeding down. In general, it will be admitted by all that the property interests of man and woman, except as affected by marriage, are identical. The greater portion of the law and of politics concerns matters in which the claims of man and woman are not antagonistic. In all our international, and in the greater part of our national affairs, the best thing for men is the best thing for women. In the establishment of peace or the declaration of war, men have certainly as much at stake as women. In the adjustment of the tariff, in the disposition of public lands, in the regulation of national banks, of internal revenue, of civil service, of commerce and navigation, of municipal government, men have no interests distinct from those of women. Those decisions and that legislation which advance the prosperity of men, advance equally the prosperity of women, whether they are active business managers or mere owners of property. In these matters, perhaps, the question of sex enters not at all. In most of them a majority of women take no interest, nor does it seem essential that they should. They are matters on which twenty men may throw as much light as ten men and ten women. A man may be profoundly ignorant of the temperament and nature of woman, and yet be wise in respect to laying taxes on iron and steel; but if women are to inform themselves and to vote on the few questions which directly concern them, they must do it also on the many questions which concern them but indirectly. In giving an account of her labors, one of the female-suffrage missionaries reported that she found among women scarcely any opposition, but a great deal of ignorance. They seemed to have heard little about the movement going on to secure them the ballot; but when she explained the case, they admitted that it was reasonable, and put their names to her petition. But after the suffrage is secured the same work of instruction must be wrought upon these women to show them how to direct their effort for the amelioration of the laws. If this missionary had made a digest of all the objectionable state laws; had shown where they were oppressive, and how they should be altered to secure justice and dignity to woman, without injuring any other class; had embodied this in a petition to the Legislature, and had then gone around among women explaining her design, and asking their signatures, would she not have helped women far more directly and speedily? I do not believe a single state Legislature exists which would dare to refuse, or which would even wish to refuse, any thing for which the women of their state should thus express a desire—the women of the state; not, of course, any mere clique of women. If they would refuse it, they certainly would not give women the ballot. If they would not let women have their way in one thing, it is not probable they would put into their hands an instrument whereby they might get their way in all things. If they would not refuse it, then women have a method whereby they can speak their minds, when they have any, and yet need not be obliged to make up their minds on points to which they are indifferent. It is only now and then that questions come up for which women naturally care. On those occasions they find no difficulty in expressing themselves. Perhaps they come out with all the more influence because they come but seldom. No one had any doubt what women thought, how they loved, on which side they stood, during the late war. Alike North and South they made themselves felt as strongly without the ballot-box as men did with it. On the question of protection or free trade they have said little; perhaps because they have not the power to vote, but perhaps also because they have little to say, and what little they have they find just as well said to their hand. On the subject of ship-building they feel no enthusiasm; the salt of San Domingo does not arouse their sympathy

But women, it is said, ought not to be in the attitude of petitioners. It is not dignified for them to beg men to do for them what they have a right to do for themselves. But they are petitioners in any case. They must beg even for the vote. Right or wrong, men have the power, and women have it not. It is no more undignified to ask man to reach you an apple from the shelf, than it is to ask him to place his footstool for you to stand on and reach it yourself. Do you say that the apple is as much yours as his, and ought never to have been put out of your reach? But it *is* out of your reach, and you can not get it unless he gives it to you. That fact is as fixed as fate, and women had as much part in fixing it so as men.

We talk as if the present state of society were the result of some arbitrary outside influence, which has repressed and altered the nature of things. Women, we say, are equal to men, but they have been subdued to inferiority by wrong training and false public opinion. Men, it is true, have done the great deeds, but women have never had a fair chance. Give them the same education and the same traditions that men have, and put men to the narrow life and petty service of women, and we should soon see what we should see.

Very true; and yet, if women are naturally equal to men, how came they to be actually unequal? Who prescribed the wrong training, and who made the false opinion, and how came women into the narrow path? Man and woman started in life together. If they were equal, why did she not show her hand? There was no public opinion then to warp her thought. Eve had just as good an education as Adam. No petty traditional cares came to belittle her purpose or to fritter away her days. That was the time for her to make a stand, if she proposed to make one at all. After all these years, it is no use to cry out that she could do all things if she only had the chance. She had the chance once, and she did not do them. This is the simple fact, and no amount of rhetoric alters it. Men have made the discoveries, and invented the machinery, and built the cities, and acquired the honors, and subdued the world, because they could. Women have not, because they could not. Men are masters of the situation because they are stronger than women, and there is no good in beating about the bush. Men have the education because they would have it. They have not the thousand small cares because they would not have them. Women have had neither the strength to grasp the one nor to reject the other. What men gave them they took, and what men refused them they went without, and they could not help themselves. Nor has any thing yet happened to invalidate this superiority. If women attempt to measure swords with men, they will be beaten. If woman could not hold her own against man in the beginning, she can not hold her own now. Things are as they are, not from any outside interference, but from their own inherent nature. There is nobody outside but God.

In competition with man, woman makes no show at all. If that is her case, she has no case. All prophecy of what she will do goes for nothing in face of the fact that for six thousand years she has not done it. No possible legislation, no conceivable contingency can give her a fairer field, a more equal position with man than she had at the beginning.

My inference is that her work lies in another direction. Her field is on another plane. I believe in her glory, honor, and immortality; and I believe profoundly and unalterably in her superiority to man, but not in the *rôle* of man.

When it is objected that if women vote on the few points in which they are interested they must also vote on the many points in which they are not interested, the reply is made that they ought to be interested in all. Women are equally concerned with men in the character of government. They ought to have an equal knowledge of, and an equal share in politics. To say that they have no desire to vote amounts to no more than did the old slaveholding assertion that the slaves did not desire to be free. Speaking of this alleged unwillingness, one of the leaders says, "As if this, being true, justified the domination of the strong, and the servile acquiescence of the weak! As if this, being true, did not prove an immense loss of self-respect, self-control, personal independence, and wholesome responsibility on the part of the women thus ignobly praised!"

But I utterly repudiate the idea that the unwillingness of women to vote implies servility or a lack of self-respect. There may be thoughtless and spiritless women who care nothing about it one way or the other, and there appear to be those who think hostility to it a winning and womanly thing. But beyond these stand the women who think, and think the other way; who, whether or not pecuniarily dependent, are mentally independent; who are resolute and self-possessed. When of such women we predicate servile acquiescence in the domination of the strong, we speak nonsense. No line of argument in the suffrage cause is more fatuous than that which assumes the women of this country to be in any sense slaves. If the laws on the statute-books were forty times worse than they are, it would be equally fatuous. Such an assumption is an insult, and no argument. It has scarcely truth enough to sting. It hardly arouses resentment; it slightly excites contempt; it never convinces the reason. It may inflame the suffering, and impose upon the weak, but it does not advance the cause in those quarters where advance must be made if the result is to be beneficial. The women of this country are as free in word and deed as the men, so far as the ballot affects freedom. Their ownership of property is in many cases as absolute, and where there is a difference, it is a difference of degree, not of kind. The wife does not hold her property free from her husband's control, but neither does he hold his free from her control. The restrictions may not be equal, but both are restricted, each by the other. By a foolishly-worded marriage-vow—a relic of barbarism—she promises to obey him; but she is just as legally married without the promise, and when she does make it, it never practically amounts to any thing. If she will, she will, and if she won't, she won't. Her obedience or her command depend upon her disposition and character, and upon those of her husband. Wives, and perhaps women, are to some extent forbidden to hold office; but it is not wholly because they are women, nor necessarily because women are considered inferior to men. Many men are equally forbidden, and some men by reason of no inferiority. All members of both houses of Congress are legally disqualified for holding office during their term of service, but it involves no discourtesy to the members. The idea which underlies the law is doubtless that one man can not well perform the two sets of duties, and it is not unreasonable to suppose that this is precisely the idea which underlies the legal disqualification of women. Looking at their actual social status in this country, it is as easy to believe that they are forbidden on account of the superior service which they render to the state in other directions, and with which office-holding might conflict, as it is to believe that they are forbidden on account of inferiority, or for the purpose of enslavement. Women know that they are not slaves. Bad as are some of the laws in some of the states, there is none in which women do not possess the essentials of liberty; none in which a woman may not exercise entire freedom of thought, of word, and, for the most part, of deed, hampered only by bonds which are the results of her own acts or character. All the laws which unjustly restrict her she may in the most public manner denounce, and use all her efforts to destroy, and to substitute for them such as are just, while the changes which have been effected in these later years show that denunciation is not the dashing of impotent rage against an immovable body, but may become a skillful instrument for fashioning the grim block into a shapely statue. To say that woman has no voice in making the laws which govern her is not correct. She has no vote, but in every other respect she has a voice as free, and clear, and penetrating as man's. To inform the mother of a family, the woman who stands at the head, ruling, guiding, watching, influencing, controlling her husband in twenty matters for one in which he controls her, taking in society precisely the position which her abilities fit her to take, that she is a slave, or even a child; to tell a woman who does *not* take the position for which she is fitted because she has not leisure, who spends the long days in serving, and cooking, and care-taking for little children who do not know enough to be thankful, and for a hard-working husband who has all his life been used to seeing women work, and is not overmuch troubled thereby, who is an equal partner in the family firm, and whose mind has equal force in the family councils; to tell a woman whose life has been one long *grind* of endurance from a tyrannical, miserly, petty husband; to tell a young girl, free and merry, or an unmarried woman of mature years, of active life, of definite purpose, or "anxious and aimless," through lack of purpose, that they are one and all slaves because they can not vote, argues an indistinctness of vision or a misuse of words that bodes ill to any cause. It gives a made-up air to the whole grievance. It looks as if there were no ground of complaint. It looks as if women were so well off that real fault could not be found with their condition, and therefore a demonstration is arranged to prove that they are logically what really every one knows that they are not, and what, without the denunciation, no one would ever suspect them of being. Unhappily, there are restrictions which ought to be removed—restrictions from which these false issues divert attention, and to whose removal they become therefore real obstacles.

It is only the most stupid and degraded of slaves who are content with slavery, who do not wish to be free. Do the advocates of woman suffrage know what they are doing when they liken their opponents to such? Do they know what sort of woman it is upon whom they attempt to fasten the stigma of servility? Do they understand the meaning of words when they assume the monopoly of self-respect and self-control, and deny their possession to all other women?

XV.
EXEMPTION OR IMPOSITION.

IN the discussion of female suffrage, we hear much about the privileges and honors of politics, little about its duties; much about the injustice which debars women from its emoluments, little about the justice which exempts women from its demands. It will not be denied that political power makes severe demands and prescribes exacting duties. To conduct this great nation, with its varied interests, its clashing nationalities, its numerous sub-governments, its wide-stretching territories—to bear it on from day to day without bankruptcy, without impinging upon other nations, without falling a prey to the conflicting claims of its own members—this is no sinecure. It employs a large class of the best men in the country, it secures the best thoughts of another large class of best men, it occupies a large share of the attention and interest of every intelligent and conscientious man, and in the last resort its call is paramount to all others. The moment that women have the power to vote, all this responsibility devolves equally upon them. It becomes at once their duty to inform themselves on every political subject, to hold themselves ready to answer the summons to all political service. It is true that men do not. Men, untaught, unaccustomed to logical thinking, prejudiced and opinionated, vote ignorantly, blindly. Intelligent and honest men decline political duty, and even plume themselves on it, though the public receive harm in consequence. But women are entering the arena not to imitate men, but to improve upon them; not to do things as they are done, but as they ought to be done. Ignorant legislation is already our great menace. Women are not to increase its quantity. They will be, equally with men, recreant to their trust unless they comprehend intelligently all the issues upon which they pronounce decision, and pronounce decision upon all the issues submitted to their judgment.

Hitherto man has done this work alone. We must give him the credit of never having asked woman to share it with him. If he has claimed its honors, he has at least borne its burdens. If he has never suffered woman to rule, he has never asked her to serve. He has repeatedly blundered into war, but he has fought it out himself.

To my thinking this is simply as it should be. I give man no credit for generosity, only for justice. He ought to do this work, for woman has another work to do, by virtue of which she stands exempt from this. Her part is more severe, more exacting, more important than his. He may well take upon himself the whole burden of business, political and pecuniary; she more than offsets it in bearing the burden of motherhood. This, with what it involves, demands, and permits, is so onerous that all other task-work laid upon her is unnatural. I would absolve her from every thing except that which ministers directly to the spiritual life of the race. Nature has spoken here with a clearness which it is impossible to mistake, with a force which it is impossible to resist.

So many witless, wicked, and unclean words have been uttered in these latter days touching woman's place, that no folly, no madness even, on the part of women ought to excite surprise. When a mother, who has brought up children to usefulness and honor, rises on the platform to give her opinion as to what is best for women, and clergymen of moderate abilities and precarious position tell her in reply that her true work is to go home and take care of her children, or that she is advocating free love, the destruction of marriage, and the dissolution of society, one feels that argument would be thrown away, and that the true womanly and fitting response would be, in the language of the poet,

> "To take them as you would mischievous boys,
> And shake their heads together."

When our religious teachers count it a praiseworthy thing to turn the most austere and momentous service of womanhood into a means of acquiring property, and hold up the example for imitation, it is idle to reproach women for infidelity. If female suffrage obtains to-morrow, its most effectual calling will have been from pulpits and religious newspapers, which denounced it. Ministers are sometimes reproached for confining themselves too closely to the sins of past ages, and letting the sins of the present go unchecked. But, listening to a suffrage sermon, one mentally exclaims, "Oh, if they only would never come nearer to us than Nebuchadnezzar!" The mouthings of mountebanks are neither here nor there; but when clergymen, even of parts and culture, undertake to preach woman, it is fearful and wonderful to see what paralysis comes upon their perception, what mildew blights their judgment, what dry-rot falls upon their reason. Men may keep up any kind of a thinking, but all they have a right to say is, "We will not be an obstacle to women. Whenever the majority signify a desire to exercise the right of suffrage, we will not resist." If they wish to preach down woman suffrage, the way is to let women alone and preach to men, curbing their selfishness, enlightening their ignorance, showing them how to be so pure, so gentle, so just, so wise, so strong that women shall be confident and comfortable, free from anxiety and toil, never tempted or forced by man's inefficiency to put their shoulder to his wheel, but, gratified, satisfied, elated with the way he does his work, and content and delighted to devote themselves to their own.

As I do not desire at present to have an ecclesiastical war on my hands, I make only this slight allusion in passing; but, from a general survey, it would not be fair to leave out the material aid which the woman party has received from the clergy, and the corresponding obstacles which its opponents have been obliged to surmount.

But fallacy can not change facts. It still remains that the one divine institution, changed by no times, weakened by no sophistry, profaned by no barter, is the family. In motive and method it most nearly approaches our ideal of God's idea. Of this, all other governments, national, state, municipal, are but a clumsy and cumbrous imitation. Crowning this fact rises another which no impertinence of repetition affects, that this is woman's kingdom. Man is an important officer, but woman is the reigning monarch. He is the prime minister whose wisdom makes the kingdom prosperous. He is the brilliant general whose exploits bring it renown. He is the unprofitable servant whose weakness drags it to the dust.

In this kingdom woman is not only sovereign, but sovereign-mother. Man's work, if necessary, she can make shift to do after a fashion. Her work he can not do at all. Whatever of toil and sacrifice a man renders for his family, a woman can also render; but beyond this she bears a burden, above this she wields a power which he can never assume. In the tabernacle of life man dwells in the outer courts, woman ministers at the holy of holies. Her influence upon humanity is so primal, so intimate, so dominant, that it might seem almost divine. She is second only to the Creator.

Herein lies her superiority. In coarse and common service, in the race of the swift and the battle of the strong, man immeasurably outstrips her. In the higher service of love, which lies above battle-field and race-course, of whose ministry God himself is the only perfect exemplar, she holds a position so advanced that man is not even her competitor.

From such a point the question is not, Have not women a right to enter upon the arena of politics? but, Have men a right to demand that women shall enter that arena? From such a point I not only admit, but, if called upon, avow, that women as truly as men have the right to vote, but, above and beyond this, they have a higher right which men can not claim—the right not to vote.

Never do I more regret the dishonor into which woman's work has fallen—or, shall I say, out of which it has not yet arisen—never appears a misapprehension of values so great and fatal as when I hear a woman publicly espouse the suffrage cause by saying, "No longer will woman be content merely to rear a family, and drudge and die." *Merely* to rear a family! When women come to look upon the rearing of a family as a small thing, we are indeed far from the kingdom of heaven. We have groveled to sad purpose if the little needs, the petty cares, the mere material service which attend all families, and which dominate so many, have made themselves to represent family life. To rear a family, to establish a home, to make domestic life what it ought to be, to give it that part in the social structure, in national excellence, in the elevation of humanity which belongs to it, and for which there is no substitute, is an object worthy the ambition and the energies of the best and wisest woman that ever was or ever will be born. The great work of both man and woman is the fashioning of immortal beings; but what can be done through business and politics, though necessary, is but feeble and far off compared with what can be done in the family. Nature, with infinite pains and infinite delicacy, has given woman a peculiar fitness for this work, and a peculiar unfitness for every other. What I want is that we should heed nature, and magnify the office of woman. My claim is that all the rough, clashing, confusing work outside and inside—not only that which men now do, but a great deal of that which is done by women, shall be assumed by men, that women may be left tranquil, and free, and fine for the delicate touches. Homes are defective, harsh, forbidding, uninfluential, because the women who should preside over them are cumbered with much serving in them. It disturbs me little to hear men say that if women vote they must also trade, and toil, and fight. Thousands of women could hardly find life more stern than it is, and it savors of hypocrisy for men to warn off from the political field by prophecies of hardship women who are already well-nigh overborne by hardship, and who only look that way longing for relief. But what shall I say when women tell me that the nature of woman demands the toil, and trade, and strife of the outside world as a higher and better thing than the mechanisms of the soul? I claim that women have a right to be independent of those upon whom they have no claim, and of the brutality of those upon whom they have a claim, but a higher and sweeter, a divine right to be dependent upon those to whom such dependence is a savor of life unto life, and for the sake of those whose dear cherishing, whose moral life, and highest happiness, and finest growth make such dependence necessary. But if women disdain their prerogative, and choose to minister unto themselves in carnal things rather than minister unto others spiritual things! Men speak often as if the responsibility and result of home and family rested on woman. I deny it absolutely, seeing nowhere in nature any indication of it, believing that the stake is too great to be left to either sex, but demands the harmonious efforts of both; and believing that man's part, though less absorbing, less difficult, and in some sense less honorable than woman's, is no less incumbent on him. Men deprecate high education for women, fancying it unfits them to be good housewives. I crave the highest, if for no other reason, that they may thus be fitted to be good housewives. Do boys need a liberal education to become skillful in their profession? Women need it as much to become skillful in theirs. No calling can absorb more wealth of resource than the woman's calling. None counts wisdom more vital, folly more fatal. All knowledge is its province. Whatever tends to enlarge the mind, as well as to increase the sympathy, belongs to woman. Politics, art, science, all are hers, subject only to her choice, subordinate always to her freedom. She may be poet, painter, philosopher, sea-captain, sempstress, lawyer, lecturer—whatever she has impulse and power to become; but none of these things shall be laid upon her, for upon her the Creator has laid another work which has the right to exclude them all. She shall have the widest scope for selection, and ample opportunity for preparation, whatever career she select; real power in any direction is power in this. And so certain is nature to secure her aims, that all the impulse which women feel in all other directions is insignificant compared with the common impulse which moves them in this. Whether a woman gathers a family around her, or whether she sits "on winter nights by solitary fires," is but an incident; but she was organized without regard to incident. Her strength and her weakness point in one direction. Humanity is her field. Deeper than her choice, more remote than her will, lie the sources of her power.

When we plan to impose upon women the whole new world of politics, from what department do we plan to release her in order to equalize the duties of men and women? My hope is that she may move surely onward, out of her foreign bondage to degrading tasks into native freedom for elevating work. I am willing even to journey through the wilderness of trade and mechanics, and to admit that, for some, there may be no other way to the Promised Land; but I can not admit that the wilderness is Canaan except in comparison with Egypt. I see in the advocacy of suffrage no attempt to lift off old burdens, but only to add new. From no kind of toil is there any movement to free woman, but only to bring her under another yoke with man. Her own load can not be lightened, and therefore she shall have a fresh weight!

Why should women persist in appraising themselves at men's valuation, and that of the baser sort of men? In savage tribes, where the standard has hardly risen above physical strength, it is not strange that women should be menial in service and soul. In this age and country, where women are often actually, and always theoretically held in honor, largely exempt from pecuniary, and always exempt from political labor, they ought to adopt the highest theory, and insist that it be carried out. They ought to insist upon freedom from toil, that they may worthily discharge the duties of their spiritual office and all mental furnishing, that their freedom may be a blessing and no bane. Instead of this, we are bidden to fall back upon the theory of savages, and look upon woman's exemptions not as preparation for, but banishment from the most honorable offices. We demand that women shall come to their own, not by enforcing, but by relinquishing their prerogative. What they do already of necessity from man's incapacity, they shall do of set purpose by reason of their own capacity. And when women, with not one jot or tittle of their own law abrogated, shall be set side by side with men, be made subject to the same tasks, liable for the same debts, and obedient to the same summons, we shall have secured the enfranchisement and the elevation of woman!

XVI.
THE ATTITUDE OF MEN.

It is reckoned a matter of course that men should oppose female suffrage. They have held power too long, and learned to love it too well, to relinquish it without a struggle. They will not willingly share that which they have hitherto monopolized.

If men were indeed tyrants by nature, this would be their natural feeling. There are stupid, ignorant, and tyrannical men enough to give rise to the statement. Such men oppose the movement with arguments whose impudence and coarseness are the shame, and doubtless the torture, of the women to whom they belong. Men who have not ability to govern themselves, who are a disgrace, a terror, or a trial to their families, are loud in their outcry against the government of women. Let us not be blind to the fact—nor yet to that other fact, that the best men too are its opponents. Men just and calm, who are never guilty of discourtesy, who are lovely and pleasant in their home lives, and who radiate light in the social circle; who are not only deferent in manner, but who practically honor women by their walk and conversation; in whose character jealousy, envy, meanness have no place—these men too, persistently, though perhaps passively, and always politely, oppose. Is it too much to say that the instinct of men is against it? They will admit its reasonableness, they will even obey orders under its leaders, but there seems to be nothing in them to respond with enthusiasm to its appeal, and they seldom take it up spontaneously.

[I believe, indeed, it is a man who announces that "there are thousands of men and women in Massachusetts who would walk barefoot from Berkshire to Barnstable, who would sacrifice party, social position, money, reputation, life itself, to establish woman suffrage in the Old Bay State to-day," and I suspect that statement must be referred to enthusiasm. The money and life are easy to believe. We can any of us pick out a dozen or two women among our neighbors who would cheerfully mount the gallows for the sake of securing the immediate passage of a certain act by the Legislature, but these very women have been so accustomed to shoes and stockings that it would be simply impossible for them to walk across Massachusetts barefoot, and they would not like to be seen doing it either!]

Masculine hostility or indifference to female suffrage may be a vice, but it may also be an instinct. Masculine vice shall receive no quarter, but instinct is divine, irrespective of sex. The hostility is at least worth taking into account. If there is a course of action to which a large class of women feel no drawing, to which another large class are opposed, and which a large class of men consider unbecoming and undesirable for women, there is surely ground for hesitation. As things are, may it not be said, in general terms, that what men dislike in women, and what women dislike in men, is unlovely? Men, we say, wish to keep women inferior for the better security of their own position, but I never saw a man evince any repugnance to a woman on account of her superiority. Men admire fine qualities, and acknowledge remarkable attainments in a woman as heartily as they do in a man. Doctors refuse to consult with female physicians, but they refuse to consult with male physicians also; and among the obstacles to female medical practice, not the least formidable is the unexpected fact that women will not have women-doctors. Artists detract from the merits of a female artist, but male artists quarrel among each other. Outside and above the circle of professional jealousy, masculine opinion is as likely to take up for the woman as the man. Assumption of superiority, boldness and badness of manner, self-laudation, men do not like. Neither do women, nor probably angels. But men are as proud of their daughters' proficiency in Latin and the higher mathematics as they are of their sons'. Yet these men, who respect the judgment of their wives, give the best possible education to their daughters, and find their most cherished, valued, and honored friends among women, retain still an insurmountable repugnance to the proposed political leveling. They are not afraid that wife or friend will be contaminated by politics. They have too much respect for both politics and women. It can not be jealousy or tyranny. They are incapable of either. To charge it to such motives does not help solve the problem. They are not to be won over with hard words. They are sensitive — men are sometimes, particularly towards women—and such allegations give them a sense of wrong, and even of outrage. They know that they are not tyrants, that they wish well to women, that they would gladly do whatever is right and wise; but they see an army of women charging fiercely for the suffrage and making the heavens ring with cries of injustice and oppression; they see another army of women, equally virtuous—and, in spite of contrary representations, I will venture to say, equally intelligent—wholly opposed to the suffrage, and they know not what they are expected to do. They hesitate from doubt as to what women want, not from anxiety for their own prestige. They may in their hearts hope the change will never come, but they would not selfishly oppose it against the protest of women.

Whatever be the cause of this antagonistic or uncertain

attitude, it can not be wise to ignore or overbear it. The leaders of the party say frankly that men will never grant the right so long as they can help it. I believe they can always help it if they choose, but even if they can not, and suffrage should be extorted, could the result be otherwise than unhappy? Antagonism between man and woman is, of all things, unnatural. Attraction is the natural relation. It seems immodest for woman to thrust herself into the ways and walks of man. Necessity is its own hard and sufficient justification; but, if I am right, the necessity is not here. Its existence is, at least, not certain. Feminine interference, when needed, is not recognised as interference, but help—is not rejected, but welcomed. If woman suffrage is to be, let it come from man's call, not from woman's clamor. Let it come because the wisdom and strength of woman are so manifest, because she is seen to be larger than her life, and because the councils of her country need her aid. If, even in the home for which she is eminently and primarily fitted, she does not take the initiative, but awaits invitation and preparation, how much less should she rush unbidden into the outer wilderness. Called by man to his public life as earnestly as he calls her to the support of his inner life, her response might well be as ready, and her aid as wholesome. Does this seem to be hyper-sentimental? But the indifference and reluctance of men and women certify that there is some sentiment, real, deep, perhaps to be found in the end inexpugnable. Certainly, whatever we shall have gained of valuable, we shall have lost somewhat of invaluable when any improvement or enlargement shall have caused that women cease to be, to the imagination of men, worshipful, retiring, inspiring, and become aggressive, pugnacious, self-centred.

XVII.
RESULTS.

But I have a profound faith in the inviolability of nature. Neither man nor woman can ever be permanently unsexed. Not all the laws of all the lands can add one cubit to the stature of either. After the agitation is soothed, and readjustment secured, men will remain men, and women women, just as much alike, just as widely unlike, and just as attractive in their unlikeness as they now are, for nature is amenable to divine and not to human will. But, while this may give heart to those who fear universal derangement and deterioration from the proposed change, it ought also to inspire caution in those who hope all things from the same source. Nature makes no allowance for ignorance, and condones no mistakes. While sciolists are experimenting, sentient beings are suffering. If to-day women should acquire legal equality with men, and customs should enforce social equality, would Heaven take heed and give us natural equality to correspond? Will divine laws be changed to match our human code? I know some say that by divine law equality is already established, which is simply saying that women are men, save for a little training. An earnest pleader, arguing in numbers, bids us

> "Remember, God bestows his care
> Of sex regardless every where."

Nothing is more palpably false. So far is God from being regardless of sex, that sex appears rather to be the key-note of creation. So far is he from bestowing his care regardless of sex, that he seems to have been careful to confer immunity upon the one and to impose tax upon the other. Looking at it without regard to spiritual compensation, God is the most partial of beings. He made one sex strong and the other sex weak, and upon the weak he laid a heavy burden, where upon the strong he laid none at all. Worse than this, he made the burden of the weaker sex inseparable, while the only burden of the stronger sex was so lightly and loosely laid that it could always be shifted to the shoulders of the weaker, and it always has, to a greater or less degree, been thus shifted, so that the weaker has borne the load of the stronger in addition to its own. With all this, he left it to no one's choice whether to be male or female, or whether to be at all, but of his own will begat he us. To man he gave not only strength, but joy; to woman, not only weakness, but suffering. Man incurs pain only through disease, the result of folly or ignorance. Woman's highest health and happiness come through the valley of the shadow of death. The harshest law that man ever framed for woman is tender and benevolent compared with the irreversible natural law under which she lives, and moves, and has her being.

Do I then arraign God? I do, if social equality is the complement of natural inequality. I do, unless political decisions shall change physical conditions; unless constitutional amendments shall emanate from the courts of heaven to correspond with mundane legislation; unless the decree that woman's arm shall do man's work is attended by another decree that it shall be endowed with man's muscle. If it is God's will that women shall be on the same footing with men; that they shall go out as men go, to earn their own living and make their own way, to bear the brunt, and form the front, and face the foe, then there is no God. There is only a great, cruel, partial, pitiless Man sitting in the heavens, whom I hate, though I can not hinder.

Happily, we are not reduced to the alternative. God moves in a mysterious, but not in an arbitrary way. It is impossible to fathom his motives, to see why evil should be the inexorable attendant of good, why good and evil should be so unequally distributed. Our popular understanding of the Hebrew explanation is as little satisfactory as the theological assertion that compensation is found in a superior moral power of endurance. The way to look for relief is not in the direction of endurance, but of delight; in the unspeakable joy of a love so intense that sacrifice becomes impossible. Be that as it may, on the hither side we are not left in doubt. Why God made us as we are no one can say. Having made us as we are, he has given sufficient intimation of our course. God—my God—says, "The woman was not made for toil. Man alone shall eat bread in the sweat of his brow. Woman shall work in calmness and repose. Hers is the flower and fruit of human power, to whose perfect unfolding all other human power shall minister." The imposition of task-work is man's doing, not God's. It is the result of imperfect, not the object of perfect development. It is something which we are gradually to throw off, not systematically to take on. We see this in the invariable tendency of man as he advances in refinement to cherish woman, in the natural content of woman to be cherished. The instinct of love, the highest instinct of all, leads a man to defend a woman from everything that is harsh, hard, repellant, and gives him a new incentive to win fame and fortune.* The woman feels no such impulse.

* One of the most brilliant of the suffrage leaders—a man, however—in a letter to a labor-congress, says: "Eagerly do I share the sentiment that every man should support some woman—his heart's mate whom he loves, and for whom he strives. The chivalry which makes the strong sex the natural protector of the weak runs in every true man's blood. * * *

"Finally, after having gallantly received her into the trade of her

Her love moves her to untiring but silent service. It is ingenious and delicate, but it craves quiet and withdrawal. It sees, and watches, and waits. It controls by indirection —not the indirection of duplicity, but of instinct and wisdom. Its audacity is in affection and amusement. Its rebuke is chiefly suggestive. Its fashioning comes in tenderness. Where a man will be downright, a woman is content to be upright.

The misery of wrong-doing points the same way as the happiness of right-doing. A woman under the yoke, whether she be overburdened with the cooking, washing, and serving of her family, or with plowing and mining—indeed, many forms of housekeeping are more onerous and less remunerative than many of the employments of men—a woman under the yoke imposed by poverty or ignorance never becomes a man, but often she does become a worn-out woman, shattered in nerves, health, temper. In some countries it goes so far that she becomes a brutalized woman. In all countries her comeliness is marred, her physical delicacy destroyed, her real service lost. Thus Nature protests against the spoliation.

When women are cursed with their granted prayer, the hardest lot will fall to those whose lot is hardest now. It is the working-woman for whom all is asked, but it is the working-woman on whom the sword will be turned. She is the unfriended or the insufficiently befriended. Working-women are chiefly those whose male relatives are unable or unwilling to support them. "The loving and beloved wife," the "petted and caressed daughter" of the strong and suc-

choice, if then you can not bear to see her soiling her white hands with its grime, and you want to get her out of it, why, seize the first golden chance to *marry* her out of it, and, my word for it, she will then graciously leave you the monopoly all to yourselves!"

But now she says she won't!

cessful man, will be scarcely conscious of any change. In her well-guarded home it matters little to her whether she is loved by law or grace. But the unguarded woman must fight her fight with the same real and relative disability as now, but with an assumed, a legal equality which precludes privilege, though it can not disarm fate. While she has no vote, no defined power, her position is a constant appeal to chivalry, a constant rebuke to brutality. When she has seized the suffrage, her brutal employer and the not too gentle by-standers will not fail to say, "Now you have got your long-sought equality, make the most of it; ask no favors, and look out for yourself." Alas! but women are women still. Change thy laws, thy state is still the same. Good men will be good, but the bad and the selfish will have no cloak for their sin. With woman somewhat deferred to, with greed somewhat held in leash by shame, the life of the weak workwoman is hard enough. Is it likely to be easier when she has dismissed the advantages while retaining the disadvantages of sex, challenged her foes to combat, and dulled the swords of her defenders?

But "there is no work in the world which a man will not do better for having a woman at his side." That, too, I dispute. There is no work which a man will not do better for having a woman awaiting him at home; but there are few men, and, indeed, few women, who can stand constant association. It is the alternation of day and night that makes both pleasant and even tolerable. It is the temporary separation that gives zest, and even worth to companionship. *Is* a man better or happier for having a woman holding the plow, or swinging the axe, or pegging the shoe, or hammering the anvil beside him, than for thinking of her, tidy, and fresh, and bright at home? Is the true ideal of home one where the man and the woman shall both be out in the world at work, and the house left empty and silent? That is no home at all. The mother's presence in the house is not the fiat of tyranny or prejudice, but the natural craving of the heart. Do you say that her life there is often but a martyrdom; that she is as heated and hurried in her kitchen as her husband in his hay-field, and gets but a begrudged tithe of his wages? I know it a thousand times; but let us not, therefore, get her out of the kitchen into the hay-field, out of the frying-pan into the fire, at any wages whatever, still less at entirely uncertain ones. What I want is to take her from both frying-pan and fire into peace of mind, and tranquillity of nerve, and perfect physical comfort. But I must confess that even with the discomposure, anxiety, and overwork too often found, home is more home with the mother in it than with the mother out. I blame no woman for leaving it. If she has partially or wholly to support herself or her children, it is for herself to choose the mode, nor shall the way be fairly blocked to any honest work; but it is only the least of two or of many evils. It is not the greatest good. Men as yet need some help to their imagination. There remains still room for a little illusion. It is better for men, it is better for women, that each somewhat idealize the other. Much is lost when life has lost its atmosphere, and is reduced to naked facts. The most real relation between man and woman involves somewhat of wonderment and mystery, leaves ever something to be divined. Dissevered and defective as society may be, the most perfect trades' union of the sexes that the philosophic brain ever devised will not so nearly compass their real unity as has been compassed by the blind instincts of the generations. The one is a clever device, but it is a device, and can not hold. The other is a hindered but healthy growth; but it is a growth, and growth means life, and life prevails.

We speak often of results as if they were immediate and indisputable. We quote Judge Howe's letter from Wyoming as if that were conclusive regarding the effects of female suffrage. In two or three years, after the novelty is over, all will be quiet, and we shall marvel at the agitations of the past. But two or three years and two or three generations will hardly settle it. Whoever realizes how radical is the contemplated change, will not fail to see that only the slow growth of character can attest success or failure. It is not whether a woman shall or shall not be justice of the peace; it is whether the plane of national life shall be higher. It is pleasant to know that a half dozen female jurors were dignified and decorous, conscientious and resolute, and that lawyers and others were courteous to them, but it is not surprising. American women are accustomed to be dignified and resolute outside of jury-boxes, and to receive deference from American men outside of court-rooms; we should be altogether struck dumb with amazement to find that their presence in a court-room caused a sudden change of front. But this does not determine whether a public abnegation of sex, an indiscriminate commingling of men and women in all the walks of life, will intensify and increase in each sex those traits which are recognized as most desirable, will establish a purer and more intellectual society, a more delicate, refined, and upright national life. We resent the exclusion of women from colleges; but when Harvard and Yale are thrown open to girls, we have not gained the victory. We have only occupied the ground. The battle is still to be fought. It is impossible not to have grave doubts of the result. I believe, first, last, and always, in the highest education for women, and it is a waste to establish girls' colleges if existing ones will equally answer the purpose. But it is a significant fact that the chief opposition to the admission of girls to a certain college came from mothers who were unwilling to have their sons attend "mixed colleges." I am told that, even in a college which has been always open to girls, there is arising among the professors a query as to whether this is, on the whole, the wisest course. Theoretically it is unobjectionable. Separation in study, association in recitation, would seem adapted to give the best results—would seem to be most in the line of nature. But if there are qualities in human nature which make such alliance impracticable; if there are underlying facts, of which no theory takes account, but which experience brings inevitably to the surface; if, for some unexplained reason, mixed colleges prove less efficient for either sex than those which are prepared for one sex alone, we must recognize the fact, and shape our institutions accordingly, at whatever inconvenience or expense. I shall be only too well content if the main obstacle do not prove to be the disinclination of girls to submit to the rigor of an honorable college curriculum. When I see how indifferent they often are to the advantages already presented; when I see how they drop out of the high schools in the second and third years; when I hear that of the thirty courses of university lectures thrown open to women at Harvard, not more than half a dozen have had a paying audience of half a dozen each, I confess I am not sanguine. It is said that the possession of the suffrage will give new ambition, and change indifference to eagerness. But it is not easy to see why suffrage should do more for women than it does for men, and, in spite of our rhetoric, it leaves men very much as it finds them. The populace of New York seem to be no more intelligent, self-controlled, patriotic, or aspiring than they were on the day they were naturalized. The ignorant, drunken, and stubborn rustic has been voting as long as the scholar and gentleman at his side. I see far more light in the direction of the Vassar College—would it were not called a college!—and the Simmons Institute than in that of the ballot-box.

There is another kind of school, whose influence is scarcely less than that of the college, which is even harder to open to girls, yet without which it would be unjust to demand from them the work of boys. A lad of fourteen, for instance, is sent alone on a pleasure-tour to New York, Cleveland, Niagara, Chicago, to travel by himself, sleep at hotels, pay his own bills, find his own trains—in short, to get out of his week's vacation all that he can. Three boys of fifteen and seventeen take their boat, tent, and provisions, and spend their vacation in coasting, rowing and sailing by day, landing at night, preparing their meals, making inland excursions, sleeping in their tents, and drinking great draughts of health, information, and sagacity. A boy of sixteen goes to Europe alone, with such help as letters and careful directions may afford, to study and travel for a year. We can hardly overestimate the self-reliance, the curious, accurate, and valuable knowledge which such experiences bring. Are they possible for girls? Must not something more than law, more even than public opinion, be changed before we shall send girls of fourteen, sixteen, and seventeen out into the world unattended, to observe, judge, and learn for themselves? Would the most profound believer in woman's equality with man send her young daughter on a pleasure-tour through the country with no other anxiety than would follow her young son on the same journey? And until we can establish equality in the whole class of conditions of which this is but a single example, is it not idle to expect equality of results?

We will have women introduced into our courts of law as jurors, and at the first blush the presiding judge feels called upon to assure them that "it would be a most shameful scandal that in our temples of justice and in our courts of law any thing should be permitted which the most sensitive lady might not hear with propriety, and witness." But does not this at once put us on unequal ground? Is not the temple of justice immediately changed to a drawing-room? It is very much to be desired that we should all and always live under the drawing-room code of politeness and propriety; but, taking society as it is, high and low, if courts of law are to be temples of justice, how is it possible to exclude from them many things which must be extremely painful to sensitive persons, whether ladies or gentlemen? Indeed, courts of law are, in some sort, receptacles for impropriety, the appointed places where hatred, envy, malice, and all uncharitableness and uncleanness must be weighed, measured, and repressed for the health of society, and we can not adopt the principle of excluding testimony on account of its disagreeableness without subjecting clients to injustice and society to injury. Thus nature rises at once stronger than legislation. When you have secured equality before the law, you have not secured equality behind the law. Though in the relations of love and friendship a man and a woman can receive and return more confidence than two of the same sex, in the relations of competition, hostility, or indifference there must be, in high-minded persons, a deference, a restraint, a reticence not always favorable to the elucidation of truth or to the arrival at durable conclusions.

That some women of ability, education, and experience are well fitted for political activity no one will deny. It is not strange that such women, warm-hearted, benevolent, and conscious of power, seeing the suffering around them, should demand amplest scope. But if their freedom involves a chain to vastly superior numbers who have neither their gifts nor their opportunities, is it too much to ask that they should forego its full possession? To say that no one will force women to vote against their will is but partial truth. When women have the power to vote, it becomes their duty. A moral coercion is put upon them which, if women are what they are represented to be, will operate, and in any event ought to operate, as effectively as physical force. I preach no such doctrine as that women ought to "trust" their husbands, fathers, and brothers. No one should intrust to another what he ought to do himself. Men are not given to women to be trusted, but to be trained. They may, indeed, be trusted as a part of their training—as Dr. Arnold trusted little Arthur to big Tom Brown, not to protect Arthur, but to save Tom. It is simply that women can not do every thing; that they have at least no more fitness than men to mould affairs, and a great deal more fitness than men to mould the human race; that men, with all their failures, succeed better in the lower work of politics and business than they do in the higher work of humanity; and that it is, therefore, better that politics should be left to men than that men should be left to themselves. Moreover, the freedom of the many requires the repression of the few in only one direction. Every weapon of warfare but one they may wield without stint. They may promulgate their views, exert their influence to the height of their ability and desire, through pulpit, press, and platform. In politics they can command every thing but office—I believe, indeed, they are not wholly excluded from office; and surely it is not office for which we are making all this ado. Some of the most influential men in the old anti-slavery times did not vote, and were as morally ineligible to office as are women legally; and some of the most influential anti-slavery reformers were women. Let a woman have real power, and no party but will be glad to avail itself of her pen and voice, and to pay her all personal honor, and ample pecuniary reward. If she have a taste for mechanics, or medicine, or law, for learning or science, let her cultivate it to the last degree of excellence, assured that she who attains skill in any department is not only enriching her own life, but is helping all women; for no argument is so incontrovertible as success. Every woman who does good work of any kind—without or within, on land or sea—every woman who commands high wages for her work; every woman who invents some new method of usefulness; every woman who succeeds in a trade or occupation hitherto unappropriated by women; every woman who successfully conducts business, not because she particularly likes it, nor because it is necessary to herself, but for the encouragement and assistance of those to whom some business is necessary—all these are rendering to their sex and to society invaluable service. Every woman who goes honorably through a difficult course of mental or mechanical training gives an incentive to all women. Neither literary nor political intelligence, nor practical skill, unfits a woman for home. They make her more ready of hand, more fertile in resource. Handicraft is not woman's best preparation for her natural work, but neither is it the worst. When it is seen that the highest education does not make a woman pedantic and angular, but rather endows her with grace and tact; that political knowledge, patriotic interest, and practical skill do not make her opinionated, bellicose, self-asserting, but forbearing, appreciative, considerate, comprehensive, prejudice against learning and politics will vanish. And the highest universities calling to woman, and every facility for trade and traffic afforded her, will never compel, will only invite and allure. It can all be gained without diminishing the freedom, imposing upon the conscience, adding to the burden, or arousing the opposition of any woman, but not without attracting the attention, and tempting the admiration and emulation of all. And if, by-and-by, science and art assume the alien work which now weighs woman down, and leisure, and observation, and thought shall make her insight, her judgment, her quick sympathy so valuable that men seek her co-operation in all their plans, then such co-operation will become but a part of her natural function, and suffrage—if it shall be called suffrage—will come harmoniously and beneficently. But to come now with hatred, and hooting, and howling from lewd fellows of the baser sort, against the wish and the conviction of a majority of both men and women, to a class already overburdened with unnatural work, and in a society which has as yet but a rude and vague conception of the difference between male and female work—this is a process so unnatural that I see not how the effects can avoid becoming disastrous except by becoming insignificant.

Yet, if women insist upon the suffrage, men must grant it. If women claim the consequences and the burdens, how can they justly be hindered from exercising the powers? But we have a right to demand that men shall not yield it at the call of any clique, committee, or convention, but only of a certified majority of women. They shall make sure that women do want it, and not impose a burden on the mistaken supposition that they are granting a request.

With women, the danger is that the case go by default. The hardship to which many women are subjected is real, the remedy proposed is superficially reasonable, its advocacy is persistent and palpable; opposition, from the nature of things, is more or less passive. Men are strong and dominant, and they vote. Women have as good a right to vote as men. Let them vote, and they also will become strong and dominant. Thus lightly, and without at all comprehending the extent of the revolution which must follow if the suffrage amounts to any thing, women may assume, or permit to be imposed upon them, a task from which they will find it difficult to disembarrass themselves.

In the mean time, is it not possible for women to forget

the foolish and exasperating arguments which have been turned against them, and yet to respect the opposition out of which those arguments sprung, and which is infinitely wider and deeper than they? Never a cause escaped wholly undisgraced by its own followers. False assumptions and degrading implications are no new things under the sun. But truth is ever to be sought along the pathway of error. Let us cease to take the wings of the morning and fly to the uttermost parts of the earth to find reasons for the existing state of society, but admit simply and frankly at the outset that things are where they are because they are what they are. We shall then be in the line of discovery and advancement. If the equality of man and woman is the problem of the race, we have no data to reason from. The past is wholly inconsequent, and the future is but guess-work. But if we relinquish the idea of equality, and substitute for it unity, apprehending the perfect being as man created by God male and female, and not two men or two women, even the fighting facts of history cluster into symmetry, the harshest discords soften into harmony, and out of the depths of failure and anguish comes the certain promise of peace.

Looking back along the progress of the centuries, we find that woman has attained power and pre-eminence chiefly in the realms of the spirit. Man has subdued the world, but woman has subdued man. Mind and muscle have won his victories; love and loveliness have gained hers. No monarch has been so great, no peasant so lowly, that he has not been glad to lay his best at the feet of a woman. Is there no significance in this? Does it mean simply that men have been trained to material victory, women to spiritual conquests? As well might we adopt the famous theory that language was invented by a convention of learned societies assembled for that purpose.

The degradation and suffering of woman does not contradict, but confirm this hypothesis. In the race as well as the individual, spiritual development comes not first. The sweetest saint in the calendar was a little animal for the first months of his life. In the ruder stages of the human race physical life is high, but spiritual life is faint and feeble. Woman, man's inner, finer, dearer self, is held in abeyance. She can be only spiritually discerned, but his spirit is scarcely yet roused into life, and she becomes but a hewer of wood and a drawer of water; though even then the light which he can not see shines sometimes into his closed eyes and warms his torpid soul; then, out of a barbaric past, down the gloomy ages, trembles a legend of truth and tenderness that makes all ages kin. In the lowest, as in the highest states of life, man treats woman precisely as he treats his own spiritual nature. If all his powers are bent to self-indulgence or to self-glorification, woman does but minister to his pleasures, or emphasize his grandeur. As he rises in the scale, she rises in his estimation. The more noble, truthful, self-sacrificing, benevolent he becomes, the more tenderly he cherishes, the more devoutly he serves where once he exacted and despised. Then the story of the Genesis is evolved. Out of his love springs her life. She who was his prey becomes his protector. She saves him from himself. Fenced in by his care from outward hurt and hinderance, she guards him, consciously or unconsciously, from his baser impulses, from his downward tendency, from his reckless strength and regnant will.

Thus it has been, and thus it shall be under the sun. The plant which flowered to grace, and color, and fragrance amid the confusions of the past, drew its life from no chance source, struck its roots into no shallow soil. Thorns and brambles abound, and many a heart will faint before the wilderness shall blossom into the garden of the Lord. A thousand seeds may be planted, and a thousand saplings transplanted, and no one of them utterly fail; but it is this one growth, springing spontaneously from the soil, tender, yet hardy, as brave as beautiful, that shall rise, and broaden, and bourgeon into the tree of life, whose leaves are for the healing of the nations.

THE END.

VALUABLE STANDARD WORKS

FOR PUBLIC AND PRIVATE LIBRARIES,

PUBLISHED BY HARPER & BROTHERS, NEW YORK.

☞ *For a full List of Books suitable for Libraries, see* HARPER & BROTHERS' TRADE-LIST *and* CATALOGUE, *which may be had gratuitously on application to the Publishers personally, or by letter enclosing Five Cents.*

☞ HARPER & BROTHERS *will send any of the following works by mail, postage prepaid, to any part of the United States, on receipt of the price.*

MOTLEY'S DUTCH REPUBLIC. The Rise of the Dutch Republic. By JOHN LOTHROP MOTLEY, LL.D., D.C.L. With a Portrait of William of Orange. 3 vols., 8vo, Cloth, $10 50.

MOTLEY'S UNITED NETHERLANDS. History of the United Netherlands: from the Death of William the Silent to the Twelve Years' Truce—1609. With a full View of the English-Dutch Struggle against Spain, and of the Origin and Destruction of the Spanish Armada. By JOHN LOTHROP MOTLEY, LL.D., D.C.L. Portraits. 4 vols., 8vo, Cloth, $14 00.

NAPOLEON'S LIFE OF CÆSAR. The History of Julius Cæsar. By His Imperial Majesty NAPOLEON III. Two Volumes ready. Library Edition, 8vo, Cloth, $3 50 per vol.
Maps to Vols. I. and II. sold separately. Price $1 50 each, NET.

HAYDN'S DICTIONARY OF DATES, relating to all Ages and Nations. For Universal Reference. Edited by BENJAMIN VINCENT, Assistant Secretary and Keeper of the Library of the Royal Institution of Great Britain; and Revised for the Use of American Readers. 8vo, Cloth, $5 00; Sheep, $6 00.

MACGREGOR'S ROB ROY ON THE JORDAN. The Rob Roy on the Jordan, Nile, Red Sea, and Gennesareth, &c. A Canoe Cruise in Palestine and Egypt, and the Waters of Damascus. By J. MACGREGOR, M.A. With Maps and Illustrations. Crown 8vo, Cloth, $2 50.

WALLACE'S MALAY ARCHIPELAGO. The Malay Archipelago: the Land of the Orang-Utan and the Bird of Paradise. A Narrative of Travel, 1854-1862. With Studies of Man and Nature. By ALFRED RUSSEL WALLACE. With Ten Maps and Fifty-one Elegant Illustrations. Crown 8vo, Cloth, $3 50.

WHYMPER'S ALASKA. Travel and Adventure in the Territory of Alaska, formerly Russian America—now Ceded to the United States—and in various other parts of the North Pacific. By FREDERICK WHYMPER. With Map and Illustrations. Crown 8vo, Cloth, $2 50.

ORTON'S ANDES AND THE AMAZON. The Andes and the Amazon or, Across the Continent of South America. By JAMES ORTON, M.A., Professor of Natural History in Vassar College, Poughkeepsie, N. Y., and Corresponding Member of the Academy of Natural Sciences, Philadelphia. With a New Map of Equatorial America and numerous Illustrations. Crown 8vo, Cloth, $2 00.

2 Harper & Brothers' Valuable Standard Works.

LOSSING'S FIELD-BOOK OF THE REVOLUTION. Pictorial Field-Book of the Revolution; or, Illustrations, by Pen and Pencil, of the History, Biography, Scenery, Relics, and Traditions of the War for Independence. By BENSON J. LOSSING. 2 vols., 8vo, Cloth, $14 00; Sheep, $15 00; Half Calf, $18 00; Full Turkey Morocco, $22 00.

LOSSING'S FIELD-BOOK OF THE WAR OF 1812. Pictorial Field-Book of the War of 1812; or, Illustrations, by Pen and Pencil, of the History, Biography, Scenery, Relics, and Traditions of the Last War for American Independence. By BENSON J. LOSSING. With several hundred Engravings on Wood, by Lossing and Barritt, chiefly from Original Sketches by the Author. 1088 pages, 8vo, Cloth, $7 00; Sheep, $8 50; Half Calf, $10 00.

WINCHELL'S SKETCHES OF CREATION. Sketches of Creation: a Popular View of some of the Grand Conclusions of the Sciences in reference to the History of Matter and of Life. Together with a Statement of the Intimations of Science respecting the Primordial Condition and the Ultimate Destiny of the Earth and the Solar System. By ALEXANDER WINCHELL, LL.D., Professor of Geology, Zoology, and Botany in the University of Michigan, and Director of the State Geological Survey. With Illustrations. 12mo, Cloth, $2 00.

WHITE'S MASSACRE OF ST. BARTHOLOMEW. The Massacre of St. Bartholomew: Preceded by a History of the Religious Wars in the Reign of Charles IX. By HENRY WHITE, M.A. With Illustrations. 8vo, Cloth, $1 75.

ALFORD'S GREEK TESTAMENT. The Greek Testament: with a critically-revised Text; a Digest of Various Readings; Marginal References to Verbal and Idiomatic Usage; Prolegomena; and a Critical and Exegetical Commentary. For the Use of Theological Students and Ministers. By HENRY ALFORD, D.D., Dean of Canterbury. Vol. I., containing the Four Gospels. 944 pages, 8vo, Cloth, $6 00; Sheep, $6 50.

ABBOTT'S FREDERICK THE GREAT. The History of Frederick the Second, called Frederick the Great. By JOHN S. C. ABBOTT. Elegantly Illustrated. 8vo, Cloth, $5 00.

ABBOTT'S HISTORY OF THE FRENCH REVOLUTION. The French Revolution of 1789, as viewed in the Light of Republican Institutions. By JOHN S. C. ABBOTT. With 100 Engravings. 8vo, Cloth, $5 00.

ABBOTT'S NAPOLEON BONAPARTE. The History of Napoleon Bonaparte. By JOHN S. C. ABBOTT. With Maps, Woodcuts, and Portraits on Steel. 2 vols., 8vo, Cloth, $10 00.

ABBOTT'S NAPOLEON AT ST. HELENA; or, Interesting Anecdotes and Remarkable Conversations of the Emperor during the Five and a Half Years of his Captivity. Collected from the Memorials of Las Casas, O'Meara, Montholon, Antommarchi, and others. By JOHN S. C. ABBOTT. With Illustrations. 8vo, Cloth, $5 00.

ADDISON'S COMPLETE WORKS. The Works of Joseph Addison, embracing the whole of the "Spectator." Complete in 3 vols., 8vo, Cloth, $6 00.

ALCOCK'S JAPAN. The Capital of the Tycoon: a Narrative of a Three Years' Residence in Japan. By Sir RUTHERFORD ALCOCK, K.C.B., Her Majesty's Envoy Extraordinary and Minister Plenipotentiary in Japan. With Maps and Engravings. 2 vols., 12mo, Cloth, $3 50.

ALISON'S HISTORY OF EUROPE. FIRST SERIES: From the Commencement of the French Revolution, in 1789, to the Restoration of the Bourbons, in 1815. [In addition to the Notes on Chapter LXXVI., which correct the errors of the original work concerning the United States, a copious Analytical Index has been appended to this American edition.] SECOND SERIES: From the Fall of Napoleon, in 1815, to the Accession of Louis Napoleon, in 1852. 8 vols., 8vo, Cloth, $16 00.

Harper & Brothers' Valuable Standard Works. 3

BALDWIN'S PRE-HISTORIC NATIONS. Pre-Historic Nations; or, Inquiries concerning some of the Great Peoples and Civilizations of Antiquity, and their Probable Relation to a still Older Civilization of the Ethiopians or Cushites of Arabia. By JOHN D. BALDWIN, Member of the American Oriental Society. 12mo, Cloth, $1 75.

BARTH'S NORTH AND CENTRAL AFRICA. Travels and Discoveries in North and Central Africa: being a Journal of an Expedition undertaken under the Auspices of H.B.M.'s Government, in the Years 1849–1855. By HENRY BARTH, Ph.D., D.C.L. Illustrated. 3 vols., 8vo, Cloth, $12 00.

HENRY WARD BEECHER'S SERMONS. Sermons by HENRY WARD BEECHER, Plymouth Church, Brooklyn. Selected from Published and Unpublished Discourses, and Revised by their Author. With Steel Portrait. Complete in Two Vols., 8vo, Cloth, $5 00.

LYMAN BEECHER'S AUTOBIOGRAPHY, &c. Autobiography, Correspondence, &c., of Lyman Beecher, D.D. Edited by his Son, CHARLES BEECHER. With Three Steel Portraits, and Engravings on Wood. In 2 vols., 12mo, Cloth, $5 00.

BELLOWS'S OLD WORLD. The Old World in its New Face: Impressions of Europe in 1867–1868. By HENRY W. BELLOWS. 2 vols., 12mo, Cloth, $3 50.

BOSWELL'S JOHNSON. The Life of Samuel Johnson, LL.D. Including a Journey to the Hebrides. By JAMES BOSWELL, Esq. A New Edition, with numerous Additions and Notes. By JOHN WILSON CROKER, LL.D., F.R.S. Portrait of Boswell. 2 vols., 8vo, Cloth, $4 00.

BRODHEAD'S HISTORY OF NEW YORK. History of the State of New York. By JOHN ROMEYN BRODHEAD. 1609–1691. 2 vols. 8vo, Cloth, $3 00 per vol.

BROUGHAM'S AUTOBIOGRAPHY. Life and Times of HENRY, LORD BROUGHAM. Written by Himself. In Three Volumes. 12mo, Cloth, $2 00 per vol.

BULWER'S PROSE WORKS. Miscellaneous Prose Works of Edward Bulwer, Lord Lytton. 2 vols., 12mo, Cloth, $3 50.

BULWER'S HORACE. The Odes and Epodes of Horace. A Metrical Translation into English. With Introduction and Commentaries. By LORD LYTTON. With Latin Text from the Editions of Orelli, Macleane, and Yonge. 12mo, Cloth, $1 75.

BULWER'S KING ARTHUR. King Arthur. A Poem. By EARL LYTTON. New Edition. 12mo, Cloth, $1 75.

BURNS'S LIFE AND WORKS. The Life and Works of Robert Burns. Edited by ROBERT CHAMBERS. 4 vols., 12mo, Cloth, $6 00.

REINDEER, DOGS, AND SNOW-SHOES. A Journal of Siberian Travel and Explorations made in the Years 1865–'67. By RICHARD J. BUSH, late of the Russo-American Telegraph Expedition. Illustrated. Crown 8vo, Cloth, $3 00.

CARLYLE'S FREDERICK THE GREAT. History of Friedrich II., called Frederick the Great. By THOMAS CARLYLE. Portraits, Maps, Plans, &c. 6 vols., 12mo, Cloth, $12 00.

CARLYLE'S FRENCH REVOLUTION. History of the French Revolution. Newly Revised by the Author, with Index, &c. 2 vols., 12mo, Cloth, $3 50.

CARLYLE'S OLIVER CROMWELL. Letters and Speeches of Oliver Cromwell. With Elucidations and Connecting Narrative. 2 vols., 12mo, Cloth, $3 50.

CHALMERS'S POSTHUMOUS WORKS. The Posthumous Works of Dr. Chalmers. Edited by his Son-in-Law, Rev. WILLIAM HANNA, LL.D. Complete in 9 vols., 12mo, Cloth, $13 50.

4   Harper & Brothers' Valuable Standard Works.

COLERIDGE'S COMPLETE WORKS. The Complete Works of Samuel Taylor Coleridge. With an Introductory Essay upon his Philosophical and Theological Opinions. Edited by Professor SHEDD. Complete in Seven Vols. With a fine Portrait. Small 8vo, Cloth, $10 50.

CURTIS'S HISTORY OF THE CONSTITUTION. History of the Origin, Formation, and Adoption of the Constitution of the United States. By GEORGE TICKNOR CURTIS. 2 vols., 8vo, Cloth, $6 00.

DRAPER'S CIVIL WAR. History of the American Civil War. By JOHN W. DRAPER, M.D., LL.D., Professor of Chemistry and Physiology in the University of New York. In Three Vols. 8vo, Cloth, $3 50 per vol.

DRAPER'S INTELLECTUAL DEVELOPMENT OF EUROPE. A History of the Intellectual Development of Europe. By JOHN W. DRAPER, M.D., LL.D., Professor of Chemistry and Physiology in the University of New York. 8vo, Cloth, $5 00.

DRAPER'S AMERICAN CIVIL POLICY. Thoughts on the Future Civil Policy of America. By JOHN W. DRAPER, M.D., LL.D., Professor of Chemistry and Physiology in the University of New York. Crown 8vo, Cloth, $2 50.

DAVIS'S CARTHAGE. Carthage and her Remains: being an Account of the Excavations and Researches on the Site of the Phœnician Metropolis in Africa and other adjacent Places. Conducted under the Auspices of Her Majesty's Government. By Dr. DAVIS, F.R.G.S. Profusely Illustrated with Maps, Woodcuts, Chromo-Lithographs, &c. 8vo, Cloth, $4 00.

DOOLITTLE'S CHINA. Social Life of the Chinese: with some Account of their Religious, Governmental, Educational, and Business Customs and Opinions. With special but not exclusive Reference to Fuhchau. By Rev. JUSTUS DOOLITTLE, Fourteen Years Member of the Fuhchau Mission of the American Board. Illustrated with more than 150 characteristic Engravings on Wood. 2 vols., 12mo, Cloth, $5 00.

DU CHAILLU'S AFRICA. Explorations and Adventures in Equatorial Africa: with Accounts of the Manners and Customs of the People, and of the Chase of the Gorilla, the Crocodile, Leopard, Elephant, Hippopotamus, and other Animals. By PAUL B. DU CHAILLU. Numerous Illustrations. 8vo, Cloth, $5 00.

DU CHAILLU'S ASHANGO LAND. A Journey to Ashango Land, and Further Penetration into Equatorial Africa. By PAUL B. DU CHAILLU. New Edition. Handsomely Illustrated. 8vo, Cloth, $5 00.

EDGEWORTH'S (MISS) NOVELS. With Engravings. 10 vols., 12mo, Cloth, $15 00.

GIBBON'S ROME. History of the Decline and Fall of the Roman Empire. By EDWARD GIBBON. With Notes by Rev. H. H. MILMAN and M. GUIZOT. A new Cheap Edition. To which is added a complete Index of the whole Work, and a Portrait of the Author. 6 vols., 12mo, Cloth, $9 00.

GROTE'S HISTORY OF GREECE. 12 vols., 12mo, Cloth, $18 00.

HALE'S (MRS.) WOMAN'S RECORD. Woman's Record; or, Biographical Sketches of all Distinguished Women, from the Creation to the Present Time. Arranged in Four Eras, with Selections from Female Writers of each Era. By Mrs. SARAH JOSEPHA HALE. Illustrated with more than 200 Portraits. 8vo, Cloth, $5 00.

HALL'S ARCTIC RESEARCHES. Arctic Researches and Life among the Esquimaux: being the Narrative of an Expedition in Search of Sir John Franklin, in the Years 1860, 1861, and 1862. By CHARLES FRANCIS HALL. With Maps and 100 Illustrations. The Illustrations are from Original Drawings by Charles Parsons, Henry L. Stephens, Solomon Eytinge, W. S. L. Jewett, and Granville Perkins, after Sketches by Captain Hall. 8vo, Cloth, $5 00.

HALLAM'S CONSTITUTIONAL HISTORY OF ENGLAND, from the Accession of Henry VII. to the Death of George II. 8vo, Cloth, $2 00.

Harper & Brothers' Valuable Standard Works. 5

HALLAM'S LITERATURE. Introduction to the Literature of Europe during the Fifteenth, Sixteenth, and Seventeenth Centuries. By HENRY HALLAM. 2 vols., 8vo, Cloth, $4 00.

HALLAM'S MIDDLE AGES. State of Europe during the Middle Ages. By HENRY HALLAM. 8vo, Cloth, $2 00.

HILDRETH'S HISTORY OF THE UNITED STATES. FIRST SERIES: From the First Settlement of the Country to the Adoption of the Federal Constitution. SECOND SERIES: From the Adoption of the Federal Constitution to the End of the Sixteenth Congress. 6 vols., 8vo, Cloth, $18 00.

HARPER'S NEW CLASSICAL LIBRARY. Literal Translations. The following Volumes are now ready. Portraits. 12mo, Cloth, $1 50 each.

CÆSAR.—VIRGIL.—SALLUST.—HORACE.—CICERO'S ORATIONS.—CICERO'S OFFICES, &c.—CICERO ON ORATORY AND ORATORS.—TACITUS (2 vols.).—TERENCE.—SOPHOCLES.—JUVENAL.—XENOPHON.—HOMER'S ILIAD.—HOMER'S ODYSSEY.—HERODOTUS.—DEMOSTHENES.—THUCYDIDES.—ÆSCHYLUS.—EURIPIDES (2 vols.).—LIVY (2 vols.).

HUME'S HISTORY OF ENGLAND. History of England, from the Invasion of Julius Cæsar to the Abdication of James II., 1688. By DAVID HUME. A new Edition, with the Author's last Corrections and Improvements. To which is prefixed a short Account of his Life, written by Himself. With a Portrait of the Author. 6 vols., 12mo, Cloth, $9 00.

HELPS'S SPANISH CONQUEST. The Spanish Conquest in America, and its Relation to the History of Slavery and to the Government of Colonies. By ARTHUR HELPS. 4 vols., 12mo, Cloth, $6 00.

JAY'S WORKS. Complete Works of Rev. William Jay: comprising his Sermons, Family Discourses, Morning and Evening Exercises for every Day in the Year, Family Prayers, &c. Author's Enlarged Edition, revised. 3 vols., 8vo, Cloth, $6 00.

JEFFERSON'S DOMESTIC LIFE. The Domestic Life of Thomas Jefferson: compiled from Family Letters and Reminiscences by his Great-Granddaughter, SARAH N. RANDOLPH. With Illustrations. Crown 8vo, Illuminated Cloth, Beveled Edges, $2 50.

JOHNSON'S COMPLETE WORKS. The Works of Samuel Johnson, LL.D. With an Essay on his Life and Genius, by ARTHUR MURPHY, Esq. Portrait of Johnson. 2 vols., 8vo, Cloth, $4 00.

KINGLAKE'S CRIMEAN WAR. The Invasion of the Crimea, and an Account of its Progress down to the Death of Lord Raglan. By ALEXANDER WILLIAM KINGLAKE. With Maps and Plans. Two Vols. ready. 12mo, Cloth, $2 00 per vol.

KINGSLEY'S WEST INDIES. At Last: A Christmas in the West Indies. By CHARLES KINGSLEY. Illustrated. 12mo, Cloth, $1 50.

KRUMMACHER'S DAVID, KING OF ISRAEL. David, the King of Israel: a Portrait drawn from Bible History and the Book of Psalms. By FREDERICK WILLIAM KRUMMACHER, D.D., Author of "Elijah the Tishbite," &c. Translated under the express Sanction of the Author by the Rev. M. G. EASTON, M.A. With a Letter from Dr. Krummacher to his American Readers, and a Portrait. 12mo, Cloth, $1 75.

LAMB'S COMPLETE WORKS. The Works of Charles Lamb. Comprising his Letters, Poems, Essays of Elia, Essays upon Shakspeare, Hogarth, &c., and a Sketch of his Life, with the Final Memorials, by T. NOON TALFOURD. Portrait. 2 vols., 12mo, Cloth, $3 00.

LIVINGSTONE'S SOUTH AFRICA. Missionary Travels and Researches in South Africa; including a Sketch of Sixteen Years' Residence in the Interior of Africa, and a Journey from the Cape of Good Hope to Loando on the West Coast; thence across the Continent, down the River Zambesi, to the Eastern Ocean. By DAVID LIVINGSTONE, LL.D., D.C.L. With Portrait, Maps by Arrowsmith, and numerous Illustrations. 8vo, Cloth, $4 50.

6   Harper & Brothers' Valuable Standard Works.

LIVINGSTONE'S ZAMBESI. Narrative of an Expedition to the Zambesi and its Tributaries, and of the Discovery of the Lakes Shirwa and Nyassa. 1858-1864. By DAVID and CHARLES LIVINGSTONE. With Map and Illustrations. 8vo, Cloth, $5 00.

MARCY'S ARMY LIFE ON THE BORDER. Thirty Years of Army Life on the Border. Comprising Descriptions of the Indian Nomads of the Plains; Explorations of New Territory; a Trip across the Rocky Mountains in the Winter; Descriptions of the Habits of Different Animals found in the West, and the Methods of Hunting them; with Incidents in the Life of Different Frontier Men, &c., &c. By Brevet Brigadier-General R. B. MARCY, U.S.A., Author of "The Prairie Traveler." With numerous Illustrations. 8vo, Cloth, Beveled Edges, $3 00.

M'CLINTOCK & STRONG'S CYCLOPÆDIA. Cyclopædia of Biblical, Theological, and Ecclesiastical Literature. Prepared by the Rev. JOHN M'CLINTOCK, D.D., and JAMES STRONG, S.T.D. *3 vols. now ready.* Royal 8vo. Price per vol., Cloth, $5 00; Sheep, $6 00; Half Morocco, $8 00.

MOSHEIM'S ECCLESIASTICAL HISTORY, Ancient and Modern; in which the Rise, Progress, and Variation of Church Power are considered in their Connection with the State of Learning and Philosophy, and the Political History of Europe during that Period. Translated, with Notes, &c., by A. MACLAINE, D.D. A New Edition, continued to 1826, by C. COOTE, LL.D. 2 vols., 8vo, Cloth, $4 00.

MACAULAY'S HISTORY OF ENGLAND. The History of England from the Accession of James II. By THOMAS BABINGTON MACAULAY. With an Original Portrait of the Author. 5 vols., 8vo, Cloth, $10 00; 12mo, Cloth, $7 50.

NEVIUS'S CHINA. China and the Chinese: a General Description of the Country and its Inhabitants; its Civilization and Form of Government; its Religious and Social Institutions; its Intercourse with other Nations; and its Present Condition and Prospects. By the Rev. JOHN L. NEVIUS, Ten Years a Missionary in China. With a Map and Illustrations. 12mo, Cloth, $1 75.

OLIN'S (DR.) LIFE AND LETTERS. 2 vols., 12mo, Cloth, $3 00.

OLIN'S (DR.) TRAVELS. Travels in Egypt, Arabia Petræa, and the Holy Land. Engravings. 2 vols., 8vo, Cloth, $3 00.

OLIN'S (DR.) WORKS. The Works of Stephen Olin, D.D., late President of the Wesleyan University. 2 vols., 12mo, Cloth, $3 00.

OLIPHANT'S CHINA AND JAPAN. Narrative of the Earl of Elgin's Mission to China and Japan, in the Years 1857, '58, '59. By LAURENCE OLIPHANT, Private Secretary to Lord Elgin. Illustrations. 8vo, Cloth, $3 50.

OLIPHANT'S (MRS.) LIFE OF EDWARD IRVING. The Life of Edward Irving, Minister of the National Scotch Church, London. Illustrated by his Journals and Correspondence. By Mrs. OLIPHANT. Portrait. 8vo, Cloth, $3 50.

POETS OF THE NINETEENTH CENTURY. The Poets of the Nineteenth Century. Selected and Edited by the Rev. ROBERT ARIS WILLMOTT. With English and American Additions, arranged by EVERT A. DUYCKINCK, Editor of "Cyclopædia of American Literature." Comprising Selections from the Greatest Authors of the Age. Superbly Illustrated with 132 Engravings from Designs by the most Eminent Artists. In elegant small 4to form, printed on Superfine Tinted Paper, richly bound in extra Cloth, Beveled, Gilt Edges, $6 00; Half Calf, $6 00; Full Turkey Morocco, $10 00.

RAWLINSON'S MANUAL OF ANCIENT HISTORY. A Manual of Ancient History, from the Earliest Times to the Fall of the Western Empire. Comprising the History of Chaldæa, Assyria, Media, Babylonia, Lydia, Phœnicia, Syria, Judæa, Egypt, Carthage, Persia, Greece, Macedonia, Parthia, and Rome. By GEORGE RAWLINSON, M.A., Camden Professor of Ancient History in the University of Oxford. 12mo, Cloth, $2 50.

Harper & Brothers' Valuable Standard Works. 7

RECLUS'S THE EARTH. The Earth: a Descriptive History of the Phenomena and Life of the Globe. By ÉLISÉE RECLUS. Translated by the late B. B. Woodward, and Edited by Henry Woodward. With 234 Maps and Illustrations, and 23 Page Maps printed in Colors. 8vo, Cloth, $5 00.

SMILES'S LIFE OF THE STEPHENSONS. The Life of George Stephenson, and of his Son, Robert Stephenson; comprising, also, a History of the Invention and Introduction of the Railway Locomotive. By SAMUEL SMILES, Author of "Self-Help," &c. With Steel Portraits and numerous Illustrations. 8vo, Cloth, $3 00.

SMILES'S HISTORY OF THE HUGUENOTS. The Huguenots: their Settlements, Churches, and Industries in England and Ireland. By SAMUEL SMILES. With an Appendix relating to the Huguenots in America. Crown 8vo, Cloth, $1 75.

SHAKSPEARE. The Dramatic Works of William Shakspeare, with the Corrections and Illustrations of Dr. JOHNSON, G. STEEVENS, and others. Revised by ISAAC REED. Engravings. 6 vols., Royal 12mo, Cloth, $9 00.

SPEKE'S AFRICA. Journal of the Discovery of the Source of the Nile. By Captain JOHN HANNING SPEKE, Captain H. M.'s Indian Army, Fellow and Gold Medalist of the Royal Geographical Society, Hon. Corresponding Member and Gold Medalist of the French Geographical Society, &c. With Maps and Portraits and numerous Illustrations, chiefly from Drawings by Captain Grant. 8vo, Cloth, uniform with Livingstone, Barth, Burton, &c., $4 00.

SPRING'S SERMONS. Pulpit Ministrations; or, Sabbath Readings. A Series of Discourses on Christian Doctrine and Duty. By Rev. GARDINER SPRING, D.D., Pastor of the Brick Presbyterian Church in the City of New York. Portrait on Steel. 2 vols., 8vo, Cloth, $6 00.

STRICKLAND'S (MISS) QUEENS OF SCOTLAND. Lives of the Queens of Scotland and English Princesses connected with the Regal Succession of Great Britain. By AGNES STRICKLAND. 8 vols., 12mo, Cloth, $12 00.

THE STUDENT'S SERIES.
France. Engravings. 12mo, Cloth, $2 00.
Gibbon. Engravings. 12mo, Cloth, $2 00.
Greece. Engravings. 12mo, Cloth, $2 00.
Hume. Engravings. 12mo, Cloth, $2 00.
Rome. By Liddell. Engravings. 12mo, Cloth, $2 00.
Old Testament History. Engravings. 12mo, Cloth, $2 00.
New Testament History. Engravings. 12mo, Cloth, $2 00.
Strickland's Queens of England. Abridged. Engravings. 12mo, Cloth, $2 00.
Ancient History of the East. 12mo, Cloth, $2 00.
Hallam's Middle Ages. 12mo, Cloth, $2 00.
Lyell's Elements of Geology. 12mo, Cloth, $2 00.

TENNYSON'S COMPLETE POEMS. The Complete Poems of Alfred Tennyson, Poet Laureate. With numerous Illustrations by Eminent Artists, and Three Characteristic Portraits. 8vo, Paper, 75 cents; Cloth, $1 25.

THOMSON'S LAND AND THE BOOK. The Land and the Book; or, Biblical Illustrations drawn from the Manners and Customs, the Scenes and the Scenery of the Holy Land. By W. M. THOMSON, D.D., Twenty-five Years a Missionary of the A.B.C.F.M. in Syria and Palestine. With two elaborate Maps of Palestine, an accurate Plan of Jerusalem, and several hundred Engravings, representing the Scenery, Topography, and Productions of the Holy Land, and the Costumes, Manners, and Habits of the People. 2 large 12mo vols., Cloth, $5 00.

TICKNOR'S HISTORY OF SPANISH LITERATURE. With Criticisms on the particular Works, and Biographical Notices of Prominent Writers. 3 vols., 8vo, Cloth, $5 00.

TYERMAN'S WESLEY. The Life and Times of the Rev. John Wesley, M.A., Founder of the Methodists. By the Rev. LUKE TYERMAN, Author of "The Life of Rev. Samuel Wesley." Portraits. 3 vols., Crown 8vo.

8 Harper & Brothers' Valuable Standard Works.

VÁMBÉRY'S CENTRAL ASIA. Travels in Central Asia. Being the Account of a Journey from Teheran across the Turkoman Desert, on the Eastern Shore of the Caspian, to Khiva, Bokhara, and Samarcand, performed in the Year 1863. By ARMINIUS VÁMBÉRY, Member of the Hungarian Academy of Pesth, by whom he was sent on this Scientific Mission. With Map and Woodcuts. 8vo, Cloth, $4 50.

WOOD'S HOMES WITHOUT HANDS. Homes Without Hands: being a Description of the Habitations of Animals, classed according to their Principle of Construction. By J. G. WOOD, M.A., F.L.S. With about 140 Illustrations. 8vo, Cloth, Beveled Edges, $4 50.

WILKINSON'S ANCIENT EGYPTIANS. A Popular Account of their Manners and Customs, condensed from his larger Work, with some New Matter. Illustrated with 500 Woodcuts. 2 vols., 12mo, Cloth, $3 50.

ANTHON'S SMITH'S DICTIONARY OF ANTIQUITIES. A Dictionary of Greek and Roman Antiquities. Edited by WILLIAM SMITH, LL.D., and Illustrated by numerous Engravings on Wood. Third American Edition, carefully Revised, and containing, also, numerous additional Articles relative to the Botany, Mineralogy, and Zoology of the Ancients. By CHARLES ANTHON, LL.D. Royal 8vo, Sheep extra, $6 00.

ANTHON'S CLASSICAL DICTIONARY. Containing an Account of the principal Proper Names mentioned in Ancient Authors, and intended to elucidate all the important Points connected with the Geography, History, Biography, Mythology, and Fine Arts of the Greeks and Romans; together with an Account of the Coins, Weights, and Measures of the Ancients, with Tabular Values of the same. Royal 8vo, Sheep extra, $6 00.

DWIGHT'S (REV. DR.) THEOLOGY. Theology Explained and Defended, in a Series of Sermons. By TIMOTHY DWIGHT, S.T.D., LL.D. With a Memoir and Portrait. 4 vols., 8vo, Cloth, $8 00.

ENGLISHMAN'S GREEK CONCORDANCE. The Englishman's Greek Concordance of the New Testament: being an Attempt at a Verbal Connection between the Greek and the English Texts: including a Concordance to the Proper Names, with Indexes, Greek-English and English-Greek. 8vo, Cloth, $5 00.

FOWLER'S ENGLISH LANGUAGE. The English Language in its Elements and Forms. With a History of its Origin and Development, and a full Grammar. Designed for Use in Colleges and Schools. Revised and Enlarged. By WILLIAM C. FOWLER, LL.D., late Professor in Amherst College. 8vo, Cloth, $2 50.

GIESELER'S ECCLESIASTICAL HISTORY. A Text-Book of Church History. By Dr. JOHN C. L. GIESELER. Translated from the Fourth Revised German Edition by SAMUEL DAVIDSON, LL.D., and Rev. JOHN WINSTANLEY HULL, M.A. A New American Edition, Revised and Edited by Rev. HENRY B. SMITH, D.D., Professor in the Union Theological Seminary, New York. Four Volumes ready. (*Vol. V. in Press.*) 8vo, Cloth, $2 25 per vol.

HALL'S (ROBERT) WORKS. The Complete Works of Robert Hall; with a brief Memoir of his Life by Dr. GREGORY, and Observations on his Character as a Preacher by Rev. JOHN FOSTER. Edited by OLINTHUS GREGORY, LL.D., and Rev. JOSEPH BELCHER. Portrait. 4 vols., 8vo, Cloth, $8 00.

HAMILTON'S (SIR WILLIAM) WORKS. Discussions on Philosophy and Literature, Education and University Reform. Chiefly from the *Edinburgh Review*. Corrected, Vindicated, and Enlarged, in Notes and Appendices. By Sir WILLIAM HAMILTON, Bart. With an Introductory Essay by Rev. ROBERT TURNBULL, D.D. 8vo, Cloth, $3 00.

HUMBOLDT'S COSMOS. Cosmos: a Sketch of a Physical Description of the Universe. By ALEXANDER VON HUMBOLDT. Translated from the German by E. C. OTTÉ. 5 vols., 12mo, Cloth, $6 25.

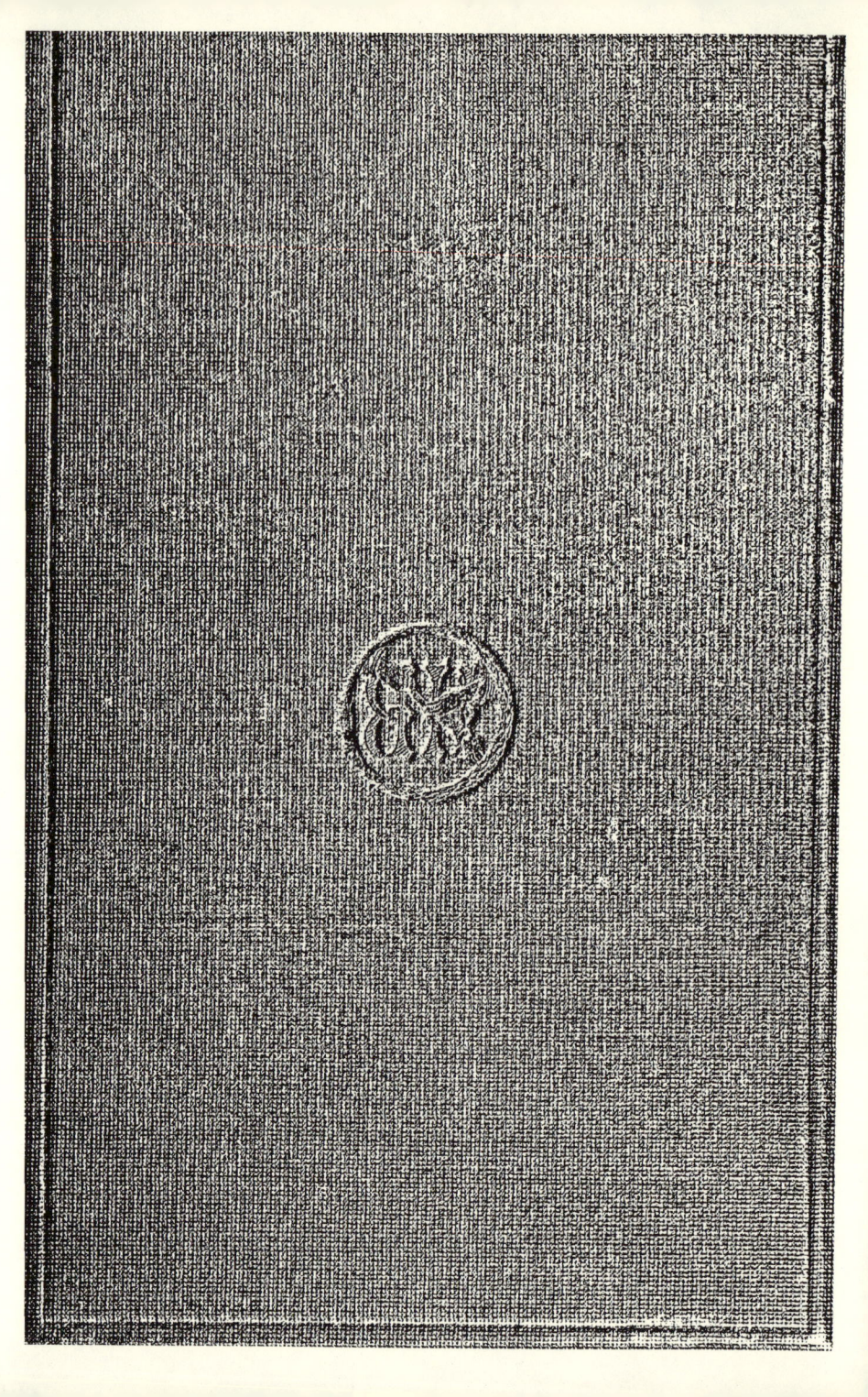

This volume from the
Cornell University Library's
print collections was scanned on an
APT BookScan and converted
to JPEG 2000 format
by Kirtas Technologies, Inc.,
Victor, New York.
Color images scanned as 300 dpi
(uninterpolated), 24 bit image capture
and grayscale/bitonal scanned
at 300 dpi 24 bit color images
and converted to 300 dpi
(uninterpolated), 8 bit image capture.
All titles scanned cover to
cover and pages may include
marks, notations and other
marginalia present in the
original volume.

The original volume was digitized
with the generous support of the
Microsoft Corporation
in cooperation with the
Cornell University Library.

Cover design by Lou Robinson,
Nightwood Design.

Made in the USA
Lexington, KY
05 January 2011